Culture and Ideology
in Higher Education

CULTURE AND
IDEOLOGY IN
HIGHER EDUCATION

Advancing a Critical Agenda

Edited by
WILLIAM G. TIERNEY

New York
Westport, Connecticut
London

Library of Congress Cataloging-in-Publication Data

Culture and ideology in higher education : advancing a critical agenda
  / edited by William G. Tierney.
       p.   cm.
  Includes bibliographical references and index.
  ISBN 0–275–93469–1
  1. Education, Higher—United States—Aims and objectives.
  2. Education, Higher—Social aspects—United States.
  3. Marginality, Social—United States.   4. Critical theory.
  I. Tierney, William G.
  LA227.3.C85   1991
  378.73—dc20   90-40708

British Library Cataloguing in Publication Data is available.

Library of Congress Catalog Card Number: 90-40708
ISBN: 0–275–93469–1

First published in 1991

Praeger Publishers, One Madison Avenue, New York, NY 10010
An imprint of Greenwood Publishing Group, Inc.

Printed in the United States of America

The paper used in this book complies with the
Permanent Paper Standard issued by the National
Information Standards Organization (Z39.48–1984).

10 9 8 7 6 5 4 3 2 1

CONTENTS

ACKNOWLEDGMENTS

Sally Kelley and Nancy Gearhart provided technical assistance and coordination for this text that was invaluable. My research assistant, Craig Heller, faithfully read and commented on each chapter, which helped move the process along. Dan McLaughlin read parts of the book and provided much needed advice. Each of these individuals has my gratitude.

Part I   THE RESEARCH
FRONTIER

1 BORDER CROSSINGS: CRITICAL THEORY AND THE STUDY OF HIGHER EDUCATION

William G. Tierney

In his book about the hill country of Thailand, Charles Nicholl writes of a Frenchman, Harry, who has lived and traveled in the jungles of Thailand and Burma all of his adult life. The author asks the Frenchman if he misses his home and what it feels like to be a perpetual alien, a constant traveler. Harry replies, "Sont tous les marginaux, comme moi. People on the borderline, you know?" (Nicholl, 1989, p. 132).

The Frenchman's response does not so much speak of the physical geography of foreign territory as it highlights the cognitive landscape that makes him feel as if he is on the border, among the marginal, ever removed from constancy and acceptance. Because he lives in Thailand, Harry is forever a foreigner by custom, belief, language, and religion. Harry is incapable of coming in from the frontier, but we find him comfortable as a traveler. Also, we listen as he describes how we are all—"sont tous"— living on the border, whether we need passports or not.

The chapters in *Culture and Ideology in Higher Education* also speak about cultural borders, but these boundaries are of a different kind; the travelers, too, are not like Harry, although the authors of the chapters in this volume are most definitely traversing new territory. This book concerns the border zones of academe. We will raise questions about how academe's borders have been shaped and formed. We will argue that most previous research about postsecondary education has overlooked or suppressed border areas and consequently marginalized different constituencies. In doing so, we will agree with Rosaldo:

More often than we usually care to think, our everyday lives are crisscrossed by border zones, pockets, and eruptions of all kinds. Social borders frequently become salient around such lines as sexual orientation, gender, class, race, ethnicity, nationality, age, politics, dress, food or taste. Along with "our" supposedly transparent cultural selves, such borderlands should be regarded not as analytically empty transitional zones but as sites of creative cultural production that require investigation. (Rosaldo, 1989, p. 208)

In this chapter, I will offer the reader a brief outline of how previous researchers have conceived of academe's geography, and then discuss the perspective we will advance in the ensuing chapters. I will discuss the organizational borders that have been conceived about colleges and universities, and speak about those who inhabit border areas.

THE RESEARCH FRONTIER

In Chapter 2 Yvonna Lincoln takes issue with the questions raised by higher education researchers. Through an analysis of the literature of (1) leadership and (2) students, Lincoln argues that higher education researchers have failed to come to terms with why particular individuals are relegated to the margins of academe—women, people of color, and part-time faculty, for example. She argues that, in general, previous research efforts have not grappled with the larger social contexts in which institutions are situated, but rather have defined "problems" in terms of particular variables of a population under study. In doing so, researchers have perpetuated the false belief that organizational reality is mutually understood and interpreted by all of the organization's participants. Further, Lincoln underscores that often researchers have concentrated on issues of effectiveness and efficiency in academe rather than having a central concern with issues of social justice and democracy.

Lincoln's concern with the topics that higher education researchers have chosen for study leads to a discussion of the methodological choices we have made. Most previous research in higher education, she points out, has been grounded in the basic tenets of logical positivism. William Foster comments on the overarching tenet of the positivist approach:

Logical positivism asserted that only scientific knowledge, which was verifiable in principle, was true knowledge and could be expressed in logical and therefore true form. This removed a good deal of human affairs from the realm of truth; values, ethics, and morality would simply become matters of assertion or preference. (Foster, 1986, p. 35)

Lincoln critiques the positivist approach by taking up where Foster leaves off. She points out the centrality of one's values and interpretations when one undertakes higher education research. Rather than denying that the researcher has values, Lincoln suggests that all research is value-laden.

In general, the scaffolding for such research, as the ensuing chapters demonstrate to varying degrees, derives from qualitative methodologies and designs that allow those under study the ability to speak about "their" perceptions and realities. Critical theorists assume that researchers must insert themselves in the research process, and engage in praxis-oriented research projects that seek to give voice to the disempowered and bring into question the borders we have created around our research.

In the rejection of the logical positivist approach to the study of higher education, the book's authors argue for a radical alternative. Each of the authors will work from a perspective informed by critical theory. Because of the relatively unfinished nature of critical theory, one of the challenges theorists face is finding a mutual language and understanding of what is meant by critical theory. That is, theories develop and change over time; in comparison to logical positivism, critical theory has had a relatively short history in which to explicate all of its epistemological underpinnings. Of consequence, all its finer points and issues have not been worked out.

The higher education literature includes only a dearth of studies that have employed critical methodologies and frameworks. This book seeks to further our understanding of what is meant by a critical approach to the study of higher education. In order to do so, however, we must first have a general understanding of what is meant by critical theory. A caveat is in order. In what follows, my purpose will not be to offer a full discourse concerning critical theory; several excellent recent works already have plowed that turf (Bernstein, 1976; Fay, 1987; Giroux, 1983; Kellner, 1989). However, I will offer five broad axioms with which each of the authors of this book has operated, and which influence our interpretation of educational institutions and research.

Any discussion of critical theory takes as its point of departure the founding of the Institute for Social Research—the "Frankfurt School"—and, among others, the work of Adorno, Horkheimer, Marcuse, Fromm, and eventually Habermas. Although the Institute's roots began in Frankfurt, Germany in the 1920s, because of the rise of Nazism the Institute eventually moved to Columbia University, then to Los Angeles, and again to Frankfurt in 1951. It is interesting to note that the genesis of the term "critical theory" took place when the members arrived in the United States.

The Institute's members felt compelled to use a code word because of their commitment to Marxism and America's abhorrence of anything related to socialist revolution and the Soviet Union (Kellner, 1989, p. 44).

Although theorists began with a primarily Marxian analysis of capitalism and modernity, in recent years they have struggled to come to terms with what critical theory means in a postmodern era. They also have redefined how they interpret Marxism. Nevertheless, the overt political aspect of critical theory and its constant struggle to understand how society operates have remained part of critical theory's central core. As Fay notes, "Critical social science is an attempt to understand ... the oppressive features of a society such that this understanding stimulates its audience to transform their society and thereby liberate themselves" (Fay, 1987, p. 4). Viewed in this light, the first central difference between logical positivism and critical theory arises: *critical theorists want to understand the world in order to change it.*

A second crucial difference concerns how critical theorists conceive of knowledge. Knowledge is a power-laden concept that helps define reality. Young elaborates, "Those in positions of power will attempt to define what is taken as knowledge, how accessible to different groups any knowledge is, and what are accepted relationships between different knowledge areas and between those who have access to them" (quoted in Wexler, 1987, p. ix). Thus, *critical theory views the production of knowledge as socially and historically determined and as a consequence of power.*

Knowledge, then, is neither neutral nor situated within traditional disciplines. As Kellner observes, "It traverses and undermines boundaries between competing disciplines, and stresses interconnections" (Kellner, 1989, p. 7). If knowledge is not oriented in the disciplines, and if it is contextually framed, then the role of the critical researcher will be fundamentally different from that of the logical positivist. If we assume that our understanding of knowledge is historically determined and socially constructed, then we must investigate the borders of knowledge not as cemented concepts that are objectively defined, but as malleable explanations which, as a function of power relations in society and different perspectives of the researcher and the researched, constantly undergo reinterpretation. Further, if the researcher's purpose is to change the world rather than merely study it, then the stance the researcher takes vis-a-vis his or her subject of study will be different. Simply stated, the researcher cannot be objective, detached, or neutral.

The point is not that authors must write polemics or fictions, but rather that they must reconceptualize their positions within a research project, and inform the reader about the nature of their assumptions and biases. "The usual notions of evidence, accuracy and argumentation," Rosaldo adds, "continue to apply for their studies" (Rosaldo, 1989, p. 69). A major difference, however, between positivist research and critical interpretations is that the critical researcher assumes that one's findings are tentative and provisional. The accumulation of knowledge is not necessarily cumulative so that it can be added together into a unified summation.

For the purpose of this book, we have taken Rosaldo's point one step further. We have inserted ourselves into the text in a variety of manners. Most obviously, the frequent use of the first person acknowledges the author's presence in the research project. The chapters also consider particular problems of academe by utilizing current qualitative research designs and methods. Jacoby's charge, then, that much academic writing is "technical and unreadable" (Jacoby, 1987, p. 141) and Wexler's criticism that most radical critiques employ the logic of "quantitative correlational studies" (Wexler, 1987, p. 82) will not apply in the chapters that follow. To summarize, *the role of the researcher to the researched is brought into question and examined.*

Each of the axioms underscores a similar point about those issues that are objects of study and those individuals who are "research subjects." The purpose of research is to change the world; the assumption is that knowledge is not objective, and the researcher's interpretations, however carefully made, are provisional and subjective. The question naturally arises: to what end are we to change the world? If knowledge is not objective, and researchers hold subjective views, toward what goal is critical theory aimed? An understanding of power is necessary to answer both questions.

Power is often used by those who are powerful to oppress those who are not. The purpose of critical theory is to interpret power not as a weapon that the powerful wield, but as a process of enablement in which the voiceless and oppressed are empowered to act on their own behalf. When individuals have become empowered, the possibility then exists for them to challenge those situations and individuals that oppress them. *Empowerment concerns the liberation of individuals, so that they are capable of understanding their relationship to the world and complex organizations in which they reside.*

Throughout the 1980s, the concept of "empowerment" became a catch-all phrase, so that one heard community activists speak of "empowering the people" as well as credit card companies that sought to increase their clientele by "empowering you with greater purchasing power." Both Ronald Reagan and Jesse Jackson sought to "empower" their supporters.

The use of the word "empowerment" by so many politically different groups and individuals is an example of the appropriation of discourse for whichever point a group or individual desires. Buying a Diner's Club credit card has little, if anything, to do with the manner in which we will use the term "empowerment" in this book.

Empowerment is a complex process that takes place within a matrix of specific cultural relations. Individuals do not empower other individuals irrespective of the situations in which they find themselves. Empowerment is not something that one individual gives to another. Instead, empowerment is a process whereby individuals come to self-understandings of their place in society. Empowered individuals are able to see how the larger society has formed, shaped, and mangled their own lives and interpreted realities. These same individuals are then able to re-form and reshape their lives, and those of their families and friends.

Seen in this light, empowerment is not something to be given, seized, or shared. Although it is possible to create the conditions for empowerment to take place, individuals cannot transform others. The concept of organizational heroes or "great men" is substituted with a portrait of countless individuals in organizations who work actively, constantly, and seek to make empowerment possible (Tierney, forthcoming a). Necessarily, empowerment does not result from a single action or a causal process. Simply because one learns to read or registers to vote does not mean that the individual is empowered. Similarly, empowerment is not prescriptive; individuals cannot follow "five steps to empowerment." To reiterate, then, empowerment is a multivariate phenomenon that takes place within specific cultural, racial, and gender- and class-related borders (McLaughlin, 1990). Individuals can struggle to generate the conditions for empowerment, but ultimately, those who are dispossessed and voiceless take control of their own lives; empowerment is not something that is rendered unto them.

With regard to education, critical theorists point out that the purpose of schooling is not merely to provide jobs or to create good citizens. Indeed, one central arena where the conditions for empowerment can be constructed is within educational institutions. As Giroux notes, critical theory

does not equate the struggle for public life with the narrowly defined interests of one group, irrespective of the nature of their power or the legitimacy of their interest. This is a pedagogy which links schooling to the imperatives of democracy, views teachers as transformative intellectuals, and makes the notion of democratic difference central. (Giroux, 1989, p. 6)

Education is a transformative activity that creates conditions of empowerment through a central concern for social justice and democracy. As we shall see, the contexts and constituencies in academe have both liberating and constraining aspects that make empowerment possible or futile. The researcher's quest is to unearth the forces that deny voice to the powerless. Once those forces are understood, the task is to create the conditions for change. We now turn to a discussion of the contexts of academe to shed light on how we have framed its borders.

ACADEMIC BORDERS

In *Borderlands/La Frontera*, Gloria Anzaldua writes, "Borders are set up to define the places that are safe and unsafe, to distinguish *us* from *them*"(Anzaldua, 1987, p. 3). As the authors in this book will show, in academe we have created organizational borders that distinguish some activities and not others, that make particular individuals prominent and others invisible. The creation of these borders occurs by way of an organization's ideology. In Chapter 3, in a discussion about institutional ideology, I write that ideology "helps determine how culture is enacted and how the institution's identity is defined." The point to be stressed is that the task for the researcher and organizational participants is to come to terms with an institution's ideology, and to struggle to break down those ideologies and cultural artifacts that prevent individuals from creating the conditions for empowerment (Giroux, 1989, p. 11).

The two institutions discussed in Chapter 3 have radically different ideologies, and of consequence, the organizational borders and constituencies differ. One college, Working Class State, reflects the demands of the state for a particular kind of educational experience that molds students and teachers in a manner that reinforces a "working-class" ethos. Education is equated with employment. The second college, Testimony State, offers an ideology with an explicit concern for empowerment as I have defined the term in the discussion above.

Sheila Slaughter extends the discussion of ideology in Chapter 4 with an analysis of the discourse and belief systems of university presidents. The testimony of presidents before Congress is the data Slaughter deconstructs. Rather than confine her analysis to a college or university, the author investigates the borders of the system of academe. What comes into focus through this study is what academe's leaders believe to be important and, of consequence, what is of little import. Slaughter contends that, by unearthing the ideological apparatus of a university or the system of higher education, we are able "to come to a better understanding of the ways in which ideas are used to legitimate structures of privilege and power and, often inadvertently, to mask inequities and injustices."

Thus, we hear a consistent argument in Chapters 3 and 4 concerning the nature of ideology. All organizations and systems have ideologies, whether or not individuals are aware of them. Ideologies are belief systems that are enacted on culture's surface. Although we suggest that overarching ideologies often support the interests of the dominant, of the "best and brightest" as Slaughter points out, we do not argue that ideology must always be shaped by those in power. Indeed, by our discussion of the forces at work in institutions specifically, and more generally throughout the system of higher education, we stress the interests that ideologies mask so that we may change those ideologies. Rather than fixed and determined, we see the cultures of organizations and systems and their ideologies as fluid and transitory. As Slaughter notes, "Individuals are comprehended as complex and contradictory, agents not objects, while social structure is understood as fluid."

In Chapter 5 Patricia Gumport extends Slaughter's analysis with a discussion of the consequences for an organization when funded research becomes ideologically "imperative." Through a case study, Gumport offers examples of two facets of an organization that face significant change when university participants decide to become upwardly mobile and seek major contracts for research. A two-tier system—those who are grant-active, and those who are not—is put into place. Gumport asserts that a wide gulf then exists between the "haves" and the "have-nots," in terms of "office/lab space, research resources, and teaching loads, as well as varying senses of efficacy versus alienation within the campus community."

Graduate education also undergoes a change. Embracing the ideology of research means that graduate programs able to attract significant research contracts—often in the sciences—will prosper. Other graduate programs unable to attract outside funding—many times in the humanities—will not flourish. The purpose of Gumport's analysis is to highlight the consequences to an organization when it embraces a particular ideology and defines its borders in a particular manner.

William Foster, in Chapter 6, creates a bridge between Parts 2 and 3. In our delineation of academe's borders, Gumport, Slaughter, and I point out problems of legitimacy, status, and privilege. From these chapters, one might be led to conclude that our analyses end in despair or nihilism. Given what we know about the constraints and power of ideologies, what might be done? Indeed, Slaughter's presidents and Gumport's university seem indicative of the way we think of higher education in the late twentieth century.

Foster provides an answer with an example for one area in academe—postgraduate education. He utilizes the notion of *agency* as an analytic tool that can be used to reconceptualize postgraduate education. *Agency*, to Foster, means that "individuals with particular professional backgrounds are agents of social change, can indeed make a difference in their social networks, and are fundamentally committed to creating practices intended for social progress." In this light, organizations allow much room for creative action and struggle on the part of individuals, yet the organizations' participants are not free to change their lives or organizations at will.

Essentially, individuals interact in an organization that has an ideology that permeates the culture. The interaction between individuals and the social system produces and reproduces the organization's structure and ideology, according to Foster. Social change, then, does not occur because of heroic individuals, or because of rationally determined processes and goals. Instead, change takes place by the continuous interaction of structure and individual. The question then becomes, if social change is possible within ideologically formed organizations and systems, what kinds of individuals populate academe's borders, and how might we reconceive their experiences?

PEOPLE ON THE BORDERLINE

As Gumport's analysis suggests, some people in academe are marginalized and made invisible, while others are celebrated as organizational heroes. Chapter 7 offers a twofold portrait concerning those who are marginalized. First, Ken Kempner writes about an organization—the community college—that is at the border of academe's system. The ideology of power and privilege that Slaughter highlights in Chapter 4 necessarily places community colleges and those who populate them at the outer extremes. Even in my own study, the public state institutions, Working Class State and Testimony State, are "closer in" from the border than Kempner's community college.

Furthermore, within "Hill Community College," we see that differences again have been made between the haves and the have-nots. Thus, even in an institution on the systemic border, we see that organizational borders exist. The differences, however, are not between those who do research and those who do not; instead, among other differences we see conflicts between students who opt for vocational programs and those who follow an academic track, and clashes between those faculty who teach vocational courses and those who offer academically oriented courses. The conflicts that erupt at Hill are ideologically oriented and take place over the mission of the institution. As Kempner notes:

Community colleges are sites where proponents of opposing economic and social ideologies compete for dominance.... Such conflict is evident at specific locations within colleges, most notably vocational education, transfer, basic skills, and continuing education programs.

Kempner frames his analysis around a discussion of false consciousness. He raises the question of how a general acceptance of organizational orthodoxy takes place, and why organizational beliefs go unchallenged by some and are debated by others. In doing so, the chapter leads the reader to think about processes of human agency and possibilities for reform.

Sears, Otis-Wilborn, and Marshall bring a discussion of organizational reform efforts to the forefront in Chapter 8. Like Slaughter, who spoke about ideologies supporting the needs of the "best and the brightest," in this chapter the authors speak about teacher education reform and the assumption that the choice of those who would make the best teachers "was premised on the axiom: The brightest students make the best teachers." The question, of course, is how we define "brightest."

The authors spent six years studying a teacher education program at one university. In their case study, they point out the epistemological assumptions on which the program is based and how such assumptions privilege those who are in control. Utilizing the work of the French sociologist Pierre Bourdieu, the authors point out in great detail the political function of education by its unequal distribution, legitimation, and transmission of particular forms of cultural capital. Those students who are defined as "the best and the brightest" are the ones who come from the upper echelons of society and have internalized the knowledge base, values, and language of the controlling cultural group. We see how "low-ability" students, or those who do not come from schools in upper-class neighborhoods, are excluded from the program because they do not fit the definition of "best and brightest." In essence, those who do not possess the requisite cultural capital are placed on the other side of the border.

Chapter 9, "The Public Interest and Professional Labor," returns us within academe's borders. A commonplace assumption of academe is that the notions of public interest, expressed in the ideals of public service and objectivity, are central to faculty life. From this perspective, the work of the faculty advances without pressure from outside interests, and it is believed that the advancement of knowledge serves society. Rhoades and Slaughter bring both assumptions into question.

They examine the discourse of academics and administrators about intellectual property rights at one public research university. Their chapter points out that, when knowledge advances, it most often serves "society" as defined by those in power. Rules that govern technology transfer and public property rights are devised so that they serve corporate America. Power concerns not only individuals' ability to influence decisions; power also exists with regard "to structures that mediate social relations." They conclude that the ways in which individuals formulate discussions around such topics as technology transfer frame how academics think about and serve society.

In the final chapter, Anthony D'Augelli moves back to the borderline. He discusses those individuals who are perhaps academe's most invisible constituency—gays and lesbians. As a community psychologist, D'Augelli discusses his experiences in implementing a Freirian-based class devoted to lesbian and gay development. Again, the notion of human agency comes into play. "I'm going to try to have an effect on the amount of homophobic comments I hear," says one student as the class finishes, "I will no longer keep silent." Another student adds, "The course has put me in touch with some of the greater injustices that will prevent me from ever just fading back into the closet."

In his class, D'Augelli is enacting what Henry Giroux has called "a border pedagogy of postmodern resistance" (Giroux, 1989, p. 6). Because Giroux's notion is central to this book's framework, I will close this section by quoting him at length:

It is a pedagogy that is attentive to developing a democratic public philosophy that respects the notion of difference as part of a common struggle to extend the quality of public life. The notion of border pedagogy presupposes not merely an acknowledgement of the shifting borders that both undermine and reterritorialize different configurations of power and knowledge, it also links the notion of pedagogy to a more substantive struggle for a democratic society. It is a pedagogy that attempts to link an emancipatory notion of modernism with a postmodernism of resistance. (Giroux, 1989, p. 7)

CONCLUSION

This book is an invitation to the reader to rethink some of the most basic assumptions of higher education. What is the relationship of academe to society? How might we think of a "productive" faculty member? How do words like "ideology," "culture," and "human agency" operate? As an invitation, the book is not a definitive statement about critical theory and academe, but rather an initial comment. Indeed, our intent is to foment discussion rather than passive acceptance of what we posit. The chapters that follow highlight different areas within higher education; several other fruitful areas await analysis. An examination of minority participation in postsecondary education, the structure of disciplinary forms of knowledge, and faculty socialization processes are examples of the kinds of inquiry that demand investigation (Tierney, forthcoming b).

All of the following chapters reconceptualize how we think about the borders of academe. The authors continually move back and forth between the organization and society. In our travels, we discover borders and people whom we did not know existed. Ultimately, critical theorists hope to change those forces of oppression that exclude individuals and groups.

As we approach the twenty-first century, higher education is encountering attacks from many different camps. Conservatives lament that colleges and universities have not helped society become more "productive." Social reproductionists have argued that education can do little more than mirror the demands of the corporate order. Liberals have become despondent at the seeming failure of academic programs to redress the ills of society. Fiscally minded administrators have thrown up their hands in confusion at how to balance budgets with inadequate resources. The overwhelming sentiment is one of despondency.

In this book, we offer a different analysis. To be sure, in chapters such as Slaughter's and Gumport's the reader will discover how those in power insert their ideas into academe's fabric. However, in other chapters, such as Foster's and D'Augelli's, we uncover a politics of hope, of possibility. Essentially, we all raise a similar question: If particular forces are indeed at work in academe, what actions can be undertaken to transform the organization? These actions must be understood with a theoretical framework. As Bernstein notes, "What is required is a fundamental reexamination of the very categories by which we understand human action. . . . The root issues concern the most basic questions about what human beings are, what they are in the process of becoming, and what they may yet become" (Bernstein, 1976, p. 227). In moving back and forth between theory and action, we offer an antidote to those who despair about academe; we point out the difficulties that exist and the possibilities that might occur.

REFERENCES

Anzaldua, Gloria. (1987). *Borderlands: La frontera. The new mestiza*. San Francisco: Spinsters/Aunt Lute.

Bernstein, Richard. (1976). *The restricting of social and political theory*. Philadelphia: University of Pennsylvania Press.

Fay, Brian. (1987). *Critical social science: Liberation and its limits*. Ithaca, NY: Cornell University Press.

Foster, William. (1986). *Paradigms and promises: New approaches to educational administration*. Buffalo, NY: Prometheus Books.

Giroux, Henry A. (1983). *Theory and resistance in education: A pedagogy for the opposition*. South Hadley, MA: Bergin & Garvey.

———. (1989). Border pedagogy in the age of postmodernism. *Journal of Education, 170*(3), 162–181.

Jacoby, Russell. (1987). *The last intellectuals: American culture in the age of academe*. New York: Basic Books.

Kellner, Douglas. (1989). *Critical theory, Marxism, and modernity*. Cambridge, England: Polity Press.

McLaughlin, D. (1990). From the editor. *Journal of Navaho Education, 7*(2), 2.

Nicholl, Charles. (1989). *Borderlines: A journey in Thailand and Burma*. New York: Penguin Books.

Rosaldo, Renato. (1989). *Culture and truth: The remaking of social analysis*. Boston: Beacon Press.

Tierney, William G. (forthcoming a). Advancing democracy: A critical interpretation of leadership. *Peabody Journal of Education*.

———. (forthcoming b). *The worlds we create: Organizational aspects of Native American participation in higher education*.

Wexler, Philip. (1987). *Social analysis of education: After the new sociology*. New York: Routledge & Kegan Paul.

2 ADVANCING A CRITICAL AGENDA

Yvonna S. Lincoln

My thesis is a very simple one: I do not believe that epistemology is a bloodless abstraction: the way we know has powerful implications for the way we live. I argue that every epistemology tends to become an ethic, and that every way of knowing tends to become a way of living. I argue that the relation established between the knower and the known, between the student and the subject, tends to become the relation of the living person to the world itself. I argue that every mode of knowing contains its own moral trajectory, its own ethical direction and outcomes.

Parker J. Palmer, 1987

I begin with the assumption that, in general, the higher education community has proceeded on the premise that if a research question is addressed in its most theoretically, conceptually, and methodologically elegant and "correct" manner, then the results are the best obtainable. In a preliminary way, this chapter challenges that premise, suggesting instead that the questions asked determine what can be known about an entity, and that the place from which an observer observes determines what can be observed. This is because we look through lenses that represent a set of values and attempt to take "pictures" of a phenomenon at a given moment in time. We also have acted as though those photographs ("perspectives") could, when merged and ordered taxonomically, provide us with a composite photograph that would reveal everything we needed to know about the thing investigated.

The taxonomic, aggregationist model of knowledge portrays only one of many potential representations of knowing and knowledge. The latest work on IQ clues us that intelligences, and therefore probably knowledges, are not necessarily linear, taxonomic, or hierarchical. Still, we have operated on what we took to be the best model available for investigating the unknown, the scientific method model. However, we probably ought not to continue to assume that it is still the only model when the academic disciplines are grappling with others that are contenders for legitimacy, and when scientists are beginning to understand that scientific knowledge generated by one model is not the only form of knowledge available to us. George Keller (1985) observed that higher education researchers have very precise answers to possibly the wrong questions, and as higher education researchers, we might be better off with less precise answers and better questions than the reverse (Keller, 1985, 1986). What I shall try to do is review the literature in the two areas; suggest questions that remain unanswered; introduce the critical perspective; and pose questions that the critical perspective raises, which address both our unanswered questions and the role of the university as a moral and potentially transformative agent.

THE LITERATURE AND A FEW GOOD QUESTIONS

In a preliminary way, I have reviewed two areas of literature, the first on leadership in colleges and universities, and the second on college students.[1] These two particular bodies of literature were chosen for several reasons. First, they are a literature that is read by the author, since I teach in these areas. Second, they represent problem areas, in that the literature has not proven particularly useful in solving long-term dilemmas, either regarding the nature of leadership, or with respect to how certain kinds of students might enjoy increased retention rates in higher education, or how institutions might reduce costly attrition and hold on to dwindling numbers of traditional-aged college students. Third, they are important areas because both leadership and student attrition/retention interact with other policy arenas (e.g., state, legislative, and federal, most especially student financial aid). Research on these areas is a hotly contested debate, and thus, it tends to have high visibility in research and administrative circles.

The Leadership Literature

A simple but straightforward place to begin with the literatures is to ask, "What do we now know?" That question ought to suggest what we know, what we do not know, and how others might frame similar questions, which will be the last topic undertaken.

With respect to leadership, we know a good bit. Higher education researchers have been enriching the literatures with extensive descriptions, ethnographies, and cultural "thick descriptions" (Geertz, 1983, pp. 24–25) as a way of returning to "grounded theory." An increasing number of scholars have tried to utilize new and emerging constructs to understand and elucidate power, leadership, and the contexts in which leadership occurs (Chaffee, 1984; Knight and Holen, 1985; Chibucos and Green, 1989; Young et al., 1989; Conger, Kanungo, et al., 1988; Birnbaum 1988a, 1988b, 1988c, 1988d). Studies of organizational culture (Chaffee and Tierney, 1988; Smith and Peterson, 1988; Masland, 1985; Kolman and Hossler, 1987), and studies of symbolism and organizations as "enacted" social constructions (Tierney, 1987, forthcoming) are beginning to have an influence on the ways in which leadership is defined and researched (Birnbaum, 1989a, 1989b; Chaffee, 1989).

Critical understandings have tended to come in generations. Birnbaum's review of the implicit leadership theories of college presidents notes that there are major categories of leadership research (Birnbaum, 1989b, pp. 126–127). These categories are, in part, generational; that is, they tend to represent successive generations of research thought and research sophistication pursued when the limits of previous research become understood. So, for instance, early research theories focused on *trait theories*, presumably characteristics of "great men" acknowledged to be leaders; a second generation of leadership studies focused on *power and influence theories* as a way of comprehending the extent and uses of power leaders were able to command, and the ways in which they exercised the same over persons presumed to be followers; a third generation of leadership studies focused on *behavioral theories*, emphasizing leader behavior, and so on (Birnbaum, 1989b, p. 126).

As leadership theories evolved, so did understandings of organizations. Early organizational management studies focused on *time and motion* studies. Such studies were succeeded by studies of efficient *organizational forms* (with, for instance, a high emphasis on bureaucracy as the peak of efficiency and rationality in organizational functioning). Those studies were superseded eventually by the *human relations* school. This last school is rapidly being overtaken, I would argue, by an emphasis on culture and on organizations as anthropological artifacts, as moral entities, and as political systems in which human activity is voluntarily directed for a range of self-actualizing needs.

There remain, however, enough unanswered questions that we still cannot provide adequate descriptions of the human organizations we inhabit, or of the kinds of leaders they have, successful and unsuccessful, and we cannot prescribe exactly what kind of leader a given organization should have (a normative rather than a descriptive statement, but one that is of critical import to search and screen committees charged with identifying and hiring leaders). Higher education researchers cannot unanimously agree on what leadership *means* in any heuristic sense. Succeeding generations of leadership research have defined the term differentially, so researchers typically clarify exactly what they mean by leader and leadership early on in a publication, if it is not clear from the context.

Researchers do not, additionally, have a very comprehensive sense of when, where, under what circumstances, and by whom leadership occurs. We have focused systematically on those persons formally charged with managing (usually hierarchical, bureaucratic) organizations, and we have failed to notice they are not the only persons exhibiting leadership behaviors. We have systematically ignored others whose roles were too informal for our notice. The emphasis on formal organization has centered most of our research on groups who have been routinely managed by white, Anglo-Saxon males, and as a result, our research has centered, as Bleier (1986) noted, around the social and class preoccupations of that group.

The epistemological and ontological stance of much of this research has been realist and positivist in orientation. The focus on describing and creating a theoretical base for a single, "true" reality has created most of the gaps in our knowledge bases. Our emphasis on understanding higher education structures from the perspectives of those who lead them has sometimes left us with inadequate knowledge from those who do not, or who hold power as lower-order participants. Although we have asked good questions about the apparent forms, researchers in general have probed little into the less-apparent structures from which proceed more rigid social relations. Thus, although the conventional researcher might ask, "What is leadership, and how does it function to be successful or unsuccessful in a given context?" a critical perspective questioner might ask, "What are the underlying values, forms of discourse, and organizational and social structures that function to preserve the possibility of leadership in some types of leaders (dominant culture males, for instance), and that work to subvert the leadership of others (from marginal cultures)?" The first question poses the possibility that, once the "right" form of leadership is found for a given context, it will work whoever practices it. The second question acknowledges the possibility that contexts reify pervasive social structures that prevent some persons from exercising leadership, whatever their skills or talents.

The College Student Literature

The research on college students is even more plentiful than the research on leadership in higher education.[2] We have extensive databases that now describe who current college students are: their demographic distributions (Estrada, 1988; Carnegie Foundation, 1989); their mobility patterns (Carnegie Foundation, 1989); their vocational interests (Katchadourian and Boli, 1985); how many of them are minorities and how those minorities are faring;[3] information about the new majority in higher education, women (Solomon, 1985; Komarovsky, 1985); how the socio-economic status levels of this generation compare to the last (Smart and Pascarella, 1986, 1987); what some of the factors in college leaving and attrition might be (Tinto, 1987, 1988; Terenzini et al., 1985); and what strong factors are associated with degree completion and retention (Smart and Pascarella, 1987).

We know a good bit about college choice among undergraduates; how students rate the effectiveness of the instruction received (Wilson, 1988); the socio-economic status differentials that typically exist between students who choose various kinds of institutions, and whose academic aptitude may not resemble those of more traditional college-aged students (Cross, 1971). We understand a good bit more about the needs and developmental stages of adult learners than we ever have before (Weidman and White, 1985; Steltenpohl and Shipton, 1986; Brazziel, 1987), and something about the impact of financial aid on coming, going, and minorities (Olson and Rosenfeld, 1984; Jackson, 1988; Stampen and Fenske, 1988; Hansen, 1989).

However, we have little idea how to "match" students with institutions. Also, researchers cannot say, for instance, how to assure that a risky student will complete his or her degree. This is particularly critical, since postsecondary institutions have minority enrollments that are low at best, since those who do begin postsecondary work often drift away, and since minority persons will comprise 35 percent of the labor force in the year 2010. If we are to continue to fuel the information society's managerial and technological needs, who will do the work if minorities are not educated for those roles?

The troubling business about this extensive research comes in the form of a comment made to the author personally by a researcher who has made this particular subset of higher education research his life's work. He said, with a mixture of sorrow and chagrin, "I think I'm coming to the conclusion that we have gone as far as we can go with this line of inquiry. We are going to have to rethink the questions we've been asking, and we're going to have to change *strategies* for getting them answered." Perhaps without realizing it, my good friend has happened onto a sound philosophical truth: any model or paradigm for research can entertain some questions with great facility and power, and cannot entertain other questions—perhaps equally significant—well or at all. When the inquiry model we are using fails to respond to a different array of questions, then we need to shift models. We can look more broadly at the ways of knowing that we have available to us. One of those ways of knowing is the so-called "critical perspective."

THE CRITICAL PERSPECTIVE'S AGENDA

Critical theory begins with an explanation—as do all social or scientific theories—of "the way things are."[4] Critical social theorists characterize these givens in the following manner:

Assume for the moment that a society is marked by fundamental structural conflict and that this conflict produces deep suffering in its members. Indeed, assume further that this conflict has reached such a proportion that it threatens to lead to the breakdown of society—that, in other words, the society is in crisis. Moreover, assume that one of the causes of this situation is the systematic ignorance that the members of this society have about themselves and their society—that, in other words, one of the causes of the crisis and its attendant suffering is what has been traditionally called the false-consciousness of some or all of its members. Furthermore, assume that the sufferers themselves wish their suffering could cease. Lastly, assume that the social order is such that if the sufferers came to have a different understanding of themselves, they would be able to organize themselves into an effective group with the power to alter their basic social arrangements and thereby to alleviate their suffering. (Fay, 1987, pp. 27–28)

Almost "any critical theory is propagated with the idea that it will itself be the catalytic agent in the overthrow of a given social order" (Fay, 1987, p. 28), once it is able to provide for, in turn, enlightenment—or the removal of false or divided consciousness, empowerment—or the enabling of the audience for them to act on their new consciousness, and emancipation—the removal of the original social order which is the root cause of the original suffering, and its radical restructuring.

Giroux (n.d.) regards the social crisis as precipitated by a modernist (e.g., positivist) world view whose

claim to authority partly serves to privilege Western, patriarchal culture, on the one hand, while simultaneously repressing and marginalizing the voices of others who live outside of the dominant centers of power, that is, those others who have been deemed subordinate and/or subjected to relations of oppression because of their color, class, ethnicity, race, or cultural and social capital. In postmodernist terms, the political map of modernism is one in which the voice of the other is consigned to the margins of existence, recognition, and possibility. (Giroux, n.d., pp. 1–2)

Giroux regards the social crisis, in part, as both stemming from, and historically located within, education, which serves to oppress and repress "voices" outside the dominant culture. Although other sources (e.g., Marx) have criticized other social institutions (e.g., the world of work, production and the formation of capital markets, or marriage), the most vocal, serious, and articulate of contemporary critics have addressed themselves to the social structures of education.

Critical social science is characterized by differing interpretations, but typically the critical perspective embraces four sub-theories. They include a theory of false consciousness, which proposes how a group's self-under-standings fail to account for their experiences; a theory of crisis; a theory of education; and a theory of transformative action, which details what is to be altered, for whom, and how (Fay, 1987, pp. 31–32).

The theory of crisis and the theory of transformative action are especially useful in the context of literature on leadership and college students. A critical perspective on leadership, for instance, might ask: Do leaders, leadership styles, and ways of managing higher education contribute to the marginalization of groups? Are there deep social structures that leaders consciously or unconsciously support and that act to preserve the dominance of some groups while systematically oppressing others? Are there ways in which leaders can act to transform institutions toward more just social ends?

With respect to college students, probably the greatest social crisis facing the higher education community has been the seeming inability or unwillingness to welcome and educate racial and ethnic minorities (Arbeiter, 1987; Franklin, 1987). Since these segments of the population are growing faster than traditional college populations (white, middle class), there exists some moral responsibility to see that such minorities take their rightful places in an educated society. We are failing on that social objective, failing badly, and it is generating a social crisis between the "haves" and the "have-nots." The historical account of the development of this crisis is less important than the "structural basis of the society"—a point to which researchers rarely ever turn. Structural analyses of higher education as a social and cultural enterprise often reveal that its major function is sorting and certifying certain classes of persons (more often white, and middle to upper class) for professional, managerial, and technical positions—positions that act to concentrate wealth, power, and influence in the hands of those who often have it already (Silva and Slaughter, 1984).

The sub-theory of transformative action would "isolate those aspects of a society which must be altered if the social crisis is to be resolved" and indicate who might be the agents of this anticipated social rearrangement (Fay, 1987, p. 32). This suggests a research agenda for those who would be a part of the transformation of institutions of higher education. To adopt the stance and language of more radical critical theorists, oppressive and repressive structures operating within higher education would be identified and structurally recreated in order to provide opportunities for students to enter, engage, and confront their false consciousness.[5]

A LARGER CRITICAL AGENDA

A revivified social science would contain not only conventional (i.e., positivist) accounts of phenomena, but also be open to the validity of various radical social critiques. As one of the radical critiques, critical social science suggests a whole range of questions that cannot be explored well within the bounds of conventional scientific inquiry, but that can be addressed robustly using the critical perspective. The following section suggests a critical agenda for future research.

First question: *What are the underlying structures—the processes and unexamined social arrangements—of institutions of higher education that act to reproduce larger social structures? Do those structures act to oppress and/or marginalize certain classes of persons?* Examining the leadership literature with this question in mind forces one to confront the issues of why there are so few women in administration, so few minority persons, and why those who are there speak of barriers, discrimination, hostility, the "glass ceiling," being closed out of the networks, and other horrors that their white or male counterparts rarely endure. The research on college students, particularly women and minority college students, would lead one to ask, why is it that the climate is so chilly, and/or why do so few survive to the "finish line" (degree completion)? What structures hinder or impede progress? What processes act to marginalize minorities either with respect to leadership, or with respect to attainment of the degree that would almost guarantee access to middle- and upper-level professional positions?

Second question: *Does the university's role in knowledge production and transmission function in reifying certain world views and dismissing to marginality others?* Studies on primatology, sex roles, sex, and gender (Bleier, 1984, 1986; Haraway, 1986), and explorations of the rise and role of social scientists as policy experts (Silva and Slaughter, 1984; Slaughter, 1988), demonstrate how the knowledge production functions act as ideological filters within institutions. As Bleier notes:

In the absence of knowledge about female primates based on observations of their behaviors, primatologists then felt free to speculate about (that is, to construct) female primates *in ways which allowed their imagined behaviors and characteristics to fit existing male-centered theories of human cultural evolution and thus to embellish, naturalize, and reinforce the social construction of human female and male genders and of relations of domination and subordination.* (Bleier, 1986, p. 9, emphasis added)

Primatology and sex role research is one excellent example of how knowledge production has functioned to re-create and reify social structures and constructs that appear to support the interests of the dominant class, a largely male "privilege[d] Western, patriarchal culture" (Giroux, n.d., p. 1).

Third question: *How do reconstructions of ways of knowing bring about and provide contradiction and conflict in academic organizations?* Gumport provides us a clue in this direction with her studies of women's studies as a profession, and with an examination of the ways in which academic culture is becoming fragmented (Gumport, 1989b). Although it is widely presumed that ethnic and women's studies are subspecialties of larger academic disciplines (Clark, 1970), it can be argued that such "new disciplines" have at their core radically different ways of knowing (Palmer, 1987). Disagreement regarding the way we know or come to know (epistemology) has radical implications for the unity of the academic community. This is especially true if Palmer is correct in stating that epistemology carries with it an implied ethic, encapsulating a moral dimension of life (Palmer, 1987; this is a point I have also argued in Lincoln and Guba, 1989). The *conflict* felt by individuals torn between their "home" disciplines and their substantive and/or political commitments, and the *contradiction* between disciplinary dictates regarding ways of knowing, and intuitive, self-revealed ways of knowing have, together, the potential to create a revolution and transformation in the academy.

It is probably possible to use the conflict and contradiction (Gumport, 1989a, 1989b) over the discourse of science, knowledge production, and ways of knowing to leverage higher education out of its current state of "divided consciousness," but before that can be accomplished, we will probably need to understand the nature of the conflict/contradiction that confronts us. It is likely the case that we as teachers could also use this conflict or contradiction as a critical perspective teaching/modeling device, if we understood more about it. We have only begun, however, to understand that the phenomenon exists; we have no idea what its boundaries or parameters might be.

To relate this question to the larger leadership research, we as researchers might well ask, from a critical perspective, how the leadership of our institutions supports, rewards, searches out, and encourages those who might study this phenomenon, understand the conflict and contradiction, and utilize it to raise critical awareness on the part of students. Put into one wag's terms: Have you hired a critical theorist, a constructivist, or a feminist today? Have you promoted or tenured one this year?

With respect to college students, we as teachers in higher education do not know—at this time—how to enact, on behalf of students, a curriculum that would emancipate them in any critical sense. We can teach them to think critically, but we cannot teach them (that is to say, we have no *program* for teaching them) to liberate themselves. (The old liberal arts curriculum was supposed to do this, but it clearly is not working for a large segment of higher education.) As professors, we have no clear-cut idea of how to employ the contradiction and conflict that is even now present in academia as a model for helping students to understand social structures that impinge on and act to oppress their own lives.

Fourth and final question: *Who are to be the transformative agents for higher education?* Since the critical perspective demands a critical pedagogy, it can be safely assumed that at least one set of transformative agents would come from the professoriate. It is they who are in charge of the curriculum, and they who engage in the most extensive contact with students.

However, we might well look at leaders in higher education—presidents, deans, chairpersons—to see what roles they might play in the transformation of the academy, and in the provision of the means, materials, and models for transformative leadership. Transformative leadership is a topic currently under investigation, and although leadership is rarely engaged from a critical perspective, speculating on what it might mean in terms of a critical academy might be profitable.

Agents also of change are students themselves, in at least two ways. First, they provide the experience that is "official" curriculum content, the "voices" that have been marginalized (this is particularly true with racial and ethnic minorities and with women), and they bring one or more popular (albeit marginalized) cultures to institutions of higher education, which can become the subject of ideological critique. Second, within the critical perspective, they are co-producers of knowledge (with teachers) and, therefore, central to the process of their own educations. Without their understanding of how they have been marginalized, no critical pedagogy can take place.

CONCLUSION

I have suggested that we have, as a community, asked and answered elegant questions about the structures and processes of higher education. Yet, despite our research, we have little to guide us in decision-making, virtually no way to hold on to students who should be getting the best we have to offer, and theories that provide little practical help in administration, leadership, pedagogy, or matching students with institutions. We mostly operate by the seat of our pants. I am not suggesting, however, that we need more elegant, predictive, or prescriptive theories. What I am suggesting is that we take a longer and deeper look at the institutions we have studied, to see what we might have missed.

I myself am not a critical theorist, as readers of the chapter will probably recognize immediately, nor do I make any pretense of being one. I am, more properly, a constructivist—a "naturalistic inquirer," a phenomenologist. As such, I believe reality is a multiple (rather than singular), enacted, social construction. Constructions can be simplistic or sophisticated, and may be enlarged and refined as information and/or understanding expands. Thus, "false" (simplistic, naive, misinformed, or inadequate) consciousnesses could be replaced or reconstructed by more socially aware (critical, informed, transformative, liberating) and/or consensual constructions. I am, however, as reluctant to accept the critical theorists' "explanations" *as the sole explanation* as I am to accept the conventional scientists' "explanations" for "how things really are." Each is no more than *one* lens through which we might see. The point, of course, is *purpose*—To what purpose is the research to be put?—and *fit*—How well do the assumptions of the research model (paradigm) fit the phenomenon under investigation?

What ties me to the critical perspective in some intellectual sense is both the intuition that critical theorists are asking some good questions (some of which I have tried to raise here), and the conviction that institutions of higher education are no longer acting as democratizing, emancipatory, or transformative forces in American life. In short, the ideological critique that the critical perspective mounts against the academy—or that it should be mounting—is a persuasive one to me, and I have tried to utilize two bodies of literature widely researched to demonstrate that institutions are in a social crisis, that this crisis is in part due to the academy's dominant epistemology (objectivism), and that structural analyses such as those suggested in the final section might well reveal in what ways the higher education community could transform institutions of higher education so as to enable them to act in more empowering and emancipatory ways.

I have tried to indicate that, in terms of change, you cannot get there (to transformation) from here (current mainstream research). One profitable detour could well be questions that the critical perspective poses.

NOTES

1. I simply surveyed a contemporary selection of materials, from the most typical journals in the field of higher education, and from several recent book-length publications. The journals included *The Journal of Higher Education*, *The Review of Higher Education*, and *Change* magazine, as representative of widely read periodicals, and were reviewed backwards for five years (to 1984). These are read, typically, by scholars and researchers, and by those trained in and practicing higher education administration.

2. For the same journals, and for the same years (1984–1989).

3. See, for instance, Allen, 1987, 1988; Arbeiter, 1987; Coles, 1988; Crosson, 1988; Estrada, 1988; Fields, 1988; Fiske, 1988; Hodgkinson, 1985; Jackson, 1988; Loo and Rolison, 1986; Nettles, Thoeny, and Gosman, 1986; Olivas, 1988; Pascarella, Smart, and Stoecker, 1989; Richardson, Simmons, and de los Santos, Jr., 1987; Skinner and Richardson, 1988; Winn, 1985.

4. Ferreting out a comprehensive statement of the critical theorist's position is not always simple. Many writers and theoreticians who consider themselves critical theorists do not provide comprehensive statements regarding their philosophy. Also, it is not possible to say that all critical theorists either believe the same set of axioms applies to their belief systems, or that one set of axioms captures subtle differences in philosophy between various researchers and theoreticians. For that reason, I have simply adopted the convention of working with the most comprehensive statement to date—Fay, 1987. Working backward from various research

works and theoretical pieces, utilizing content analysis to extrapolate the undergirding assumptions, is one way to proceed when working with a new philosophical system. The process of "discovering" the axioms of logical positivism, a task to which I turned my attention some years ago (see, for instance, Guba and Lincoln, 1981; Lincoln and Guba, 1985), turned out to be quite a feat. Even philosophers do not agree among themselves about what constitutes the central or core beliefs of the logical positivists. In my and Guba's early work, we simply tried to analyze (via content analysis) what the undergirding assumptions of contemporary scientific method might be. Later, we adopted the conventions of philosophers, and talked about the axiomatic assumptions of conventional science in terms of its ontology, epistemology, and methodology, and the implications of the world view of logical positivism for each of those critical arenas in conventional inquiry.

5. The term "false consciousness" (or "divided consciousness") has problems all its own. It suggests that there is a "true," or "right," consciousness, thereby revealing the typically realist ontology of most critical theorists. There is no theoretical or substantive necessity for the critical perspective to adopt a realist stance (see, for instance, Fay's arguments, 1987, p. 37ff.), and I do not. I prefer the assumption that some consciousnesses are more sophisticated, enlightened, empowering, or emancipatory than others, but that multiple sets of consciousness (constructions) can exist, depending on where one resides in the social structures under investigation. The presumption that there exists one "true" consciousness creates a system whereby some do not have the "true" consciousness, but a few do. Thus, "true consciousness" begins to mark a "priesthood" of truth in much the same way that scientific method has done so in the past decades. My preference is to see many consciousnesses (or constructions) of varying degrees of sophistication, to see truth as that consensual construction to which we can agree (or agree to disagree), and to deny the possibility that only a few hold the critical "keys to the kingdom." For a more extended discussion of the critical theorists' position on ontology, see Guba, 1990.

REFERENCES

Allen, Walter R. (1987). Black colleges vs. white colleges: The fork in the road for black students. *Change, 19*(3), 28–31, 34.
―――. (1988). Improving black student access and achievement in higher education. *Review of Higher Education, 11*(4), 403–416.

Arbeiter, Solomon. (1987). Black enrollments: The case of the missing students. *Change*, *19*(3), 14–19.

Birnbaum, Robert. (1988a). Administrative commitments and minority enrollments: College presidents' goals for quality and access. *The Review of Higher Education*, *11*(4), 435–457.

———. (1988b). Consistency and diversity in the goals of campus leaders. *Review of Higher Education*, *12*(1), 17–30.

———. (1988c). *How colleges work: The cybernetics of organization and leadership*. San Francisco: Jossey-Bass.

———. (1988d). Presidential searches and the discovery of organizational goals. *Journal of Higher Education*, *59*(5), 489–509.

———. (1989a). Presidential succession and institutional functioning in higher education. *Journal of Higher Education*, *60*(2), 123–135.

———. (1989b). The implicit leadership theories of college and university presidents. *Review of Higher Education*, *12*(2), 125–136.

Bleier, Ruth. (1984). *Science and gender: A critique of biology and its theories on women*. New York: Pergamon Press.

——— (Ed.). (1986). *Feminist approaches to science*. New York: Pergamon Press.

Brazziel, William F. (1987). Forecasting older student enrollment: A cohort and participation rate model. *Journal of Higher Education*, *58*(2), 223–231.

Carnegie Foundation for the Advancement of Teaching. (1987). Minority access: A question of equity. *Change*, *19*(3), 35–39.

———. (1989). Student migration patterns: What they mean for states. *Change*, *21*(3), 29–34.

Chaffee, Ellen Earle. (1984). Successful strategic management in small private colleges. *Journal of Higher Education*, *55*(2), 212–241.

———. (1989). Leadership in higher education: Variations on a theme. *Review of Higher Education*, *12*(2), 167–175.

Chaffee, Ellen E., & Tierney, William G. (1988). *Collegiate culture and leadership strategies*. New York: American Council on Education/Macmillan.

Chibucos, Thomas R., & Green, Madeleine F. (1989). Leadership development in higher education: An evaluation of the ACE Fellows Program. *Journal of Higher Education*, *60*(1), 21–42.

Clark, Burton. (1970). *The distinctive college*. Chicago: Aldine.

Coles, Robert. (1988). Hispanic dreams/American dreams. *Change*, *20*(3), 12–13.

Conger, Jay A., Kanungo, Rabindra N., and Associates. (1988). *Charismatic leadership: The elusive factor in organizational effectiveness*. San Francisco: Jossey-Bass.

Cross, K. Patricia. (1971). *Beyond the open door*. San Francisco: Jossey-Bass.

Crosson, Patricia H. (1988). Four-year college and university environments for minority degree achievement. *Review of Higher Education*, *11*(4), 365–382.

Estrada, Leonardo F. (1988). Anticipating the demographic future: Dramatic changes are on the way. *Change*, *20*(3), 14–19.

Fay, Brian. (1987). *Critical social science: Liberation and its limits*. Ithaca, NY: Cornell University Press.

Fields, Cheryl. (1988). The Hispanic pipeline: Narrow, leaking, and needing repair. *Change*, *20*(3), 20–27.

Fiske, Edward B. (1988). The undergraduate Hispanic experience: A case of juggling two cultures. *Change*, *20*(3), 28–33.

Franklin, John Hope. (1987). The desperate need for black teachers: A special appeal from John Hope Franklin. *Change, 19*(3), 44–45.

Geertz, Clifford. (1983). Thick description: Toward an interpretive theory of culture. In Robert M. Emerson (Ed.), *Contemporary field research* (pp. 3–30). Boston: Little, Brown and Co.

Giroux, Henry A. (n.d.) *Border pedagogy in the age of post-modernism.* Miami, OH: Miami University.

Guba, E. G. (Ed.). (1990). *The paradigm dialogue.* Newbury Park, CA: Sage Publications.

Guba, E. G., & Lincoln, Y. S. (1981). *Effective evaluation.* San Francisco: Jossey-Bass.

Gumport, Patti. (1989a). *E pluribus unum?* Paper presented at the annual meeting of the American Educational Research Association, San Francisco.

———. (1989b). *Women's studies as a vocation.* Unpublished paper, University of California, Los Angeles.

Hansen, Janet S. (1989). A policy research agenda for postsecondary student aid. *Review of Higher Education, 12*(4), 339–347.

Haraway, Donna. (1986). Primatology is politics by other means. In Ruth Bleier (Ed.), *Feminist approaches to science.* New York: Pergamon Press.

Hodgkinson, H. L. (1985). The changing face of tomorrow's student. *Change, 17*(3), 38–42.

Jackson, Gregory A. (1988). Financial aid and minority access: Why do we know so little? *Change, 20*(5), 48–49.

Katchadourian, Herant A., & Boli, John. (1985). *Careerism and intellectualism among college students.* San Francisco: Jossey-Bass.

Keller, George. (1985). Trees without fruit. *Change, 17*(1), 7–10.

———. (1986). Free at last? Breaking the chains that bind education research. *Review of Higher Education, 10*(2), 129–134.

Knight, W. Hal, & Holen, Michael C. (1985). Leadership and perceived effectiveness of department chairpersons. *Journal of Higher Education, 56*(6), 677–690.

Kolman, Eileen, & Hossler, Don. (1987). The influence of institutional culture on presidential selection. *The Review of Higher Education, 10*(4), 319–332.

Komarovsky, Mirra. (1985). *Women in college: Shaping new feminine identities.* New York: Basic Books.

Lincoln, Yvonna, & Guba, Egon. (1985). *Naturalistic inquiry.* Newbury Park, CA: Sage Publications.

———. (1989). *Fourth generation evolution.* Newbury Park, CA: Sage Publications.

Loo, Charles, Rolison, George. (1986). Alienation of ethnic minority students at a predominately white university. *Journal of Higher Education, 57*: 58–77.

Masland, Andrew. (1985). Organization culture in the study of higher education. *Review of Higher Education, 8*: 157–168.

Nettles, Michael T., Thoeny, A. Robert, & Gosman, Erica J. (1986). Comparative and predictive analyses of black and white students' college achievement and experiences. *Journal of Higher Education, 57*(3), 289–318.

Olivas, Michael A. (1988). Latino faculty at the border: Increasing numbers key to more Hispanic access. *Change, 20*(3), 6–9.

Olson, Lorayn, & Rosenfeld, Rachel A. (1984). Parents and the process of gaining access to student financial aid. *Journal of Higher Education, 55*(4), 455–480.

Palmer, Parker J. (1987). Community, conflict, and ways of knowing: Ways to deepen our educational agenda. *Change, 19*(5), 20–25.

Pascarella, Ernest T., Smart, John C., & Stoecker, Judith. (1989). College race and the early status attainment of black students. *Journal of Higher Education, 60*(1), 82–107.

Richardson, Richard C., Jr., Simmons, H., & de los Santos, A. G., Jr. (1987). Graduating minority students: Lessons from ten success stories. *Change, 19*(3), 20–27.

Silva, Edward T., & Slaughter, Sheila. (1984). *Serving power: The making of the academic social science expert.* Westport, CT: Greenwood Press.

Skinner, Elizabeth Fisk, & Richardson, Richard C., Jr. (1988). Making it in majority universities: The minority graduate's perspective. *Change, 20*(3), 34–47.

Slaughter, Sheila. (1988). Academic freedom and the state: Reflections on the uses of knowledge. *Journal of Higher Education, 59*(3), 241–262.

Smart, John C., & Pascarella, Ernest T. (1986). Socioeconomic achievements of former college students. *Journal of Higher Education, 57*(5), 529–549.

————. (1987). Influences on the intention to reenter higher education. *Journal of Higher Education, 58*(3), 306–322.

Smith, Peter B., & Peterson, Mark F. (1988). *Leadership, organizations, and culture.* London: Sage.

Solomon, Barbara M. (1985). *In the company of educated women: A history of women in higher education in America.* New Haven: Yale University Press.

Stampen, Jacob O., & Fenske, Robert H. (1988). The impact of financial aid on ethnic minorities. *Review of Higher Education, 11*(4), 337–354.

Steltenpohl, Elizabeth, & Shipton, Jane. (1986). Facilitating a successful transition to college for adults. *Journal of Higher Education, 57*(6), 637–658.

Terenzini, Patrick T., Pascarella, Ernest T., Theophilides, Christos, & Lorang, Wendell G. (1985). A replication of a path analytic validation of Tinto's theory of college student attrition. *Review of Higher Education, 8*(4), 319–340.

Tierney, William G. (1987). Facts and constructs: Defining reality in higher education organizations. *Review of Higher Education, 11*(1), 61–73.

————. (forthcoming). Academic work and institutional culture: Constructing knowledge. *Review of Higher Education.*

Tinto, Vincent. (1987). *Leaving college: Rethinking the causes and cures of student attrition.* Chicago: University of Chicago Press.

————. (1988). Stages of student departure: Reflections on the longitudinal character of student leaving. *Journal of Higher Education, 59*(4), 438–455.

Weidman, John C., & White, Richard N. (1985). Postsecondary "high-tech" training for women on welfare: Correlates of program completion. *Journal of Higher Education, 56*(5), 555–568.

Wilson, Tom C. (1988). Student evaluation-of-teaching forms: A critical perspective. *Review of Higher Education, 12*(1), 79–95.

Winn, Marie. (1985). The plug-in generation. *Change, 17*(3), 14–20.

Young, Denise L., Blackburn, Robert T., Conrad, Clifton F., & Cameron, Kim S. (1989). Leadership, student effort and departmental program quality: An exploration of quality cross levels of analysis. *Review of Higher Education, 12*(3), 265–277.

Part II   ACADEMIC BORDERS

3 IDEOLOGY AND IDENTITY IN POSTSECONDARY INSTITUTIONS

William G. Tierney

As we approach the twenty-first century, among the most significant questions facing postsecondary institutions are questions about institutional purpose. A concern for purpose has been addressed indirectly in numerous fashions during the past decade. The higher education community has placed, for example, considerable energy into discussions about how postsecondary institutions may become more effective; by coming to terms with institutional effectiveness, we have had to take into account what we perceive an effective institution to be. In general, considerations of effectiveness have been defined in terms of organizational performance or how the institution may better serve the economic needs of society.

In this chapter, I agree with the underlying assumption of much of the recent work in higher education that coming to terms with institutional purpose is important; however, I argue that, rather than questions of effectiveness or quality, a concern with institutional purpose is essentially a moral question that demands a wider range of political and theoretical considerations than we have given. Such an argument provides a powerful understanding of institutions that are masked by traditionally "morally neutral" approaches. In doing so, I agree with Michael Katz when he says,

Universities are less able than ever to define the ways in which they are distinct from other social institutions, how the principles on which they operate differ from those in business and government, and why they should enjoy special privileges. Therefore, the next great crisis of the university may not be demographic, fiscal, or organizational. Instead, it may be moral. (Katz, 1987, p. 180)

Accordingly, I first discuss how institutional identity has traditionally been defined in the higher education literature. Clark's work about institutional saga and recent discussions about institutional missions also are discussed. I then draw upon the work of Giroux (1983), McLaren (1989a, 1989b), and Foucault (1980) to resituate the dialogue within a critical framework. I define institutional purpose neither in terms of mission nor of saga; instead, I discuss institutional ideology and how it operates as a filter that defines the activities of postsecondary institutions. I highlight the discussion by way of case studies of two public state colleges. I conclude with a discussion of the implications of a critical perspective for the study of higher education research, and I raise questions about avenues that await further analysis.

One caveat is in order. The philosophical debates concerning ideology are voluminous, confusing, and contradictory. In the pages that follow, I do not intend to trace the history of those debates. A full discussion about how various streams of philosophical thought conceptualize ideology is beyond the scope of this chapter. Instead, I utilize critical theory to highlight how ideology operates within a postsecondary institution.

RATIONALIST CONCEPTIONS OF ORGANIZATIONAL IDENTITY

The literature on organizational identity may be considered from three different perspectives. First, researchers have discussed how to define organizational identity. Second, individuals have written about institutions that have intensive cultures where "sagas" exist that define institutional purpose and action. Third, a growing number of writers have questioned the efficacy of tightly defined mission statements in light of the need of an institution to adapt to the demands of the marketplace.

Creating an Identity

Albert and Whetten have noted that, to understand an identity, three criteria need to be satisfied: define the essence of the organization; determine how it is different from others; and enable the organization to exhibit continuity over time (Albert and Whetten, 1985, p. 265). Presumably, if one cannot distinguish these three points, then the organization lacks an identity.

This perspective's assumptions are that researchers may develop empirical questions from which they may derive answers about the organization's concept of identity. For example, the manner in which an organization defines its constituency or perceives itself in relation to its environment are features that provide insight into organizational identity. The answers that the organizational participants provide may also offer clues about the threat to an organization's core identity. For instance, a small Catholic liberal arts college that has always defined itself as educating young Catholic women may develop problems of identity if the school, to increase enrollment, must suddenly attract adult men and women who are multi-denominational.

On a grand scale, organizational participants distinguish themselves from others by defining within which classificatory scheme they exist. Participants at a small Catholic liberal arts college first see themselves within the world of institutions of higher education and then within a smaller cluster of religiously based institutions. Simply by defining themselves as a religious liberal arts college poses different questions than if the college were a large, comprehensive public institution.

However, as markets have grown tighter, proponents of organizational identity have advocated greater distinctiveness, so that an institution may differentiate itself from its competitors and attract specific clienteles. Thus, a small Catholic liberal arts college may develop special majors in computer science or business, programs such as "weekend colleges," or services catering to adult students to highlight its distinctive identity and capture different markets.

The central proposition concerning organizational identity is that its loss threatens organizational health. The identity of an organization must exist over time not only so that external constituents comprehend what the institution is about, but also so that internal constituents comprehend institutional goals and purpose. Identity is particularly important for newcomers to the organization who will need to be socialized to its history and culture. If the identity is under constant threat and/or dramatic change, the assumption is that morale, and consequently productivity, will decrease. In sum, people need to understand where they have been and where they are going to be effective.

Creating a Saga

Burton Clark has written extensively about colleges and universities that have a "saga" (Clark, 1970, 1971, 1980, 1983). Clark's analysis hinges on the distinction between organizational mission and saga. As with organizational identity, a postsecondary institution with a mission is one that has a distinctive niche that separates itself from the use of other comparable colleges and universities. A distinctive mission will determine internal activities different from the use of other institutions, so that the individual's socialization and incorporation into the organization will differ from other institutions. At the same time, a mission will adapt as external forces require.

A saga is the strongest possible identity an organization may assume. "A saga," states Clark, "is a mission made total across a system in space and time. It embraces the participants of a given day and links together successive waves of participants over major periods of time. . . . [It] turns an organization into a community, even a cult" (Clark, 1980, p. 235). A college with a saga, then, resembles an institution that has a religious conviction about its beliefs. How one acts, and the activities of the organization, will be determined by the saga. Commitment will be high, and a concern for the welfare of the organization will be paramount.

The opportunities for creating a saga are most likely to occur at the inception of the organization, or when the institution is in crisis. On the one hand, the initiation of a saga is easiest when a few people become involved in the creation of a college or university. A new organization will not have established customs or structures. Individuals also may be chosen who fit the mold that the leaders want to create. In short, institutional founders appear to have the greatest leeway in choosing who they want, what they will do, and how they will conduct activities.

On the other hand, when an organization is in crisis, participants also may be willing to accept dramatic change. Simply stated, if the options for an institution are a radical reorientation or the death of the organization, most participants will opt for change. In many respects, crisis re-creates conditions of the new organization. Past practices take on less importance, and the established ways of conducting business will be put in abeyance.

The danger of having a saga is that a saga demands narrow institutional commitments. The possibility exists that, when the environment changes, the institution will not be able to adapt because of its saga. The commitment to one belief and way of conducting affairs may lead to institutional rigidity and stagnation when alternative ideas and adaptability are necessary. However, the rewards of a saga appear to be great. By creating bonds of affiliation and commitment, the organization becomes a place where members reap internal rewards and the organization achieves a distinctive identity.

Creating an Adaptive Identity

The body of literature that calls for missions sensitive to their environments and capable of adapting to the marketplace stands in contrast to the previous works that assume a clear organizational identity or saga is essential for an effective organization. Davies, for example, states, "There are very good reasons not to define institutional missions" (Davies, 1986, p. 86).

The assumption of this position is that no one benefits with a mission that is narrowly defined; potential options and possibilities that may arise will be foreclosed. The danger noted above about an institution's saga is highlighted from this perspective. The essential point for an organization is not to define itself inflexibly, but rather to develop a malleable organization that has the ability to seize opportunities that arise in the environment. Consequently, rather than clear goals, the organization should create generic statements with which everyone can agree. "Vague and vapid goals," states Chait, "that are able to attract consensus are preferable to precise aims that force choices and provoke serious disagreements" (Chait, 1979, p. 89).

The adaptive approach also has a different sense of temporality than the first two approaches. Those who believe that an institution needs to develop an organizational identity and/or saga assume that one needs to take into account the past as well as the future to understand the organization. The adaptive approach, however, eschews the organization's past and future, and concentrates on the present. To be sure, leaders must have an understanding of the past strengths and weaknesses of the organization as well as an understanding of future trends, but the emphasis is not on maintaining an identity—much less a saga—from the past to the future; instead, organizational leaders need to concentrate on capitalizing on present-day opportunities. Rather than describe what the institution wants to do, the adaptive approach emphasizes what an institution does.

The strength of this approach is that the assessment of goals and objectives is possible. Albert and Whetten have noted that the task of institutional assessment is difficult in institutions that have normative identities, such as churches and colleges. "How can you measure the effectiveness of a teacher in fostering inquisitiveness, or the effectiveness of a minister in increasing faith," they ask (Albert and Whetten, 1985, p. 284). With adaptive missions where organizational participants define themselves by what they do, assessment becomes easier. When an institution becomes more selective by changing its admissions policies, for example, or by creating new programs, the institution has changed its mission. Davies writes, "When what an institution does, or when and where and for whom it does it, changes, then the mission has changed. We are no longer peeling away layer after layer of institutional characteristics, searching for the mission. This is like removing layer after layer of an onion, searching for what makes it an onion" (Davies, 1986, p. 100). In sum, a mission should promote adaptability to the demands of the market-place; rather than promote effectiveness, sagas or institutional identities actually may hinder an institution's effectiveness.

I have elaborated on each of these views because they form the founda-tion for current thought about institutional purpose. In the next section, I shall offer a criticism of the underlying rationales of these positions, and then offer an alternative conception of institutional purpose.

A CRITICAL CONCEPTION OF
INSTITUTIONAL IDENTITY

A Critique of the Rationalist View

A critical analysis of institutional identity highlights three epistemolog-ical disagreements with the previous discussion. First, one assumption that each of the previous positions works from is that an institution's frame-work or schema is a matter of choice; the organization's participants decide whether or not to have an identity. Some institutions decide to have a saga, and others do not. Those organizations without a saga appear as free-float-ing entities where the participants freely choose what they want to be as the needs of society change. As I will elaborate in the next section, if organizations are cultures that are socially mediated, then necessarily the organization must have an underlying framework that guides activity.

The second concern with the foregoing discussion is the assumption that organizational reality is understandable by participants and researchers, and further, that everyone similarly interprets that reality. Proponents of the rationalist position assume that questions may be asked that approxi-mate "the essence" of the organization, and this "essence" is the same for all participants. A saga, for example, is the clearest example of an institu-tion where a unitary interpretation exists about the activities of the orga-nization. Curiously, even proponents of the adaptive view work from a singular conception of reality insofar as the overarching purpose of the organization is to "read" the environment accurately. Again, the assumption is that all of the participants will interpret the environment in a similar fashion.

Third, none of the positions link a discussion about institutional identity with an explicit concern for social justice or democracy. Instead, an institution utilizes a mission or saga to promote organizational health, which is equated with organizational effectiveness and performance. The assumption is that organizational identities, missions, or sagas are morally neutral. Presumably an institutional saga that espouses the exclusion of particular groups from the community is as moral as a saga that advances democracy. Nowhere in discussions about organizational sagas or the needs of the organization to adapt do we hear a concern voiced for social justice. As Robert Paul Woolf notes, the result is "a covert ideological rationalization for whatever human or social desires happen to be backed by enough money or power to translate them into effective demands" (quoted in Katz, 1987, p. 178).

In sum, the previous positions have only surface disagreements; their epistemological suppositions are quite similar. The positions differ with one another only by advocating how an institution should define itself in relation to the marketplace. One group assumes that a tightly defined identity will enable consumers to choose them for their distinctiveness; the other group posits that a lack of identity will allow the organizational participants to adapt more quickly to the changing needs of the environment. Nevertheless, each position works from an identical standpoint. Reality may be understood by all participants, and they are free to choose the identity they desire. As a concrete entity, organizational reality is not only understandable, it also lends itself to a unitary discourse mutually understood by all who seek to interpret it.

The Critical View

A critical view of educational organizations offers a quite different analysis of organizational purpose and identity from that of the rationalist perspective. To begin, critical theorists tie their investigations to a concern for social justice and democracy. Critical theorists work from the assumption that the world is marked by enormous suffering and injustice. Instead of trying to increase organizational effectiveness or neutrally describe the organizational world, the aim of critical theory is to understand the oppressive aspects of society so that those features may be transformed by those who are oppressed. Educational organizations, then, are more than training grounds for future jobs. Henry Giroux notes:

Theory, in this case, becomes a transformative activity that views itself as explicitly political and commits itself to the projection of a future that is as yet unfulfilled. . . . Rather than proclaiming a (rationalist) notion of neutrality, critical theory openly takes sides in the interest of struggling for a better world. (Giroux, 1983, p. 19)

In doing so, critical theorists disagree with the rationalist assumption that an organization exists as a reified, rational object that can be neutrally studied by the researcher. Instead, critical theorists think of the organization as a social construction of society and the participants within the organization. Based in a dialectical interplay between college community and society, the organization's purpose acts not merely as a reflector of societal mores, but also as a democratic change agent that has transformational possibilities. The role of the critical theorist is to *explain* the organizational world, *criticize* it, and *empower* its audience to overthrow it (Fay, 1987, p. 23). Also, the critical theorist's explanation of the organizational world is rooted in both the interpretive understandings of the participants and the researcher.

Given the idea that the world is socially created, the critical theorist takes issue with the rationalist premise that organizational reality is mutually understood by all who seek to understand it. Critical theory's underlying assumption is that the organization's culture focuses the participants' understanding of their relationship to society through an organizational web of patterns and meanings. In this light, organizational reality is not a grand narrative to which all participants subscribe to achieve organizational effectiveness; reality, circumscribed by culture, is embedded in relations of power and conflict.

Culture may be defined as "the particular ways in which a social group lives out and makes sense of its 'given' circumstances and conditions of life" (McLaren, 1989a, p. 171). Culture is interpretive, the product of the social and ideological relations in which it is inscribed. As Rosaldo notes, "Culture requires study from a number of perspectives, and these perspectives cannot necessarily be added together into a unified summation" (Rosaldo, 1989, p. 93). Thus, educational organizations exist as a complex of dominant and subordinate cultures, wherein different groups struggle to gain voice so as to define and legitimate their own interests and realities.

Within an organization's culture, a dominant ideology exists that helps determine how culture is enacted and how the institution's identity is defined. Ideology is the set of doctrines, the framework, through which the organization's participants make sense of their own experiences; culture is the manifold ways in which these meanings are enacted.

Ideology is neither a master framework mindlessly passed from generation to generation nor is it simply created in the mind of the organization's leader and then imposed throughout the organization. To the contrary, ideology is contested within an organization's culture to the extent that different constituencies arrive at the organization with oppositional beliefs and practices. As Burbules notes, "ideology represents a framework of explanation and justification which accommodates persons to their position vis-a-vis one another in society; and it often does so no less in the minds of the advantaged than of the disadvantaged" (Burbules, 1986, p. 106).

The view advanced here substantially differs from Marx's notion of ideologies as distortions of reality (Marx, 1970; Mannheim, 1936). Insofar as rationalist notions of reality are rejected, critical theorists do not assume that an organization's ideology necessarily permeates a false sense of reality; consequently, ideology is not something to be overcome and defeated. To speak of concerted human action within an organization is to speak of culture, and every culture has an ideology that helps produce meaning. As Siegel states, "The critical task is not to forswear ideology, which is impossible, but to adopt the best ideology one can" (Siegel, 1987, p. 155).

Thus, another difference arises between the rationalist and critical perspectives. The rationalist perspective assumes that organizational identity is a matter of choice; one chooses whether to have a tightly defined mission or not, and so on. The critical perspective assumes that organizational ideologies exist, and that a central challenge for organizational participants is to make sense of the ideologies such that all participants are given voice and empowered. From this perspective, an organizational saga is of concern not because of its inability to adapt to the demands of the marketplace, but because an institution with a saga has the potential to silence those voices that disagree with the overarching ideology, or the ideology shapes the perceptions of the participants to such an extent that they accept their role in the organization because they believe no alternatives exist.

The task for an organization's participants is to avoid an ideological hegemony, where only one definition of reality is allowed to exist. The struggle will be to allow for the full range of organizational discourse to take place so that the status quo is not maintained. Participants are constantly engaged in unmasking the ideological determinants of the organization and questioning how different ideologies mute the voices of the powerless and sustain the power of the dominant. The question then hinges on how one comes to understand ideology, and once it is understood, how one changes it? We turn to an analysis of two institutions—Working Class State College and Testimony State College—in an attempt to answer this question.

INSTITUTIONAL IDEOLOGIES AT TWO PUBLIC STATE INSTITUTIONS

During the academic year 1987–88, I interviewed approximately 250 people on seven campuses about curricular decision-making. (For a full version of the case studies, the methodology employed, and an analysis of curricular decision-making, see Tierney, 1989). What follows are portraits of two of those institutions. The point of presenting two ostensibly similar institutions—two small, public state colleges—is to highlight the quite different ways the participants at each institution define and come to terms with institutional ideology, and as we shall see, people learn about ideology on culture's surface.

Working Class State College

Working Class State College is an institution like many others—a normal school begun after the Civil War that changed to a teacher's college, then to a college, and now has the unsure status of a university. Student enrollment is over 2,000. As a public institution, it is part of a state system with a faculty of almost 200 that has a collective bargaining agreement. Working Class has an aging faculty, many of whom will retire within the next five years. Most students come from throughout the state, although the preponderance are regional sons and daughters. The president has "swept house," and the top administration is virtually new.

Because Working Class is part of a state system, it has environmental pressures and constraints that private institutions do not face. Yet, in the minds of the organization's participants, the college also has the latitude to create the kind of institution it wants to be. "I think we should become the best public institution in the state," said an administrator. "We didn't use any of the old documents or histories when we were writing our mission statement," confided Working Class's chair of the accreditation report. "We're deciding now what we want to be in the future." "We excel in international studies and I think we should play that up more," commented another individual. "There are untapped markets out there waiting for us, if we're willing to get off our butts," added a fourth person.

In one sense, newcomers appear free to define for themselves "what this place is about." A new faculty member, for example, compared Working Class with his previous institution: "I was at a conservative Christian college before coming here. I don't see much of a difference between there and here. I'd say our mission at both places is to teach. Same kind of students. Same mission." Another individual assumed that a mission of public institutions was self-evident: "We're a public state college; that's our mission—a teaching place that trains working class kids." A third person was puzzled with the question: "Our mission? We don't talk about that very much. We teach. Maybe it's changing because we're supposed to do some research now, too. But I'm a science teacher who teaches kids; that's how I think about it." A fourth individual who had been at Working Class for over a decade noted, "Our mission is changing, but it's not something we hold long discussions about. We just change."

The participants learn about the institutional ideology, then, in an indirect manner. They are neither given formal orientations that concern "what this place is about," nor do faculty believe that they work within particular constraints. The participants at Working Class almost act as if they can create the ideology for the institution *tabula rasa*. The accreditation team, for example, was not using previous mission statements as they tried to define the future of Working Class. One individual went so far as to compare a religious institution where he had been with Working Class State. If an organizational participant cannot find a difference between the mission of a secular public state college and a religious institution, then upon what basis do the organizational participants come to understand ideology?

One way that faculty learn about ideology concerns what the curriculum will be called upon to do, and at Working Class, the curriculum is seen as a functional vehicle for providing young adults with gainful employment. Employment, however, is defined in quite particular terms. Individuals neither expect that the students will become professionals nor that graduates will find "working-class" jobs. "My dad worked in a factory," commented a student, "and I'm not going to." A faculty member noted, "Lots of these kids are first-generation college-goers. We're providing them better jobs than if they'd gone straight to work." A parent commented, "My kid won't be a surgeon, but he'll sure get a good job when he graduates. Computers or something." Thus, one clear sign about the institution is that the participants see their role as training traditionally aged, working class students for employment that might be considered lower-middle income.

One learns about the institution's culture and ideology not only by understanding what people believe they do, but also by listening to others' concepts of what the institution should do. Working Class State resides in an area with high unemployment and little idea of how to stem the economic depression that besets the city. Union workers have gone on strike at a factory, and management has replaced them. For all intents and purposes, it appears after more than a year's strike that the workers have lost their jobs. Management has no intention of hiring the workers back. New industry is not coming into the area; instead, small businesses are leaving the town.

Most people credit the president of Working Class State with improving the town–gown relationship. "Everybody attends his Christmas party," related one faculty member. "He's at so many of our social events that he's really like one of us," noted a citizen of the town. Yet for all of the socializing, little educational relationship takes place between the town's citizens and the college. One individual said, "If we want a course in photography or painting or something we can just call up continuing education and they'll try to get it for us." However, an unemployed worker said, "The college doesn't help. They walk a fine line because they don't want to [annoy] management. We need retraining, some type of economic development plan, but the college isn't interested. We don't know what to do." Another local worker said, "You'd think because the faculty is in a union that they'd support us, but they don't. They don't have anything to do with us up there in their ivory tower."

Is it the duty of a public state college to cater its curriculum to a local clientele? Not necessarily. As we shall see in the next section, Testimony State College attracts students from all over the state. Yet it appears at Working Class State that decisions are made with little explicit reference to either an overt ideological assessment or a discourse that actively interprets the organization's culture. Ostensibly, the state founded public institutions to serve the needs of the citizens and the state. To be sure, how one interprets who the citizens are, and who makes up the state, will vary dramatically depending upon one's background and interests. The unemployed worker mentioned above succinctly pointed out one interpretation. If the faculty were to be involved actively with the strike, the business leaders would undoubtedly feel that the college was not serving the needs of the state, and that the college was hindering economic development and the growth of business. Conversely, because of the faculty's silence, the strikers seem to feel that Working Class State is not speaking in their interests. Either way, how faculty and administrators act toward the community—how they define words such as "community"—assesses the relationship between college and community. What is not apparent at Working Class State is the awareness that such assessments are taking place. Ideology is implicit, and because it is implicit, the participants are incapable of defining the institution except in the most generic of terms.

Yet the generic terms provide us with insight into the institutional ideology. We have seen what the participants believe the institution should do for its clientele; the participants follow a similar line of thinking with regard to how they feel the institution should be evaluated. When asked how they assessed the curriculum, individuals responded in the following way: "Do our students get jobs? That's the question to ask, and the answer is yes." A second person commented, "We've changed so that kids get jobs." "When a kid finishes," stated another faculty member, "he'll find a good job that he wouldn't have gotten if he hadn't come here. A college education—computers, teaching, business administration—that kind of thing prepares students for the work world." In effect, Working Class State College has taken assessment out of the hands of the faculty and put it into the hands of the employers.

At Working Class, assessment has little, if anything, to do with knowledge in an emancipatory sense; rather, knowledge concerns skill development. I want to stress that I am not suggesting that learning a skill is unimportant or wrong. To be sure, students from all walks of life will learn tasks that they may find economically satisfying. The question to be asked, however, is whether or not the purpose of a postsecondary education is complete when someone learns a task that will afford employment. From a critical perspective, the response is that students should not only learn specific skills: they should also be empowered to reflect on their own lives and ascertain how history and society have situated them in particular racial, class, and sexual spheres.

The point to be made here is the influence of society in determining the ideological framework of the institution that defines what a curriculum is, how it will be evaluated, and who will evaluate it. At a public institution that educates primarily working-class students, the curriculum revolves around preparation for the work world. The students at this institution come from and will return to working-class towns and cities. How faculty form the curriculum and what they believe knowledge is certainly takes into account the composition of the student body. The relationship of the organization's culture to its environment takes on increased importance.

Obviously, "Working Class State College" serves the people of the name I have given the college—the working class. By educating for jobs, the college faculty is in many respects reinforcing the ethos of the parents of students. "We knew our boy would get a job when he's done here," commented one father. The boy's mother added, "His brother graduated and he's doing well. He's got a job." The question is how faculty at Working Class State can provide gainful employment to its students while at the same time expose the invisible structures of the curriculum and the kinds of knowledge produced in the classroom, so that students understand and come to terms with the socio-economic contexts in which they are embedded. In the next case study, we will see one answer that a similar institution provides to the question.

Testimony State College

Testimony State College was created slightly more than 20 years ago. Until recently, the institutional participants had to wage a constant battle with the state legislature to keep the institution open. Recently, however, calls for closure have evaporated, in large part because student enrollment has increased to 3,000. Students from throughout the country also have applied to the institution because of the positive publicity the school has received. In-state tuition is about $1,200. Over half of the student body majors in the arts and humanities. The state has never allocated much money for the institution, so the physical plant appears a bit spartan. However, the college resides in an area of natural splendor. The faculty has a good reputation as teachers; students appear to be involved actively in their educations. Indeed, one of the more important aspects of the educational experience at Testimony is the nature of the student–faculty relationship that emphasizes the importance of learning and values.

A long-time faculty member noted, "Our mission is to provide an opportunity for a liberal arts and science education through a delivery system that practices values that are fundamental to a democratic society." An administrator agreed by saying, "Half of [the faculty] would describe this as a moral curriculum. That's our mission. The way students learn and develop a voice is what makes us different."

Individuals learn about the mission as soon as they consider applying for faculty positions. "I went to AAHE [American Association of Higher Education] and interviewed forty-five people," commented a faculty member, "and almost to a person, every individual said that the ad in the *Chronicle* [*Chronicle of Higher Education*] described the kind of values that they wanted. And we were the only institution where they had applied."

Another individual outlined the process:

Most people talk about research at other interviews; we don't do that. For the people I talk with, they want to teach. The ad self-selects. We explain that teaching is interdisciplinary; we ask people to write an essay on their philosophy of education. We explain that they may be torn in both directions—teaching and research—but that we are a teaching school.

A new faculty member confirmed the speakers' observations: "I was attracted to the term they used for what I teach, 'political economy,' and that they stressed interdisciplinary and multi-cultural work. Even though we weren't paid to do research, I knew we'd be stimulated by one another." These statements highlight the fact that people begin to create impressions about the institution prior to their arrival on campus. When they arrive on campus, their impressions are expanded and affirmed by events such as faculty parties, where individuals give testimony to the uniqueness of the college. A faculty member of seven years elaborated:

It has taken a long time to understand what this place is about, the mission of this place. I like going different places. This is the fifth college I've taught at, and it is the most difficult to understand. I remember a party one time and it was almost a series of testimonials. One after another faculty member got up and said "what this place means to me." I was aghast! It was very, very discomfiting. For everybody else it was routine. They had seen the light, the truth, and I was just one of the novitiates.

An individual who has been at Testimony for five years concurred: "There's a particular way to do things here. Because they had been under the gun so long, there has been a siege mentality built up. We give particular respect to the people who have survived, to our founding fathers and mothers." Another relatively new person pointed out, "Look at our catalogue. The first thing it says about individual faculty members is the year they came here—not what they teach, not where they got their degree, but the year they came. Doesn't that say it all?" A third person looked at my interview schedule and said, "I've had an office in every building you're going to today. All of us move our offices every year so that we remain a community. It's a pain to move every year, but it's a conscious effort, telling us what we do, the importance of collegiality and relating with all of the faculty, not just a chosen few." Needless to say, if a president of another college tried to implement a plan where all faculty members had to move their offices every year, the president would encounter fierce opposition. The example from Testimony State accentuates the need to contextualize events. At Testimony State, when faculty switch offices, the action appears consistent with the culture and ideology of the institution. At another institution, such an action would most likely appear aberrant, if not absurd.

On the other hand, a professor also mentioned that the first comment about a faculty member in the catalogue is how long he or she has served at Testimony and that "says it all." Yet many other institutions also print an individual's length of service at the college, and no one pays much attention to that fact. At Testimony State, however, the fact is an important symbolic component of the culture, and it plays a critical role in helping members define the institution.

Another way individuals come to understand their relation to the institution is through teaching. One professor commented:

We need to understand both the agencies and objects of power. I don't concern myself much with the students except to the extent that the psychiatrist is concerned with the patient. I want something to occur in our encounter. I want students to find out how tough it is to gain knowledge, what a discipline means. I want them to discover the question a discipline can't answer. If a student develops a sense of limitations, then I've succeeded.

Later on in the discussion he added:

If you want to change the curriculum, then change the way the faculty deal with one another. That's partially the answer to how to change the curriculum. It must also be interdisciplinary. See, it has a lot to do with the structure in which you find yourself. It is inextricably and unknowingly bound to structures of power, which we can only partly understand.

Needless to say, the metaphors and language this individual utilized were quite different from those that faculty at Working Class State used when they spoke about the curriculum and their role in changing it. This individual did not think of providing students with answers, or preparing them for the work force. Instead, he proffered questions that had no answers. Although many other faculty thought of the student/faculty relationship in terms of psychology, most other individuals used the language of human growth and development, instead of a focus on the language that takes place during the encounter.

The manner in which the individual spoke reflects the culture of the organization. Again, the faculty at Working Class State used a different language when they spoke about the curriculum and pedagogy. At Testimony, however, other people spoke in a manner consistent with the above speaker. For example, another individual at Testimony State defined a successful faculty member by saying, "It's someone who is really interested in teaching, in forcing students to go beyond the narrow confines of the discipline. It's being interested in broad academic matters and not just being a typical faculty member holed up in your office writing articles." "To seminar is a verb for us," related another individual. "Teaching here is uniquely our own." An administrator commented that a faculty leader was someone "who understands the faculty's relationship here."

Contradictions also arise. No culture is monolithic. One faculty member confided about what was "really" going on:

I'll tell you what it's really like here. One-third of the faculty work terrifically hard; one-third—and I'm in this category—work hard, like at other institutions; and the other third are on leisure time—they'll tell you they're busy, but . . . if you were here on a Friday, you'd see a lot less people around. Testimony's challenge is to keep people motivated and not to burn out.

Another faculty member appeared disappointed when asked if some faculty were on "leisure time" but said, "I suppose so, but you shouldn't try to paint Testimony as some kind of academic utopia. We have the same struggles as elsewhere, just different interpretations." Later in the conversation the individual elaborated by saying that Testimony was not an island unto itself. "Faculty come from other institutions, have private lives with their own inherent pressures and struggles, and are initially socialized in graduate school just like faculty at other institutions." The individual shrugged and said, "We're swimming against the tide, and we're doing a good job of it, too. Testimony has an in-bredness that we try to foster, nurture. Are we perfect? No. But we're constantly working at building our own institution."

DISCUSSION

Let me briefly review points I have made thus far. Three primary ways in which higher education researchers have considered organizational identity concern: (1) how to construct an identity, (2) how to define an institutional saga, and (3) how to enable the organization to adapt to the demands of the marketplace. The approaches differ with one another on the surface; for example, one group claims that a tightly defined identity is important, and another group argues that a loosely defined identity is paramount. However, the epistemological suppositions of the approaches are quite similar.

The rationalist perspective assumes that the organization's reality is understandable and that all participants interpret that reality similarly.

Organizational identity is a matter of choice; the group decides whether to have a tightly or loosely defined mission. Each approach also eschews any moral commitment on the part of the organization; while the proponents of institutional saga may not be as vocal in their concern for organizational effectiveness as the other two approaches, all of the rationalists disregard a concern for social justice or empowerment. In essence, a mission, identity, or saga need not take into account explicit values when the organization's participants decide what they want to be.

A critical approach starts with the assumption that values are central to understanding organizational reality. The point is not that human nature is either good or bad, but that analyses of organizational life must not reify institutions as if they existed and changed free of ideological constraints. As Heydebrand notes, organizational reality is "a concrete process of historical emergence in which practical human activity continuously produces and reproduces the material, social, and cultural worlds in which we live" (Heydebrand, 1983, p. 308). In other words, organizational reality is a collection of historically produced social structures and patterns of behavior that operate in a dialectical fashion between individuals in the organization and the greater society. Although individuals make choices in organizations, they are not free to remake reality as they see fit; one does not simply decide to have a loose or tight identity. Underneath the surface of an organization's culture, an ideology is at work that both shapes and is shaped by the cultural actions of the participants.

What are we to make of the portrayals of Working Class State and Testimony State Colleges? How might we think about these institutions as they struggle to define themselves in the waning days of the twentieth century? From a rationalist perspective, several analyses logically follow the portrayals. Birnbaum has commented that state colleges "are often easier to define by what they are not [not research institutions, not liberal arts colleges, not community colleges], than by what they are, because they have lost whatever distinctiveness they once possessed" (Birnbaum, 1984, p. 9). One the one hand, Working Class State College fits this analysis. The institution has an unclear identity, it has few, if any, characteristics that distinguish it from other public institutions, and although over time it has grown, does not have any sense of historical destiny. As with similar institutions in other state systems, attempts have been made at self-definition, yet these distinguishing markers usually have done little to help in the constituents' understanding of the institution.

On the other hand, Burton Clark might point to Testimony State as a good example of a public institution that has attained a saga. The institution was created with a distinctive identity by a small group of people. The mission has created a unique niche for the college in the environment; in turn, the distinctiveness has defined how the organization's internal activities are carried out. Socialization about the way the institution operates is also quite important. Unlike Working Class, for example, new faculty at Testimony feel as if they know little when they arrive, and they need to be taught about the institutional ethos. Presumably, faculty and administrators rally around a common definition of what they do, and the institution evokes an intense loyalty on the part of all participants. Although Testimony is a relatively new college, the institution's mission has remained stable, and there is no indication that it will change.

Those who advocate an institution's ability to adapt to the demands of the marketplace will note with alarm the distinctive identity of Testimony State. Given the tightly defined mission of the institution and its commitment to institutional history, Testimony runs the risk of not being able to capitalize on opportunities that arise in the environment. Although Working Class State ostensibly has a mission that allows the participants of the college to seize different challenges that occur in their environment, the institution appears unwilling or unable to go out and actively pursue opportunities. Thus, both institutions will meet with criticism from an adaptivist's viewpoint; one institution's activities are too tightly defined by the mission, and the other institution is not pro-active in its stance toward the environment. Again, what drives adaptive analysis is a concern for institutional effectiveness.

To those who see well-defined identities as necessary, Testimony State is an effective institution, yet the institution may develop serious problems if the environmental demands change. For Working Class to be a more effective institution, one may conclude, it needs to create a clearer identity and a niche for itself in the environment.

A quite different analysis occurs from a critical perspective. Four questions guide the analysis: (1) How might we think about the organizational reality of the institution? (2) How do the participants perceive the institution's ideology? (3) How does the institution's ideology and culture enable the multi-vocality of the participants to be heard? and (4) How does the educational agenda of the institution foster a critical awareness?

In some respects, one might say that Working Class State's constituents—students, parents, faculty, and administrators—all perceive organizational reality from the same vantage point. Education is equated with the ability to get a job. Any sense that education's purpose is to empower its constituents other than in economic terms appears absent. Some will argue that, insofar as Working Class graduates have better paying jobs than they would have if they had not gone to college, we may conceive of their education as an empowering act. In this light, education as an economic avenue is the route to greater individual freedom and choice. One might also conclude that the organization's participants have a potpourri of choices. The chair of the accreditation team, for example, did not use previous mission statements as team members defined the future of the institution.

From a critical perspective, however, the participants at Working Class State seem unaware of how the ideology of the institution constrains and defines what they do. McLaren notes that ideology "can either distort or illuminate the nature of reality" (McLaren, 1989b, p. 188). As a state institution, Working Class offers a unitary view of reality that distorts an educational purpose geared toward social justice or moral empowerment. Parents want jobs for their children, and their sons and daughters want work when they graduate. The definition of work, however, gets placed within the confines of class. The point I emphasize here is that a critical view demands more of an educational institution than providing employment for students. A dialectical analysis affirms the starting point of those involved, but it also works to enable individuals to understand their relationship to what they are learning.

At Working Class State, a relationship with the community is virtually nonexistent. Although the institution offers continuing education classes and the like, a concerned involvement in the economic development of the town during a recession with high unemployment is not apparent. We might say that the mission of the institution fits a quite traditional mold of educational purpose—to socialize youth into the mainstream of society and to provide students with the requisite skills for employment.

A critical analysis also rejects grand narratives that homogenize individuals into a unitary group. The concern for the critical theorist is that a range of organizational discourse is absent at Working Class State. The ideological determinants of the state appear so strong that no alternative voices are heard. We are left with a singular discourse that shows little regard either for issues of moral empowerment or justice.

A comparison with Testimony State will aid in our understanding. The participants at Testimony acknowledge the relations of power that exist in the organizations, and they struggle to allow different voices to be heard. As in any culture, norms exist. For example, student–teacher interaction is stressed, and research publications are not rewarded. Lectures are disdained, since they run counter to the institutional ethos. "A successful teacher here," observed an administrator, "will not teach like he or she does at other institutions." A professor related, "There's a way to do things. I was treated as if I had never taught before." A new professor pointed out, "I have to keep telling myself not to lecture—'to seminar'—it's a verb here—that it is tied into the nature of this college."

The ideology of the institution permeates activities such as faculty hiring, teaching, and assessment, yet the college explicitly attracts people who oppose a hegemonic voice. In contrast to Working Class, Testimony State's participants desire on-going discussions about the mission. The participants frequently evaluate their practices against the ideology that they espouse.

Yet the participants deny that they speak with one voice. They acknowledge a variety of discourses that appears within their culture, and they seek to foster the full range of those voices. "We know what we're doing," concluded one individual, "and we will continue to tear it down so that things are exposed, so that our discussion is clear." Other faculty concurred that they do not want to maintain the status quo. If anything, the status quo at Testimony State implies perpetual change.

We arrive, then, with quite different analyses of Working Class State College and Testimony State College. The participants at Working Class State operate from a singular world view heavily influenced by the structures that work to maintain the status quo. The ideological constraints of the institution muffle discord, and yet the constituents perceive that they are free to choose, uninhibited by history, society, or alternative viewpoints. Curiously, Testimony State College's participants acknowledge the parameters of ideology and culture, yet they foster greater choice than at Working Class. Cultural norms pervade the institution, but different constituencies interpret those norms in different ways.

CONCLUSION

The premise of this chapter has been that questions concerning institutional purpose warrant deeper investigation than prevailing analytic tools prescribe. Such questions should not relate to institutional performance. Rather, these questions are *moral* concerns that pertain to institutional democracy. Rossides has commented how higher education policies do not operate in a moral vacuum. He states, "Policy making is always a political act combining knowledge and value judgments in terms of ultimate images of human nature, society and history" (Rossides, 1987, p. 428). The "images" of nature, society, and history that organizational participants create pertain to their understanding of reality, ideology, and culture.

As we have seen, even two similar kinds of institutions arrive at different interpretations of reality. They enact different cultural dramas because their ideologies radically differ. Although these two case studies highlight divergent interpretations of culture, I do not claim that one institutional ideology should supplant another. The problems of Working Class State will not be solved simply by mimicking what takes place at Testimony State. Indeed, a critical analysis of organizations is a call for divergence. Chantal Mouffe is helpful on this point:

> What we need is a hegemony of democratic values, and this requires a multiplication of democratic practices, institutionalizing them into ever more diverse social relations, so that a multiplicity of subject-positions can be formed through a democratic matrix. . . . A project of radical and plural democracy requires the existence of multiplicity, of plurality, and of conflict. (Mouffe, 1988, p. 41)

How institutions enact these "democratic practices" remains to be seen. In large part, one of the primary avenues for further research will be ethnographies that extend our awareness of how institutional participants engage in democratic practices. Our understanding of ideology in organizations also remains incomplete. We need a clearer analysis, for example, of what are positive and negative ideological moments. We need to have a clearer idea of how ideological change takes place and what occurs when cultural practices diverge from institutional ideologies. A discussion about "false consciousness" and the role of the researcher is also warranted (Rosaldo, 1989). Although the critical theorist rejects causal rules about how to bring about change, we also need a better understanding of how we enact critical action and pedagogy. In short, much work remains to be done that will reconstitute the purpose of postsecondary institutions, and advance our thinking about the nature of ideology and culture in organizations.

REFERENCES

Albert, S., & Whetten, D. (1985). Organizational identity. *Research in Organizational Behavior, 7*, 263–295.

Birnbaum, R. (1984). *State colleges: An unsettled quality.* Background paper prepared for the Study Group on the Condition of Excellence in American Higher Education. (ERIC Document Reproduction Service No. ED 246 826).

Burbules, N. (1986). A theory of power in education. *Educational Theory, 36*(2), 95–114.

Chait, R. (1979). Mission madness strikes our colleges. *The Chronicle of Higher Education, 18*(36), 36.

Clark, B. (1970). *The distinctive college.* Chicago: Aldine.

———. (1971). Belief and loyalty in college organization. *Journal of Higher Education, 42*(6), 499–520.

———. (1980). The making of an organizational saga. In H. Leavitt & L. Pondy (Eds.), *Readings in managerial psychology* (2nd ed.) (pp. 232–262). Chicago: University of Chicago Press.

———. (1983). *The higher education system: Academic organization in cross-national perspective.* Berkeley: University of California Press.

Davies, G. (1986). The importance of being general: Philosophy, politics, and institutional mission statements. In J. Smith (Ed.), *Higher education: Handbook of theory and research, Vol. II* (pp. 85–108). New York: Agathon Press.

Fay, B. (1987). *Critical social science: Liberation and its limits.* Ithaca, NY: Cornell University Press.

Foucault, M. (1980). *Power/knowledge.* New York: Pantheon.

Giroux, H. (1983). *Theory and resistance in education: A pedagogy for the opposition.* South Hadley, MA: Bergin Garvey.

Heydebrand, W. (1983). Organization and praxis. In G. Morgan (Ed.), *Beyond method* (pp. 306–320). Beverly Hills, CA: Sage.

Katz, M. (1987). *Reconstructing American education.* Cambridge, MA: Harvard University Press.

Mannheim, K. (1936). *Ideology and utopia.* New York: Harcourt, Brace and World.

Marx, K. (1970). *The German ideology.* New York: International Publishers.

McLaren, P. (1989a). *Life in schools.* New York: Longman.

———. (1989b). On ideology and education. In H. Giroux & P. McLaren (Eds.), *Critical pedagogy, the state and cultural struggle.* Albany, NY: SUNY Press.

Mouffe, C. (1988). Radical democracy: Modern or postmodern? In A. Ross (Ed.), *Universal abandon? The politics of postmodernism.* Minneapolis: University of Minnesota Press.

Rosaldo, R. (1989). *Culture and truth: The remaking of social analysis.* Boston: Beacon Press.

Rossides, D. (1987). Knee-jerk formalism. *Journal of Higher Education, 58*(4), 404–429.

Siegel, H. (1987). Rationality and ideology. *Educational Theory, 37*(2), 153–167.

Tierney, W. (1989). *Curricular landscapes, democratic vistas: Transformative leadership in higher education.* New York: Praeger.

4   THE "OFFICIAL" IDEOLOGY OF HIGHER EDUCATION: IRONIES AND INCONSISTENCIES

Sheila Slaughter

In this chapter, I examine the ironies and inconsistencies of "official" higher education ideology as articulated by presidents of research universities in the congressional testimony in the 1980s. I call their testimony "official" ideology because the belief system presented by the presidents is composed by committees, voiced by formal institutional representatives in their executive capacity, and created for consumption by the general public. I begin by placing the concept and theory of ideology generally in the social science literature, and specifically in the educational literature. I argue that ideology allows us to interrogate belief systems, enabling us to come to a better understanding of the ways in which ideas are used to legitimate structures of privilege and power and, often inadvertently, to mask inequities and injustices. I locate the ideology of higher education in a sample of testimony made by Association of American Universities (AAU) presidents before U.S. congressional committees between 1980 and 1985. I approach the texts of the presidents' testimony using a deconstructionist strategy that focuses on a close reading of representative texts.

Overall, the presidential texts revealed a remarkably consistent ideology—a body of beliefs held by presidents who guide research institutions—related to higher education. These beliefs were animated by a single, central metaphor—"human capital"—and two sets of secondary and related metaphors, one of which used the language of "competition," and the other of which used the language of "diversity" and "choice." The metaphors were rich in irony. Investment in human capital was promoted as highly egalitarian, available to all students, yet most schemes for increasing federal contributions to human capital formation seemed likely to benefit students from the middle and upper-middle class. The language of competition spoke to the importance of basic research in revitalizing the private sector's ability to engage global markets competitively, but presidents expected the monies to fuel their universities' roles in enhancing international competitiveness to come largely from the public sector. Diversity and choice, ostensibly words signifying independence from government support, actually were used to demand continued resource maintenance from the federal government.

IDEOLOGY, SOCIAL SCIENCE, AND EDUCATION

The dictionary definition of ideology is relatively straightforward. Ideology is a "body of doctrine, myth, belief, etc., that guides an individual, social movement, institution or large group." However, in American social science usage, since the Second World War, the concept has become laden with additional meanings. Mainstream social science has used the concept of ideology in several ways, all somewhat negatively. Ideology frequently was used, as was the case in political science, to describe the idea systems of adversarial nations, whose beliefs were usually construed as totalitarian (Ricci, 1984). Domestically, ideology was used to describe political belief systems—for example, conservative and liberal—which were often implicitly contrasted with more rational ways of knowing, such as science. Indeed, ideology was used positively in social science, particularly in sociology, primarily when its end was being celebrated. This treatment of ideology probably reached its *apogee* in Daniel Bell's *The End of Ideology* (1960). In Bell's work, and others like it, ideology was presented as embodying idea systems fraught with partisan passion, blinded by emotional commitments to particular values that prevented adherents from seeing the facts of a social problem or situation. The alternative to political ideology (and political democracy) was presented as technocracy, in which public decisions were based on knowledge generated by scientifically trained experts.

Ironically, social scientists who called for the end of ideology were unable to see that they proposed to replace ideology with an alternative belief system. This belief system enshrined the values of meritocracy, advanced education, and technocracy guided by value-free social science. According to this ideology, the best and the brightest students achieved the highest levels of education, where they were trained to discover the laws of human behavior through the collection of empirical data that could be statistically manipulated. Students who were able to comprehend and apply advanced knowledge were the rightful decision-makers for society.

We can see the ideological nature of this belief system by inspecting its assumptions, selectivity, contradictions, and self-interest. The proponents of this viewpoint equated social science with natural science, a highly questionable assumption (Kuhn, 1962). They overlooked empirical evidence that suggested that some very bright students were systematically excluded from higher education on the basis of race, class, or gender (Astin, 1985). They did not explore the contradictions of making expertise the cornerstone of policy in a democratic society. Moreover, they were blind to the ways in which they benefited by making ideology anathema. An ideology that denigrates all ideology and presents itself as above ideology, and therefore the only reliable vehicle for guiding public policy, grants social scientists and higher education, the institution that confers certificates of scientific competence, great power and privilege.

Mainstream American social scientists tend not to see their own ideological propensities, and have instead negatively invested ideology in a variety of "others"; ideology has not been a building block of mainstream social theory. Rather, mainstream social theorists tend to speak of belief systems in terms of mores and norms, images and symbols, ceremonies and rituals, and, more recently, myths and metaphors, using linguistic and semiotic analysis to inform an *a priori* conception of the social system as good, or at least acceptable, and amenable to incremental reform. The social system itself is rarely the subject of inquiry or criticism. The central question asked about belief systems is: How do they contribute to social integration or cohesion? Generally, everyone in the social system is assumed to share the ideas embodied in the various myths and metaphors; those who do not are usually referred to as deviations or outliers, language that puts them beyond the circle of belief. Owing to their focus on integration, mainstream social scientists have a difficult time adjusting their lenses to look at systemic conflict within a society (e.g., Platt and Parsons, 1973). Similarly, they pay little attention to the relationship between belief systems and power, because they assume broad consensus about social purposes and therefore do not look for ways in which some groups might try to enforce their idea systems on others. Given the concern of mainstream social scientists with the detail of symbols, images, and icons, they often cannot step back to take in the whole edifice of ideas that these embody and probably do not want to because they might end up with ideology (e.g., Meyer and Rowan, 1977, 1978).

In contrast to mainstream social scientists, critical theorists have made much of the concept of ideology. The first well-developed postwar American critique of the notion that social science was value-free arose in the 1960s, as part of what came to be called "the end of ideology debate" (Waxman, 1968). The critique emerged out of the political ferment of the era, stimulated by the perceived failure of New Deal/Cold War social policies. The limits of a positivist, empirical social science were elaborated in great detail, and alternatives were sought out. Scholars and students interested in ideology turned to the ideas of Marx, European critical theorists, often those of the Frankfurt school, neo-Marxists, and especially to Antonio Gramsci, who brought ideology and the state into the Marxian vocabulary as concepts "relatively" independent of class and economic power (Carnoy, 1984; Dunleavy and O'Leary, 1987).

Gramsci employed the concept of ideology broadly and dialectically, rooting it in actual conflict between classes in a variety of "state apparatuses," from welfare and educational bureaucracies to ministries of commerce and planning. The state was simultaneously a multi-faceted resource, an arena of class struggle over public policy, and an actor in its own right. On occasion, the working class could effectively control parts of the state apparatus (Gramsci, 1971).

The "new sociology of education" began to draw on Gramsci's work, elaborating the part played by ideology in a single state apparatus, schools. "Reproduction theory," as it came to be known, looked at the ways in which school knowledge maintained existing and inequitable power arrangements (Olson, 1981; Wexler, 1987). Reproductionists were especially interested in discovering how schools reproduced class, race, and gender relations. Generally, they were critical of prevailing interpretations of belief structures, and they focused on conflict rather than cohesion, on systemic patterns of social differentiations rather than integration, and on the relation of broad messages contained in school knowledge to these systemic differences rather than on specific symbols and images. Schools were viewed as the primary site of ideological reproduction. Ideology was seen as one of the key elements in reproducing and maintaining an unjust social system. Ideology masked inequities and caused members of the working, lower, or under class, as well as women and ethnic and racial minorities, to see their inferior positions in the social system as the result of personal and individual failure rather than systemic problems (Bourdieu and Passeron, 1977; Apple, 1979; Willis, 1981; Weis, 1985).

However, reproductionists have not done full justice to Gramsci's theorization of ideology. Reproductionists do not usually specify class relations, but use broad and rather uninformative designations, such as "dominant" or "subordinate" classes, a terminology that makes difficult the explication of the class content of ideology. They look less at class struggle and more at the inevitable imposition of teacher ideology, a proxy for dominant ideology, on children who lack class privilege. Although teacher–student interactions are frequently the focus of study, too much attention has probably been paid to groups of students who discernibly and aggressively act out their class stance. Until recently, reproductionists focused on class at the expense of race and gender. Although reproductionists speak of the state as mediating class relations, the only state apparatus they examine is the school, and its relations to civil society are rarely explored.

For all their faults, reproduction theorists are trying to answer the most significant questions about schools: why, despite consistent efforts at reform, do schools not provide the equal educational opportunity that we expect of them? Through concepts of class, race, and gender, they link the collective behavior of groups to inequities of power inside and outside the school. Through the notion of ideology, they make school knowledge problematic, challenging mainstream ideas of knowledge as technical competence or value-free mastery of skills. All in all, reproduction theory has greatly expanded our vision of schools.

By and large, reproduction theory has looked at primary and secondary schools, and has rarely been extended to postsecondary education, with the exception of a handful of community college studies, and one or two studies of four-year schools (e.g., Weis, 1985; Holland and Eisenhart, 1990). There are virtually no studies of research universities from a broad reproductionist viewpoint, although there are some excellent feminist studies that focus on the ideology of science and the reproduction of gender relations in postgraduate work (e.g., Rossiter, 1982; Keller, 1985). Rather than using a reproductionist framework, mainstream social scientists have looked at the passing of a culture of inquiry from one generation of scholars, scientists, and professionals to another as a problem of professional socialization (Hughes, 1958; Van Mannan, 1983). In so doing, they frequently overlook the ways in which the participants' class, race, gender, and relative positions of power shape advanced education, an omission that becomes more serious as graduate education comes closer to being a mass institution, as is the case with master's degrees in some professional schools.

In this study, I use some of the features of the reproductionist framework to initiate inquiry into the ideology of higher education. I try to move beyond the structural–functionalism and structuralism that is so often manifested by both mainstream and critical theorists to a more postmodern position. I take postmodernism to be characterized by a concern with the problem of the relationship of individual and group agency to social structure in a context that particularizes phenomena and resists all-encompassing theoretical constructs. Individuals are comprehended as complex and contradictory, agents not objects, while social structure is understood as fluid. Concern with the problem of the relations of agency to social structure is evidenced by attention to historicity, to processes of social construction of experience, to patterns of power, and to the ways in which ideology, conventions of scholarship, and language usage constrain patterns of thought and belief. In other words, I take a critical stance, but try to minimize the problems associated with reproductionism and structuralism.

METHODOLOGY

Since there has been virtually no critical explication of the ideology of higher education, I had to look for a starting point. I selected presidents of AAU institutions, because they were at the apex of the higher education system and deeply involved in the procurement of resources. I examined their testimony before Congress, because the federal government provides far and away the largest share of research monies, and research activity is the key indicator of institutional prestige (Wolfle, 1977; Smith and Karlesky, 1978; Jones, Lindzey, and Coggershall, 1982). I thought that presidents' congressional testimony would provide texts that lent themselves to analysis of ideals as well as providing information about the proposed deployment of resources, with the juxtaposition of ideals and resources opening a window through which to see if presidents' belief systems legitimated structures of privilege and power while masking inequities.

Obviously, there are a number of limitations to my data set. First, I treat only the legislative branch of government; it is not possible to see if presidents express other ideologies in different arenas. Second, I can say nothing about the way in which presidents arrived at the positions they present. The process of negotiation, the politics of writing testimony, the constraints imposed by attempting to craft arguments able to influence legislators, all of whom have agendas of their own—all this escapes the data set under consideration. Third, the format and intent of congressional

Table 1
All AAU Presidents' Testimony before the Congressional Committees
on Education: Education and Labor and Labor and Human Resources,
1980–1985

Presidents' Testimony Year	HOUSE OF REPRESENTATIVES Committee on Education and Labor	U.S. SENATE Committee on Labor and Human Resources
1980	1	1
1981	6	1
1982	5	0
1983	4	2
1984	6	0
1985	0	0
	22	4

testimony frequently compels presidents to justify requests for continued or increased monies. The very nature of the hearings, then, may markedly narrow the beliefs that presidents express.

However, the data set has a number of strengths. The data were provided by a sample of AAU presidents' testimony before two congressional committees in the years 1980–1985 (see Table 1).[1] Such testimony was usually not the effort of an individual president, but was produced by committees that included experts on higher education, institutional researchers, attorneys, and presidential staff persons, and was endorsed by the president. When speaking before Congress, the presidents presented themselves as official institutional spokespersons and frequently as representatives of the organized interests of national research associations such as the AAU, American Council on Education, and the National Association of Universities and Land Grant Colleges. The testimony probably does not adequately represent the beliefs about higher education of any one president.[2] The text was developed communally by members of the graduate education establishment at the local and national levels, and very likely is a minimum consensus on publicly appropriate beliefs about higher education, especially with regard to resource deployment. The testimony is valuable precisely because it reveals the public positions around which the group could organize: it is an "official ideology."

I employed a deconstructionist strategy of analysis that focused on meaning. On the one hand, messages and metaphors were examined for internal ironies and inconsistencies, a mode of analysis that juxtaposes values and ideals with the means of realizing them, permitting us to get a glimpse of the discrepancies that are likely to occur between articulated belief systems and actual practice. On the other hand, messages and metaphors were analyzed in terms of what they said about the relationship of the institutions and actors in the text to the wider society, broadening our understanding of the text by situating it socially. I looked for general patterns of meaning and argument (ideology) across 13 instances of testimony by 12 presidents (see Table 2).[3] I identified three ideological patterns. Within these patterns, I searched for ironies, inconsistencies, and duality of meaning. In this search, I concentrated on images, symbols, metaphors, and examples. I thought analysis of figures of speech would provide clues to the values embedded in the rational, scientistic discourse of the presidents. These ideological patterns and the figures of speech that illuminated them were then placed in broad historical and social context, drawing on earlier work I have done on higher education policy (Slaughter, 1990).

Table 2
Presidents Whose Testimony Was Analyzed in "Ideology of Graduate Education: Ironies and Inconsistencies"

Committee on Education and Labor

Bok, Derek—Harvard University	1982
Bowen, William—Princeton University	1982
Brademas, John—New York University	1984
Danforth, William—Washington University	1984
Friday, William—University of North Carolina at Chapel Hill	1982
Ikenberry, Stanley—University of Illinois	1981
Jordan, Bryce—The Pennsylvania State University	1984
Olson, James—University of Missouri	1981
Posvar, Wesley—University of Pittsburgh	1983
Rhodes, Frank—Cornell University	1984
Sovern, Michael—Columbia University	1982

Committee on Labor and Human Resources

Bok, Derek—Harvard University	1983
Hansen, Arthur G.—Purdue University	1981

IDEOLOGICAL PATTERNS

Deconstructionist analysis of the testimony revealed a consistent use of a euphemism—the substitution of the phrase higher education for what was in fact graduate education—and three ideological patterns: higher education as human capital, a belief held by *all* of the presidents; beliefs about educational opportunity; and beliefs about the federal role in education. I will briefly outline the use of the euphemism and these three ideological patterns, and then deconstruct them.

Graduate Education as Higher Education

The presidents uniformly saw themselves as spokespersons for graduate education, research, and science.[4] Except in the case of student financial aid, their testimony was almost exclusively about graduate education and research, and even in the case of financial aid, they gave their greatest attention to various forms of graduate student aid. This is partly an artifact of the testimony; presidents often said they would address the question of graduate education because other presidents had represented different sectors of higher education. However, the presidents saw graduate education and research as the central functions of higher education, and the needs of the national research system determined what they sought in the way of resources and new programs, despite the fact that most of them led institutions where graduate students were but a small fraction of the student body. For the AAU presidents, then, the ideology of higher education was primarily an ideology of graduate education.

Pattern #1: Graduate Education as Human Capital

Higher education as human capital was most clearly articulated by Michael Sovern (1982), president of Columbia University.

We are increasingly challenged by international competitors. . . . If we are to succeed in international economic competition, we must increase our productivity. The two principal means to this objective are improved technology and more highly skilled manpower [sic]. These in turn are the products of research and teaching, the central missions of higher education. One sure way to lose the international economic race is to invest too little in the human capital developing in our universities and in the basic research being conducted on our campuses.

Sovern's testimony was typical of all the presidents. He deplored the decline of America's position in the global economy. He isolated worker productivity as the key problem. He saw investment in human capital, combined with investment in sophisticated technology, as the only way to increase worker and professional productivity, reasserting U.S. dominance in world markets. Therefore, he came to the conclusion that heavy public investment in universities was imperative: "The state of our national economy is first on just about everyone's list of domestic concerns. Long-term improvement depends fundamentally on the quality of America's colleges and universities."

Pattern #2: Educational Opportunity

Many of the presidents were concerned with educational opportunity. Six spoke generally of access, and six stressed the need for merit at the graduate level. In the early years of testimony, presidents talked about providing aid for the poor (or poor and middle income students), and in later years, about "needy" students. Minority students were mentioned by three presidents, minority and women students by two.

Generally, presidents took the position that broad access and funding targeted on needy students were important at the undergraduate level, while merit was paramount at the graduate level. In the words of William Bowen (1982), president of Princeton:

Excellence in graduate education is essential to teaching, to research, and to scholarship of the highest quality. Unless we find ways to encourage . . . our very best candidates to pursue advanced training, we jeopardize the quality of our research effort and we fail to educate those who have the talent to become the leaders of the next generation in the sciences, in engineering, in international studies, and in all other fields.

Frank H. T. Rhodes (1984), president of Cornell, made the distinction between the kind of graduate education described by Bowen and undergraduate education: "It is important to recognize that the rationale for a Federal role in higher education, and the appropriate policies to implement it, are fundamentally different from those underlying Federal support for undergraduate education, which properly emphasize access and choice through need-based student aid." Of the nine presidents who addressed these questions, six made similar distinctions.

However, presidents also evidenced distress over the lack of minority students, and argued for increased efforts to recruit them. As Rhodes (1984) said, "Incentives have to be offered at a reasonable level to attract the best minority college graduates into careers in teaching and research.

The results [of minority recruitment] are discouraging and they are not improving."

With regard to educational opportunity, presidents generally supported access to higher education, regardless of race, gender, or economic status, but increasingly stressed merit when it came to graduate education. They deplored the lack of minority students in graduate programs and were willing to offer incentives to attract them.

Pattern #3: The Federal Role in Education

All of the presidents spoke about the financial obligations that the federal government had to graduate universities and graduate students. Six addressed the special role the federal government performed with regard to private institutions, and one gave testimony about appropriate federal policy with regard to public institutions. The role of the federal government was spelled out by William Bowen, president of Princeton:

I have tried to suggest a set of basic principles for thinking about the federal role in education . . . . That role, as I envision it, is a limited but extremely significant one, with special emphasis on four broad areas: (1) support of basic research; (2) support of graduate education; (3) encouragement of individual opportunity and diversity within the educational system; and (4) maintaining an environment that encourages private support of education and the decentralized exercises of responsibility for educational decisions.

At a minimum, presidents expected maintenance of the federal graduate loan program, and pushed for expansion of Pell Grants and work–study for the first year of graduate education. In 1984 and 1985, they began to make a case for augmenting the loan program with substantial numbers of fellowships and grants for which there would be a national competition. Even though the presidents were addressing education rather than research in their testimony, six spoke to the need for federal support for maintenance of laboratories, libraries, and research facilities.

When presidents talked about the need for federal funding, they spoke simultaneously about the importance of autonomy. The position of Stanley Ikenberry (1981), president of the University of Illinois, is typical: "The incursion in recent years of federal regulations, well-motivated but frequently inflexible and costly, has further eroded the capability of university research scholars to maintain productive work." Even as they asked for autonomy in spending federal money, they were adamant about the way federal money should flow. As James Olson (1981), president of the University of Missouri, said: "Research is a long-term process. It cannot be turned off and on, and still provide a dependable base for the scientific and technological well-being of this Nation."

Presidents of private universities spoke frequently about the importance of student "choice" of where to attend college as well as about institutional "diversity." In essence, this meant that private institutions, which are more costly than public ones, would, according to present formulas, continue to get a greater share of student aid monies than public institutions, particularly low-tuition public schools. Presidents of public as well as private research institutions seemed to support this position.

The rationale for federal augmentation of state support for students in public universities was only articulated once, perhaps because the presidents were testifying before the national legislature. In the words of Stanley Ikenberry (1981), public universities, "serv[ed] a high proportion of low income families . . . with a commitment to low tuition as subsidized by our State [Illinois]." The federal government was expected to enhance state contributions through continued support of low-cost student loans.

In sum, the ideology of higher education expressed by the AAU presidents before Congress revealed a belief in higher education as central to human capital formation. With regard to educational opportunity, the presidents stressed access for all students, regardless of race, gender, or economic status, at the undergraduate level, but emphasized the importance of talent at the graduate level, although they recognized the need to attract more of the best minority students. With regard to the federal role in higher education, the presidents were agreed that government should offer steady support for basic research, graduate education, student choice, and institutional diversity, all while respecting institutional autonomy.

HUMAN CAPITAL AS METAPHOR AND MYTH

Human capital is an economic theory, a metaphor, and a myth. The economic theory explains the relationship of education to economic productivity. The metaphor makes an analogy between physical capital and highly trained intellectual capability. As myth, human capital theory resonates with beliefs about capital formation held by powerful persons and institutions in the wider society, thereby legitimating resource flows to higher education. At the same time that theory, metaphor, and myth explain and illuminate, they focus our understanding on certain aspects of higher education, turning our attention away from alternatives, as does all ideology. Human capital narrows our vision so we see the economic value of higher education as primary, competition as endemic in both the intellectual world and the marketplace, and the individual as an economic person, acting to maximize his or her economic interest, even in the educational arena. Any understanding of higher education that emphasizes the joyful, spiritual, or social side of intellectual endeavor is moved to the periphery of our vision, as are fields such as the humanities, social science, and education, since these are not seen as contributing directly to economic productivity.

Although all the presidents used human capital as a metaphor that explained and justified the need for societal support of higher education, only Michael Sovern, quoted earlier, actually used the words "human capital." Instead, presidents used words and phrases like "investments . . . in advanced education;" "cutting the nation's investment in human talent could not only undercut gains . . . but [could] prove contrary to long-term economic recovery;" "development of the intellectual capacity of succeeding generations . . . represents this nation's greatest resource;" "it is important to reflect upon higher education as a powerful national asset [and] resource . . . [it is] truly the foundation of our economic and industrial strength and the key to our technical progress."[5] The metaphor of human capital undergirded all aspects of the presidents' official ideology of graduate education.

Readers with a skeptical turn of mind might look at the words and phrases used by the presidents to describe graduate education as investment in human capital and argue that the presidents were making whatever case was necessary to ensure adequate funding for their institutions. I think this is undoubtedly the case, although my intuition is that the presidents were not being manipulative. I see them as absolutely convinced that investment in higher education is investment in human capital formation, an investment essential to the national welfare. It is not their sincerity or lack thereof that is the point to be made about the uniformity of their arguments for human capital. The analytical point is that the human capital argument represents a recontextualizing of higher education ideology. In the 1950s, higher education ideology emphasized national security, as witnessed by the National Defense Education Act (Clowse, 1981). In the 1960s, higher education ideology stressed increasing access as well as meeting the needs of individual students, particularly needy or minority students, as indicated by the development of the Pell Grants and a host of supplemental programs designed to enhance students' personal and educational development (Slaughter, 1985). In the 1980s, the presidents mentioned national security as well as student access and development, but their emphasis was on human capital as the key to strengthening the national economy. Although the metaphors and arguments used by presidents may come from their sense of what will play well in Congress as well as from their hearts, their language endorses the changes in national politics that place global economic success above social welfare, legitimating a conservative domestic political agenda.[6]

The presidents usually used the term human capital to refer to the economic theory. As an economic theory, human capital provides the most widely subscribed to and respected explanation of the relationship of education to economic productivity. It is rooted in what is regarded as the most mature and quantitative of the social sciences, economics, and is highly empirically elaborated.

However, human capital is more than an economic theory. It is a metaphor that derives meaning from an unarticulated comparison between people and physical capital. The metaphor likens the education system to the economic system, resting on the premise that education heightens men's and women's abilities to contribute to the production of wealth in the same way that capitalist entrepreneurs transform raw materials into profit. The metaphor represents the educational system as sharing the functions and values of a capitalist economic system, although the ability to make money in a competitive market has little to do with the technical aspects of graduate education.

Metaphorically, human capital theory, as used by the presidents, emphasized unbridled competition, especially in the global marketplace. "The U.S. . . . has an enviable reputation for the quality of its graduate education. . . . But this reputation is both more recent and more fragile than many realize, having been built largely over the past 40 years"; "in the long term, we will not have a strong economy in America with weak universities and vacant laboratories"; "the consequence of our weakening equipment crisis is that American science will lose its leading status in a variety of fields. In some fields, we are struggling just to remain competitive: Germany, Japan and the Soviet Union are beginning to overtake us"; "the equipment being used in the top-ranked universities has a median age twice that of the instrumentation available to leading industrial research labs." The sense of competition invoked by the presidents is closer to the nineteenth-century usage, captured by Tennyson's "nature red in tooth and claw," than to President Bush's late twentieth-century promise of a "kinder and gentler" society.

As a metaphor, the language of human capital encompasses more than the market system, including as well properties and values broadly salient to capitalism—for example, private ownership of goods and individualism (see quotations of presidents, p. 71, above). These values are also incorporated into human capital as a theoretical construct, and may account for some of the conceptual and methodological problems acknowledged even by its mainstream critics. Private rates of return for higher education, which come out of human capital theory, measure economic gains only in terms of individual post-tax income, less the cost of one's education, over the course of one's career. Social rates of return reflect only the pretax marginal gains of college-educated individuals. These methods of calculation maximize the benefits that accrue to private individuals and greatly minimize the benefits to society (Leslie and Brinkman, 1988). Indeed, there is no method of calculating social rates of return other than through benefits to individuals. In a sense, metaphor shapes theory, distorting our methods of measurement and our understanding of the economic value of higher education.

By drawing on human capital as their central metaphor, the presidents ironically emphasized the economic value of higher education above the human. The irony occurred at several levels. At the literal level, they sought resources for mathematics, science, and engineering, which they saw as contributing to economic productivity, and rarely mentioned the social sciences or humanities in their funding requests.[7] Symbolically, the presidents did not dwell on the liberal aspects of advanced education. Although it is conceivable that the presidents might have thought it frivolous to stress the joyful and creative aspects of higher education in an era of increasing economic competition, certainly they could have made a case for enhancing the liberal aspect of education at all levels, building on the arguments of Reagan administration pundits such as William Bennett.

Human capital theory has a mythical as well as a metaphorical dimension, if myth is used in Meyer and Rowan's sense of rational myth (Meyer and Rowan, 1978). Human capital symbolically celebrates the shared functions and values of the educational and economic systems. Indeed, the functions and values—competition (meritocratic or entrepreneurial) and personal accumulation—are very difficult to separate, and together constitute a saga of individual success in capitalist society. This symbolic sharing of myths on the part of the educational and economic system is undoubtedly very important to legitimating the presidents' claims to public and private resources. However, even as they made claims on national resources, presidents, through the structure of their imagery, gave support to a highly competitive capitalism, immune from human intervention and ameliorative state action. Historically, "unfettered" capitalism has been a very conservative capitalism (Kolko, 1967). On the key issue of resources, then, the presidents aligned themselves officially and symbolically with the ascendancy of conservatism, arguing that resources could be legitimately claimed only if associated with building a competitive economy.

EDUCATIONAL OPPORTUNITY: ABILITY, MERIT, AND TALENT

When the presidents addressed the issue of who should receive higher education and who should go on to graduate education, they continued to rely heavily on the human capital metaphor. For example, presidents spoke about its being "in the national interest, in educating . . . developing them [students] for the productive contributions required in our economy," or about agreeing that "investment . . . made in the intellectual development of the youth . . . was deemed fundamentally essential to the economic development of the U.S., to the growth of industrial productivity . . . ," or about "graduate schools as representing the continuing base of the pyramid of national progress. It is . . . that small, but important supply of talented individuals with the knowledge and technical skill . . . who give us . . . every aspect of our national need."

All students were able to enter the race for advanced education. As several of the presidents noted, higher education created opportunity that allowed "individuals from all walks of life . . . to move up the ladder of accomplishment as far as their energies and abilities will take them." However, not all students would be able to climb as high as the pinnacle of advanced degrees; there was only "a thin stream of extremely talented" students (Rhodes, 1984). Graduate education was highly competitive, reserved for "talented" students whom the presidents described as "able," "skilled," "well-prepared," and possessed of "sophisticated knowledge and skills."

The language used to depict the selection of the "best young minds" harks back to the human capital metaphor, with competition for educational success likened to economic competition. At the turn of the century, higher education and the professions that led to advanced degrees became the central arena for proving individual prowess and reaping social rewards. Indeed, the meritocratic ideology embedded in higher education served much the same function as did Social Darwinist ideology: it justified individual rewards without attending to the social structures that supported or inhibited individual effort (Fine, 1969; Wiebe, 1967). According to meritocratic ideology, those with the greatest intellectual capacity enter into strenuous competition with their fellows, in which the winner is named the fittest, or the most meritorious, and, claiming a credential rather than the means of production, goes on to a long and prosperous life. All the elements of the Social Darwinist ideology are present: native ability, individualism, hard work, and severe testing through competition that selects the most able.

What is absent in discussions of meritocracy and in the presidents' testimony are considerations of class, race, gender, and resource monopolies. As industrial competition was subordinated to monopolistic organization in the economic sector to preserve upper-class privilege, so educational competition was contained by a certification system designed by emerging professionals as a means to provide the middle class with predictable social and economic rewards (Bledstein, 1976; Larson, 1977). Certification turned on skills and attitudes possessed in abundance by the middle class—cultural literacy, numeracy, perseverance, self-confidence, appropriate assertiveness, and socially acceptable manners—and not found as frequently among immigrants, the working class, or the working poor. Professional certification became and continues to be a way of organizing knowledge that reinforces prevailing patterns of privilege. The majority of African-Americans are not middle class and have not been able to compete educationally. Indeed, percentages of African-American students at the undergraduate level have diminished since 1978 (Astin, 1985), perhaps reflecting changes in the distribution of economic and social goods to black communities.

Like institutional leaders in other sectors of society, the presidents had inconsistent positions on minorities. On the one hand, their sense of social justice made them strong supporters of increasing the numbers of African-Americans, the only minority they mentioned specifically, at the graduate level. On the other hand, their commitment to quality graduate education in times of economic scarcity made them argue for concentrating resources on the most able students. The presidents "stress[ed] that academic merit is an important facet of graduate education and must be a stronger factor in the allocation of support for graduate students" (Rhodes, 1984). They blamed the demand problem with regard to African-American students on failures of the K–12 educational system and directed their efforts to solving the problem at the postsecondary level to raiding each other's pools of African-American students, while complaining that their support for federal aid to historically African-American colleges made the recruitment of these students to AAU universities more difficult. The presidents did not consider the possibility that notions of merit might be socially constructed, and change with the ebb and flow of supply and demand for students holding advanced degrees.

The irony of a higher education ideology that regards the university as an institution that allows students to reach the outer edges of their abilities and ambitions lies not in the presidents' intentions; rather, the irony is found in their proposals for funding graduate education. The presidents generally did not advocate increased numbers of grants and fellowships until 1984, and then only for the very "talented." Instead, they pushed for increasing the levels that individual students could borrow to $10,000 per year, and for extending the limits that families could borrow to those families whose income was more than $65,000 annually.[8] Given that minority students and women hesitate to borrow large sums, that they tend to take longer to complete their advanced education than other students, and that the number of minority headed families making over $65,000 per year is exceedingly small, their proposals, in practice, were unlikely to increase access, and more likely to benefit white males from upper-middle-class homes.

THE FEDERAL ROLE IN HIGHER EDUCATION

Competition, Decay, and Collapse

The imagery used by the presidents in discussing the federal role in higher education is closely related to the language of human capital, but distinct enough to be considered in its own right. The language that characterized presidential requests for federal funding drew primarily on the imagery of competition. In essence, the presidents argued that international economic and scientific competitiveness had increased dramatically, yet universities were unable to foster competition because they were declining on a number of fronts, and therefore America's ability to emerge the victor in global economic struggles was seriously harmed. Competition provided the major chord, the decline and decay of research institutions, the minor. (Instances of presidents' use of this language are provided above, in the section on human capital, p. 72.)

The language of decline, decay, and collapse is probably a part of the rhetoric of crisis used by all public-sector institutions in approaching the state for funding. As myriad social service agencies mature and are able to exert their demands more skillfully, higher education becomes one of many claimants to public monies, and falls back on a generic rhetoric of crisis characteristic of public life. The intensity of this language may vary in relation to the dependence of the institution on public monies. Over the past two decades, higher education, especially research universities, have become increasingly dependent on public monies. "Big science" is now manifest on most AAU campuses in one form or another. The monies required merely for maintenance are enormous. The possibility of lack of increases in funding, let alone threats of withdrawal, ignites the fires of crisis.

Ironically, higher education has traditionally refused to define itself as a public institution. Instead, it has claimed special privileges by virtue of its distinctive function. Proponents of this ideology argue that the higher learning is answerable only to the laws and conventions of science and scholarship, not to partisan politics, administrative regulations, or even the courts. The word usually used to signify this difference is "autonomy" (Berdahl, 1975). Higher education, presidents and scholars have insisted, should have autonomy from the state that supports it. Autonomy is important for private as well as public institutions, since private universities, especially research universities, have become almost as dependent on state monies as public ones. Federal and state dollars now constitute close to half of the annual operating budgets for private institutions (McCoy and Halstead, 1984).

Despite aligning themselves ideologically with the private sector by claiming autonomy from the state, the presidents did not see the private sector as the key to resolving their financial difficulties. Instead, they continued to see the federal government as the primary source of funds for research because of the centrality of basic research. John Brademas (1984), president of New York University, captures this sentiment nicely:

Although financing graduate education is not the sole responsibility of any one sector of our society, it is the special obligation of the federal government to ensure stable and continuing support of graduate research. In the words of Simon Ramo of TRW, Inc., Chairman of President Reagan's Transition Task Force on Science and Technology, "The government, and no competitive industry, is the proper and natural source for funding university basic research. Because it benefits all citizens in the end, it is right for all citizens to share its costs."

There is an inconsistency in absolving the private sector of support for basic research. The rationale is that research benefits everyone, not just individuals in the private sector. However, in the short term, it is highly unlikely that the benefits of basic research are shared equally by all citizens. Although research may well benefit humanity as a whole in the long term, defined as generations, in the short term, defined as the lifetime of an individual, people like Simon Ramo are more likely to benefit than, say, a grape-worker or an auto-worker. As demonstrated by the recent court case against the agricultural research program at the University of California at Davis, small growers benefited while the grape-workers, originators of the suit, were severed from it in the interest of settlement. Even with regard to more generic benefits, such as those that stem from medical research, prosperous citizens are more likely to benefit than working-class citizens, given the increasing likelihood that the average worker will not have full medical insurance coverage.

In sum, the presidents justify their claims for federal support of graduate education by stressing the role that higher education plays in human capital formation, thereby enhancing the United States' ability to compete in global markets. They apparently see no irony in calling for increased public subvention to foster private-sector economic viability. Perhaps they are blind to this irony because of their belief that research, like private-sector economic success, ultimately redounds to the benefit of the society as a whole. In any event, their long-range vision does not allow them to see a foreground where the results of research, like the results of economic competition, are able to cause social dislocation and unemployment as well as personal pain and suffering.

Diversity, Choice, and Quality

Presidents of private and public institutions advocated using federal monies to support institutional choice and diversity, in effect increasing the share of public monies received by private institutions. At first glance, this position seems to work against the rational economic interests of presidents of public universities. However, selective graduate research institutions in the public sector probably share more common interests with similarly positioned private institutions than they do with other institutions in the public sector.

All but one of the six presidents who headed private or quasi-private institutions spoke about the special obligation of the federal government to maintain "diversity" and "choice." Two of the public-sector presidents endorsed the claims of the privates, and none contradicted them.

The meaning of these words can perhaps be better understood in context. William Bowen (1982) said of choice and diversity:

The federal investment in educational opportunity has enabled millions of lower and middle income citizens to exercise some choice in selecting those institutions best suited to their particular talents and aspirations. One of the special strengths of our American system of higher education is the diversity of institutions available to students. Just as important is diversity of students within individual institutions. The federal programs now in place make it possible for individuals from different backgrounds, with different perspectives, to learn together and from each other.

William Danforth (1984) of Washington University said:

The gap between tuitions charged by the public sector and the independent sector has widened over the last decade or so. We, of course, don't ever expect the gap to be filled by financial aid, but the [federal] programs have achieved a balance that helps not only insure access but to meet . . . differing institutional requirements and maintain some choice.

The presidents of private universities argued that their institutions offered choice and diversity, but were unclear about what those words meant, other than that private institutions were somehow different from public ones. It is unlikely that the presidents meant that choice was offered at the level of program. At the graduate level, at AAU institutions, programs are more likely to be defined by discipline than by institutional qualities. In other words, all physics programs, regardless of whether they are at private or public research institutions, are likely to be more similar than dissimilar, enabling students and faculty to participate in problems and debates germane to the field, not the institution. Perhaps the presidents meant that private institutions were better than public ones in terms of quality or excellence. However, most rating schemes show roughly equal numbers of departments at private and public universities ranked in the top 20 (Jones, Lindzey, and Coggershall, 1982). At the graduate level, at AAU universities, selection criteria between private and public universities are probably not too different. Even private funding cannot constitute the difference between public and private institutions. Public research institutions are generating large private endowments that are now beginning to rival those of private ones.

Although there does not seem to be many differences between AAU institutions at the graduate level with regard to program, quality, or funding source, presidents of independent institutions spoke about the "choice" and "diversity" offered by their schools. When the phrases are considered in the context of the claims these presidents made for special financial treatment, "choice" and "diversity," deconstructed, can be seen as a metaphor for the privilege traditionally accorded to the private sector in a capitalist society (Slaughter, 1990). "Diversity" and "choice" as metaphor for the privilege of the private sector become clearer if we think of them in terms of the human capital metaphor. The human capital metaphor, like the capitalist economic system, venerates whatever is labeled private, even if that activity includes a great deal of public support. Human capital theory emphasizes the economic gains of higher education to individuals in their capacity as private citizens, and has no measurement for social costs and benefits. So too independent institutions claim to provide diversity and choice, attributes associated with the private sector, thereby including themselves among the privileged and ignoring the large public subsidy they receive. In so doing, they render themselves eligible for larger student aid packages, but remain free from a variety of laws and regulations that apply to the public sector. At the same time, they are able to draw on most of the benefits that accrue to the public sector, such as tax-exempt status, dormitory loans, bonding powers, development grants, research monies, and the like.

The irony of this view of independent higher education is obvious and simply stated. Presidents of private institutions who emphasize the independence of their schools from government nonetheless seek to have the federal government pay a high proportion of their costs. In the same instance of testimony, Michael Sovern (1982) could celebrate the private sector:

From George Washington and Thomas Jefferson to Jimmy Carter and Ronald Reagan, America's leaders have called for more private initiative, more private responsibility and less government involvement in the affairs of the citizenry. America's independent colleges and universities have been listening . . .

and demand that federal funding of undergraduate education at private institutions be continued:

Choice and diversity are part of the imagery that contribute to our understanding of private as a metaphor for privilege, both in higher education and the wider society. The language masks the crucial contribution of the state to most central social institutions, whether in the economic or educational sector, whether the institutions are public or private. By focusing so intently on the difference between private and public, we do not see clearly the differences between institutions within each sector, and the many inequities that occur with regard to funding and opportunity. Because federal programs are constructed to provide choice and diversity for the few poor students able to meet private institutions' criterion of selectivity, we more easily overlook the fact that the majority of poor and minority students, perhaps most deserving of educational attention and resources if we are serious about equal educational opportunity, attend low cost, under-resourced community colleges from which they will probably drop out.

Certain public institutions, such as highly selective research universities, uphold the private-sector universities' claim to special privilege, because they see themselves as sharing their elite status. Indeed, the most prestigious public research universities claim honorary membership in the private sector through a number of mechanisms: constitutional autonomy, separation from other institutions in state postsecondary systems, designation as flagship institutions, special fee and funding formulas for graduate status, and the like. They, too, seek the privileges that are associated with the label private.

CONCLUSION

The AAU presidents' official ideology of higher education as expressed before Congress presented beliefs that suggested: graduate education was the most important component of higher education; higher education was central to human capital formation; equal opportunity was appropriate at the undergraduate level, merit at the graduate; federal support for basic research, graduate education, student choice, and institutional diversity should have been continued and accompanied by respect for institutional autonomy. In the abstract form, this ideology is easy to support. However, when put in social and historical context, and considered in light of resource allocations, a number of questions arise about the benefits this ideology offers to all members of the postsecondary community. Human capital, whether considered as ideology, economic theory, or metaphor, commits graduate education to supporting a strategy of economic development that places U.S.-based multinationals first on the agenda, and says little about the development of local and regional economies that support specific universities. Emphasis on economic productivity as the paramount good causes the presidents to stress the sciences and engineering at the expense of humanities and social sciences. When equal opportunity is subjected to the discipline of human capital formation, the number of students supported at the graduate level is sharply constricted, and, inadvertently, the number of minority students is decreased. The private sector is venerated, whether in the economy or in higher education, but presidents fail to see that the private sector cannot sustain itself without large infusions of public money. Viewed from a deconstructionist lens, the graduate education ideology presented by the presidents seems to serve institutional self-interest rather than public interest.

NOTES

1. The ideology shared by research university presidents was located in their testimony before two congressional committees in the years

1980–1985. Presidents of research universities were taken to be the presidents of all AAU institutions during the years under scrutiny. The presidents were identified through standard higher education directories, and their testimony before Congress through the Congressional Index Service. The congressional committees were those primarily responsible for higher education: Education and Labor, particularly the Subcommittee on Postsecondary Education, in the House of Representatives, and Labor and Human Resources in the Senate. From all AAU presidents' testimony before these committees (see Table 1), I randomly selected half, in proportion to the number of times the presidents testified, for further examination. For years, names of presidents, and committees before which they testified, see Table 2.

2. When presidents' beliefs, as expressed in testimony, are cross-checked with their public positions as evidenced in books and articles, they seem quite similar. See for example, Derek Bok, *Beyond the Ivory Tower: Social Responsibilities of the Modern University* (Cambridge: Harvard University Press, 1982); Paul E. Gray's comments in "New President is Chosen at MIT: He Warns of U.S. Technology Lag," *New York Times*, 6 October 1980; Sheldon Hackney, "Prologue," in Thomas W. Langfitt et al., *Partners in the Research Enterprise: University–Corporate Relations in Science and Technology* (Philadelphia: University of Pennsylvania Press, 1983), pp. xi–xv.

3. The 13 texts were coded for: (A) any statement dealing with societal rationales for higher education; (B) any statement dealing with the value of higher education; (C) any statement dealing with the relation of higher education to society; (D) any statement about who should get what educational benefits or services, and (E) any statements about how to realize, in programmatic, monetary, or legislative terms, the material coded in points A–D. The coding units for points A–D were paragraphs. Categories A–D are not exclusive; they both overlap and are conflated: essentially they code different facets of the societal value of higher education. All the sentences in any one paragraph that contained statements pertaining to categories A–D were entered into the computer. Category E, statements about the realization of higher education values, was coded separately. This category was not coded in sentences or paragraphs, but as economically as possible, recording only enough information to see if resources were commensurate with the emphasis placed on specific values.

4. Quantitative analysis of the text using the computer program GRAMMATIK indicated that research, graduate education, and science were the most frequently used words in the presidents' vocabularies.

5. These quotations represent all of the presidents, and were developed around the category of "human capital" rather than through focused analysis of an individual president's testimony; therefore, individuals are not cited. This technique was used whenever there were a number of quotes that illuminated a particular category.

6. The presidents' testimony, of course, says nothing about whether or not the ideology they voiced actually had any impact on specific campuses. The impact of presidential ideology calls for another study.

7. Three presidents mentioned the social sciences; no one spoke to the humanities.

8. These positions and amounts of money are taken from the presidents' testimony on implementation of their positions.

REFERENCES

Apple, Michael W. (1979). *Ideology and curriculum*. London: Routledge & Kegan Paul.

Astin, Alexander. (1985). Selectivity and equity in the public research university. In Leslie W. Koepplin & David A. Wilson (Eds.), *The future of state universities* (pp. 67–83). New York: Rutgers University Press.

Bell, Daniel. (1960). *The end of ideology*. Glencoe, IL: Free Press.

Berdahl, Robert O. (1975). *Statewide coordination of higher education*. Washington, DC: American Council on Education.

Bledstein, Burton J. (1976). *The culture of professionalism*. New York: Norton.

Bourdieu, Pierre, & Passeron, Jean-Claude. (1977). *Reproduction in education, society and culture*. Beverly Hills, CA: Sage.

Bowen, William. (1982). Testimony before Committee on Education and Labor, Subcommittee on Postsecondary Education, U.S. Congress, House of Representatives, *Impact of administration's proposed fiscal year 1983 budget on student financial aid and higher education programs*, 97th Congress, 2nd Session, March 22: 151–163.

Brademas, John. (1984). Testimony before Congress, Committee on Education and Labor, Subcommittee on Postsecondary Education, *Hearings on the reauthorization of the Higher Education Act*, U.S. House of Representatives, 98th Congress, 2nd Session, Spring: 275–281.

Carnoy, Martin. (1984). *The state and political theory*. Princeton, NJ: Princeton University Press.

Clowse, Barbara. (1981). *Brainpower for the Cold War: The Sputnik crisis and the National Defense Education Act of 1958*. Westport, CT: Greenwood.

Danforth, William. (1984). Testimony before Congress, Committee on Education and Labor, Subcommittee on Postsecondary Education, U.S. Congress, House of Representatives, *Hearings on the reauthorization of the Higher Education Act*, 98th Congress, 2nd Session, Spring: 294–299.

Dunleavy, Patrick, & O'Leary, Brendan. (1987). *Theories of the state: The politics of liberal democracy*. New York: Meredith Press.

Fine, Sidney. (1969). *Laissez-faire and the general-welfare state*. Ann Arbor: University of Michigan Press.

Gramsci, Antonio. (1971). *Selections from the prison notebooks of Antonio Gramsci*. Quintin Hoare & Geoffrey Nowell Smith (Eds. and Trans.). New York: International Publishers.

Holland, Dorothy, & Eisenhart, Margaret. (1990). *Schooling, romance and resistance: University women and the gender status quo*. Chicago: University of Chicago Press.

Hughes, Everett C. (1958). *Men and their work*. Glencoe, IL: Free Press.

Ikenberry, Stanley. (1981). Testimony before the Committee on Education and Labor, Subcommittee on Postsecondary Education, U.S. Congress, House of Representatives, *Hearings on oversight of the higher education budget*, 97th Congress, 1st session, February 24: 219–236.

Jones, Lyle V., Lindzey, Gardner, & Coggershall, Porter E. (Eds.). (1982). *An assessment of research-doctorate programs in the United States* (5 Vol.): *Biological sciences; engineering; humanities; mathematical and physical sciences; social and behavioral sciences*. Washington, DC: National Academy Press.

Keller, Evelyn Fox. (1985). *Reflections on gender and science*. New Haven, CT: Yale University Press.

Kolko, Gabriel. (1967). *The triumph of conservatism: A reinterpretation of American history*. Chicago, IL: Quadrangle.

Kuhn, Thomas. (1962). *The structure of scientific revolutions*. Chicago: University of Chicago Press.

Larson, Magali Sarfetti. (1977). *The culture of professionalism: A sociological analysis*. Berkeley: University of California Press.

Leslie, Larry L., & Brinkman, Paul. (1988). *The economic value of higher education*. New York: Macmillan.

McCoy, Marilyn, & Halstead, D. Kent. (1984). *Higher education in the fifty states: Interstate comparisons fiscal year 1982*. (4th ed.). Washington, DC: USGPO.

Meyer, John W., & Rowan, Brian. (1977). Institutionalized organizations: Formal structure as myth and ceremony, *American Journal of Sociology, 83*, 340–362.

———. (1978). The structure of educational organizations. In Marshall W. Meyer and Associates (Eds.), *Environments and organizations* (pp. 98–109). San Francisco: Jossey-Bass.

Olson, James. (1981). Testimony before Committee on Education and Labor, Subcommittee on Postsecondary Education. In U.S. Congress, House of Representatives, *Hearings on oversight of student financial aid programs*, 97th Congress, 1st Session, October 15: 27–38.

Olson, Paul. (1981). Rethinking social reproduction, *Interchange, 12*(2 and 3).

Platt, Gerald N., & Parsons, Talcott. (1973). *The American university*. Cambridge, MA: Harvard University Press.

Rhodes, Frank H. T. (1984). Testimony before the Committee on Education and Labor, Subcommittee on Postsecondary Education. In U.S. Congress, House of Representatives, *Hearings on the reauthorization of the Higher Education Act*, 98th Congress, 2nd Session, Spring: 458–465.

Ricci, David M. (1984). *The tragedy of political science: Politics, scholarship and democracy*. New Haven, CT: Yale University Press.

Rossiter, Margaret. (1982). *Women scientists in America*. Baltimore: Johns Hopkins University Press.

Slaughter, Sheila. (1985). From serving students to serving the economy: Changing expectations of faculty role performance, *Higher Education, 14*, 41–56.

———. (1990). *The higher learning and high technology: Dynamics of higher education policy formation*. Albany, NY: State University of New York Press.

Smith, Bruce L. R., & Karlesky, Joseph K. (Eds.). (1978). *The state of academic science: Background papers*. New Rochelle, NY: Change Magazine Press.

Sovern, Michael. (1982). Testimony before Committee on Education and Labor, Subcommittee on Postsecondary Education. In U.S. Congress, House of Representatives, *Impact on administration's proposed fiscal year 1983 budget on student financial aid and higher education programs*, 97th Congress, 2nd Session: 496–502.

Van Mannan, John. (1983). Golden passports: Managerial socialization and graduate education. *The Review of Higher Education, Summer*, 435–455.

Waxman, Chaim I. (Ed.) (1968). *The end of ideology debate*. New York: Funk and Wagnalls.

Weis, Lois. (1985). *Between two worlds: Black students in an urban community college*. Boston: Routledge & Kegan Paul.

Wexler, Philip. (1987). *Social analysis of education: After the new sociology*. New York: Routledge & Kegan Paul.

Wiebe, Robert H. (1967). *Search for order: 1877–1920*. New York: Hill and Wang.

Willis, Paul. (1981). *Learning to labor: How working class kids get working class jobs*. New York: Columbia University Press.

Wolfle, Dael. (1977). *Science and public policy*. Lincoln: University of Nebraska Press.

5 THE RESEARCH IMPERATIVE

Patricia J. Gumport

By way of a case study of the social relations of knowledge production, I examine how universities embrace the research imperative as a vehicle for upward mobility in the national hierarchy of academic institutions. In the first section of the analysis, I focus on the organizational consequences of this kind of institutional ambition for changing the nature of faculty relations and changing the nature of graduate education. In the second section, I address the implications of these changes for the higher education system and the academic profession, implications that entail hidden costs in the promise of the research imperative.

The point of departure for this analysis is grounded in three concepts developed by critical theorists. The first is to contextualize the concept of organization. Rather than seeing the organization as a functional unit based on economic rationality and ideological consensus (Reed, 1985, p. 73), the organization is seen as a political instrument structurally embedded within wider societal dynamics of class power and economic priorities. Analysis of organizational change then moves beyond mere rearrangements of formal structure to include scrutiny of changing social conditions that are played out in campus contexts.

The second is the concept of contradiction, which provides a means to explain structural change as arising out of opposing forces, rather than out of a centrally controlled, or linear, determinism (Reed, 1985, p. 78; Benson, 1977, p. 4). Simply stated, the idea is that contradictions may arise among causes or consequences, thereby inhibiting, if not ultimately thwarting, planned change.

The third concept is transformative purpose, wherein one aim of organizational analysis is to "undermine [a] sense of inevitability" (Benson, 1977, p. 6) and "to induce greater self-reflection" (Reed, 1985, p. 81). This concept hinges on the premise that, as people become conscious that the organization has been reified "as a determinate thing standing over" them, they will reconstruct the present order (Benson, 1977, p. 16).

These three conceptual premises anchor the analysis in a critical framework that sensitizes us to cultural dynamics in the working lives of organizational participants and that infuses some skepticism into the trajectory of institutional ambition.

ON THE MOVE UNIVERSITY

Twenty years ago this was a mediocre university. Many people hired then wouldn't stand a snowball's chance now. . . .

Former associate dean

Indeed, the rules have changed for faculty at a public university. Initially a land-grant institution with a threefold mission of teaching, research, and public service, the campus has achieved a reputation as one of the country's leading research universities. Over the past 20 years, members of the central administration explicitly shifted the campus priorities. Research, especially in the sciences, has been asserted as the organization's primary *raison d'être*, for it is perceived as the organizational lever to "success" in gaining a reputation for "excellence" in the competitive, national system.

According to interviews[1] with faculty, administrators, and students, who have been friends and foes alike, the campus has risen from "a mediocre university" to "a research-compulsive institution" in the past 20 years. Campus leaders have embraced the research imperative by internalizing a competitive ethos first and foremost to obtain greater amounts of federally sponsored research. To enhance that likelihood, administrators and like-minded department chairs have directed resources to hire "star faculty," to establish nationally visible science facilities, and to upgrade graduate programs in the sciences—all of which were intended to be mutually reinforcing in the drive for upward mobility.

The university has been "on the move." The campus boosted its rank to within the top 30 universities in sponsored research activity, receiving over

$125 million in external research funds, up from $60 million five years ago and from $40 million ten years ago (in constant dollars). This dramatic change has been well-publicized throughout the campus, not only in the campus newspapers, but displayed visually in lobbies of the library, the administration building, and the student union.

The sources of sponsored research funds have followed a pattern similar to other universities, with three-quarters of the sponsored research dollars coming from the federal government and over 50 percent coming from one agency, Health and Human Services. Other agencies funding campus research were the National Science Foundation (about one-sixth) and the rest from the Department of Defense, the National Aeronautics and Space Administration, and the Department of Agriculture. Since a large proportion of the federally sponsored and industry-sponsored research has been located in the biological sciences, some overhead from research projects has been allocated for construction of five new science buildings, two of those entirely for interdisciplinary science programs.

Even though the campus has achieved upward mobility, "the drive is still on" and the university is "still climbing," according to current administrators. Warning against complacency, a vice-provost asserted in a speech to the campus community, "Even if we make the top ten in research dollars, that doesn't mean we've achieved the upper echelon. . . ." In addition to obtaining sponsored research funds, he explained, the campus must make efforts on several fronts, including high-quality graduate programs and an up-to-date physical infrastructure. On the latter point, he added:

We need to create the kind of environment where people can carry out leading-edge research. The capital program is in place and will address many of the facilities problems. However at today's level of technology, research needs [to be] changed quickly. In order for us to stay competitive nationally, it is important for us to be able to respond quickly, to provide services from electrical outlets to installation of million dollar machines.

The momentum for national research prominence at On the Move University was consistently expressed with an urgency to keep up and to get ahead, a campus climate that is common in this era where research university leaders know that to do nothing is to fall behind and to be perceived as excellent requires being forward-looking.[2] The office of sponsored projects has been moved adjacent to the office of the dean for research and graduate education. One administrator suggested that the relocation symbolized the organizational strategy for transforming the university into a modern research complex.

Acting as coaches and cheerleaders, members of the central administration talked at length about their efforts and relative successes thus far in rallying the collective momentum of the campus. Yet, based on over 40 interviews with former administrators, current faculty, and graduate students across the disciplines, I propose that this process has been less than a collective enterprise and more a "facade of unity," as one humanities faculty member of 20 years suggested. The process has resulted in a markedly split faculty and an uneven graduate program. The change entailed differentiating among campus constituents, weeding out those who would enhance the forward drive in sponsored research from those who would be less productive by that criterion and thus less of an asset.

According to current administrators, the strategy since the 1970s has been to lead with their strength and expand from there. As the vice-provost explained: "We couldn't afford to develop everything at once so we picked a few things as priorities, mostly applied sciences." The strategy has two major components, in order of importance: hiring "star faculty" and upgrading graduate programs, mostly in the sciences. As administrators have sought to accomplish these twin aims, the enactment of them both—changing the criteria for faculty hiring and for graduate education—has entailed hidden costs in the internal dynamics of campus life. I examine them separately, even though the two are interdependent in the social relations of knowledge production.

Faculty Relations

Reorienting faculty hiring criteria to obtain "star faculty" who exemplify the research imperative has profoundly changed the campus, most importantly replacing a single faculty with a two-tier system. Although informal, the arrangement has had visible, material consequences in the daily lives of faculty with a wide gulf between the "haves" and the "have-nots." The differences included office/lab space, research resources, and teaching loads, as well as varying senses of efficacy versus alienation within the campus community.

The biggest change in faculty hiring occurred as a shift from the "zoo model" to the "star system." Before the 1970s, when a vacancy occurred, a department generally found a replacement of the same specialty to insure field coverage, with the rationale that, if a lion dies, you find another lion. Since the 1970s, the strategy was to find an exotic "beast," usually in the prime of academic life, perceived to have talent, distinctiveness, or simply success in drawing sponsored research grants. Hiring the star usually required discretionary funds from the central administration. Such funds were used to supplement the salary offer, to provide start-up research funds, to reduce teaching loads, to subsidize travel, or to provide fellowship support to attract graduate students that faculty deemed were of the highest quality.

Over the past 15 years of hiring star faculty, departments no longer covered all specialty areas, and many came to consist of clusters of research-minded faculty in emerging (especially interdisciplinary) fields. As justification, current department chairs expressed that, more than any other resource, they wanted more faculty billets to develop distinctiveness. A department at On the Move University, the chairs reported, cannot move into the top ten nationally, so it has to gain national visibility by being different. As one chair aspiring for his department to be in the nation's top 20 said, "The strategy . . . isn't to imitate the top departments, but to do something different." This strategy has worked in the life sciences more than in other departments, since reorganization of the sciences essentially created new departments, such as molecular and cellular biology.

The strategy has worked less well in most other departments, which are marked by a clear and enduring, internal division between two cohorts of faculty: those hired before 1970 and those hired after. Within and across departments, the two tiers of faculty have also been evident. Those hired before 1970, who have been seen by current administrators and new faculty as an obstacle rather than as an asset to the campus's upward mobility, and those hired since who have a primary orientation to research, especially sponsored research.

The differentiation of the two groups has been marked by labels such as, on the one hand, the "old guard," "the old and rusty," and, on the other hand, the "stars," the "hard hitters," the "younger faculty with a research orientation." An underlying pejorative attitude is made explicit since those in the older group have been referred to as "deadwood," a label many of them seem to internalize regardless of whether they spend their time engaged in teaching undergraduates rather than doing research or publishing.[3]

Since departments on this campus range in size from 30 to 60 faculty members, the nonstar faculty in larger departments have kept low profiles. This option is less of a possibility in smaller departments, as one chair at another (more elite) university reflected:

Our department is so small. We only have twenty faculty and each is precious. You can't have deadwood here. If you turned into deadwood you'd stick out like a sore thumb, plus self-pride keeps you going to do your best. . . . We do have some—a few—deadwood who are older, but the bottom floor is higher than other places, so we don't really have faculty who have gone to pasture or are just poking along.

At On the Move University, younger faculty have been considered more of an asset in the drive for upward mobility, which has entailed getting sponsored research and training research-oriented doctoral students. Younger faculty want to establish a track record, so "their research agenda is at the forefront," explained a science department chair.

Some faculty, usually scientists, have considered that this research orientation of the young stars enhances graduate education: "These faculty go out of their way to get external sponsored research funds. You can pick out the good faculty by their attitude toward research and toward graduate students. The good researchers are the good teachers." Other faculty, usually humanists and self-identified deadwood science faculty, offered the opposite opinion about the "young stars": "They are more interested in fulfilling the responsibility of their research projects than the educational experiences of the students. Superstar faculty will not bring quality graduate education."

If "voting with their feet" is any indication, as a department chair suggested, graduate students themselves reflected different opinions. A self-identified savvy doctoral student explained, "You're either a scientist or an ex-scientist. And if you're a scientist you get funding. We depend on the scientists who are driven to do research, so I have nothing to worry about." Curiously, other doctoral students, deemed by department chairs as not-so-savvy, sometimes have sought to work with deadwood faculty, even against the advice of the department chair and in the absence of funding to be a research assistant. Unlike the savvy students, those students who worked with deadwood took longer to complete their programs, and were marginalized socially and intellectually.

Administrators and new faculty asserted that the link between hiring star faculty and upgrading graduate (especially doctoral) programs has been vital to the university's drive to be upwardly mobile. Asserting the inseparability of research and graduate education has been an integral part of the competitive drive, whether actually accomplished or merely as a stated ideal. As a former dean and anthropologist suggested, merely asserting it has helped: "If you want to get into the coterie of national leadership, you must repeat the tribal mythology of 'excellence in graduate education and research' . . . . It's like a script."

As the university has worked to be upwardly mobile, administrators invested heavily in hiring research-oriented science faculty as well as in developing new graduate programs, especially in the interdisciplinary sciences. Faculty have been rewarded for this kind of participation in promotion and tenure decisions. The administration and department chairs suggested that faculty who participate in these programs are of a higher quality because they are individually selected to join a new program; "We can control which faculty we want, so there is no deadwood," a science department chair explained. A consequence of this strategy, however, has been to further formalize the differentiation of the faculty, since the bulk of the older faculty have been excluded from these newly formed groups, and thus, missed out on the intellectual and social opportunity.

While the split between the faculty "haves" and "have-nots" has been most apparent within the science departments, it has contributed to further differential valuing of faculty across the disciplines. In the humanities departments and in most of the social sciences, faculty reflected consistent "have-not" status. Their offices were located in old buildings, in over-crowded spaces without windows. (I interviewed an anthropologist whose office was actually a former janitorial closet.) The library, which is the most valuable resource for nonscientists, has not been upgraded since the neglect that occurred in the initial big science push of the 1970s. These faculty expressed a feeling of organizational distance between themselves and the administration, as well as between themselves and the star scientists who have accused them of "not pulling their weight" in seeking external funds to support their research and their doctoral students.

Moreover, the "have-nots" reported an erosion of their departmental autonomy, as funds were increasingly moved to the discretionary budget of the central administration. While the promise of the campus's overall upward mobility was to supplement their departmental budgets, the subsequent realities included no new faculty billets, the imposition of efficiency and productivity criteria in promotion and tenure, and a sense that the institutional ambitions to be at the forefront of science did not match with their sense of what it meant to be active scholars and good teachers. Overall, for these faculty, the organizational change to embrace the research imperative has caused them to "hunker down," as if trying to weather a storm.

Graduate Education

As I have suggested, the surge for upward mobility as a research university has also entailed changes in the nature of graduate education, not just its context but its conduct. The biggest change has been shifting from large-scale, part-time master's and small-scale, doctoral programs across a wide range of disciplines to capital-intensive, big (and interdisciplinary) doctoral science programs, which stress working on the faculty's sponsored research. Simultaneously, with the exception of a few targeted social sciences, such as cognitive and information science, the nonscience graduate programs have foundered. These programs have had insufficient funds, and students have taken longer to complete their Ph.D.s, spending the bulk of their time engaged in teaching labor rather than research training. Doctoral students tended to stay on one of two tracks, either as research assistants (RAs) or as teaching assistants (TAs), reflecting a differentiation that paralleled the faculty superstars versus deadwood.

A major focus for "upgrading" graduate programs has occurred in the biological sciences, which has undergone three curricular revisions (in 1966, 1977, and 1984) in an effort to be "on the frontiers of knowledge." The most recent revision carved up the biological sciences into 13 discipline-based departments and 17 interdisciplinary programs. As a rationale for eliminating and establishing different graduate programs, the dean of graduate education explained, "These science programs are necessary to respond to society's felt needs at the research level." His office has given these science chairs extra funds to develop new brochures that advertise the star faculty and research focus of the graduate programs, as well as extra funds to recruit Ph.D. students, flying them in from across the country to persuade them to attend On the Move University.

The finance of graduate education has been a central component of institutional efforts to upgrade the quality of the students they can attract. Institutional funds were established to supplement RA stipend levels that come from federally sponsored research projects. Some funds from the university were also allocated to supplement the stipends for state-funded teaching assistantships. Those departments with the highest undergraduate course enrollments got the greatest number of TAs. However, according to a former associate dean of the graduate college, each department had to negotiate the TA stipend level with the graduate dean annually. Those departments that tried to compete with offers from better universities got a higher stipend level. According to a former associate dean, a great discrepancy across departments has resulted, along with a sense of "personal deals" and a "deliberate ambiguity to cloud the numbers so people don't know." The amount of the stipend for nine months ranged from a TA at under $7,000 to an RA of $8,500, but in the sciences the RA stipend rose to $11,000, and it automatically included summer funding.

The procedure of negotiating stipend levels with the graduate school administration has been controversial, since greater amounts of university funds have been set aside to directly finance graduate students. The old procedure was different, as a former associate dean remembered, "The fact is there was a small, finite pot [of money], so I watched the inadequate financial resources go . . . ." As administrators in the graduate college, "we were there to essentially serve as the academic conscience of the university—a watchdog." The graduate college only "monitored" the finance of graduate education, but it was "handled" by the department, both for recruiting new students and for supporting continuing students. Under the revised plan, the administration held more money back as discretionary resources for some university-funded fellowships or for RA positions. Last year, some proportion of indirect cost recovery was also held to finance 100 first-year doctoral fellowships at $10,000/year plus $300,000 to be used at the administrators' discretion "to attract outstanding graduate scholars."

Most of these funds have gone to the finance of graduate education in the sciences, leaving humanities fields to rely on TA allocations that were state and institutionally funded. In a field like history, the graduate program thrived in the late 1980s, in contrast to 15 years ago, when its financial base of TA support had dwindled. The department has produced only nine doctorates since 1970, ranging from six-and-one-half years to 15 years in time to completion. In the 1970s, with the lull in doctoral training, the graduate program in history was not really functioning, except for a few part-time master's students. The chair of the department said, "We considered why a nonelite university should even have a history program when we cannot place our students." Their answer then and now is that the graduate program was a way to attract the better faculty/scholars, who "wanted graduate students as cheap teaching labor to cover for them" and who "wanted to work with graduate students." Since then, during the 1980s, the history department was able to get the program going again, mostly owing to increased undergraduate enrollment in history classes resulting in increased TA allocations. Although the TA funding enabled them to admit new students, it was "a mixed blessing," said the department chair, because students enter the program unprepared: "We need the bodies to staff the sections even if they are not ready. And many of them are not. . . ."

There is a noteworthy exception to this pattern in the history department. An internationally renowned renaissance scholar was wooed to the university a few years ago. To sweeten this star's offer, the dean of the graduate school arranged for him to have a few graduate fellowships annually, which he runs like a research team of RAs, not TAs. It has been a tightly integrated, small group that meets formally and informally with great frequency. Known as his students, the doctoral students have isolated themselves from the rest of the department because "we don't have time to network locally"; they have internalized a sense of privilege and forthcoming entitlement in the job market. At the same time, they seem to have gained a genuine apprenticeship in a way that none of the other nonscience doctoral students I interviewed had experienced. This anomaly in the history department reveals the possibility that changes in material conditions by the central administration can actually alter what is commonly considered to be disciplinary norms or disciplinary cultural practices in doctoral education.

Although we commonly think of the process of graduate education as being radically decentralized, the central administration has taken advantage of opportunities to encourage a brand of training that goes hand-in-hand with sponsored research activities of faculty. Noting that doctoral students could use some extra assistance in learning how to be researchers, a campus administrator advocated that "the existing but unused mechanisms for providing greater integration of graduate education and research efforts deserve high priority." He suggested developing a computerized database for students with examples of student research proposals that have been successful in national and intramural competition, offering the rationale that "while it is the primary responsibility of the faculty to assist graduate students in preparing proposals and seeking research grants, countless students come to the graduate college for such advice and assistance."

The lag time between achieving high quality in faculty research and high quality in graduate programs was mentioned often, as if the path to success is clearly laid out in steps. Faculty research has been explicitly in the forefront of leading administrators' agendas, and promoting it has required full-time students in doctoral programs. The cycle works like this, as a science department chair explained:

You get RAs to do the work you don't want to do. That enables you to get publications. The publications enable you to get more research funds and more prominence and then you can attract better graduate students. . . . The better students go to where the better faculty are unless the stipend differences are so large they can't ignore it.

Similarly, a former associate dean lamented:

The university president says we're building the Harvard of the [geographic region]. We can try to buy a few bright students who'd come to a department several cuts below [a top university] but it's difficult. The very best students always go to the very best places.

With all this emphasis on science and applied science, some faculty and former administrators asserted that the other programs (especially in the humanities) floundered as did the overall nature of doctoral education. They said that the research enterprise had become the campus's main identity at a cost to graduate education and humanistic values. A former associate dean of the graduate school noted, "Graduate education went downhill and became subservient to the research enterprise. The only way to get graduate education stable funds was to link it to research funding. I'm embarrassed to say this but graduate education is research now."

As this university has become upwardly mobile, faculty in nonscience disciplines expressed concern that the emphasis on research training had been at the expense of breadth and thinking skills. "A person might be taught to think, but I'm not so sure it happens here in the sciences," because of the emphasis on "technical skills," stated an anthropologist. A former top administrator also expressed concern, "As a research-compulsive institution, can it stay true to graduate education? If not, it will have failed."

A related fear expressed by some faculty is that the university will "sell its soul" to external sponsors, by establishing interdisciplinary science programs that will become the core of the campus, rather than buffering the core from sponsors' agendas. Their concern is that embracing the research imperative has "pulled graduate education away from being an educational enterprise" and toward being "a research factory engaged in research training." The objection is not to research per se, for the Humboldtian ideal of doctoral education has included research training from the outset. Rather, they object to a particular kind of research, that is research driven by industrial interests subsuming the academic, educational enterprise. On this campus, the whole push for interdisciplinary sciences has been funded by governmental and industrial sponsors seeking applications in national defense and product development.

On the Move University is a vivid example of a university trying to change itself. As is common in the course of deliberate attempts at organizational change, underlying conflicts and different sets of interests become apparent: between faculty and administration, among administrators, among faculty, among faculty and students, among graduate students, and so forth. While I do not wish to generalize from the case of On the Move University, it is valuable for raising questions about whether these dynamics exist at other universities and what their consequences might be.

As I have suggested, for an organization to embrace the research imperative, the shift marks a potential change in the nature of social relations on campus. This case revealed how central administrators and like-minded faculty determined to move in the competitive system—by abandoning the zoo model of field coverage in favor of hiring and rewarding "star faculty," by linking externally sponsored research and graduate education as an ideal, and by creating centralized discretionary funds that enable a "higher quality" of full-time doctoral research assistants to provide the labor for sponsored research projects. The enactment of institutional ambition entailed changing the nature of faculty relations and changing the context and conduct of graduate education, two sets of organizational dynamics with implications beyond the quality of life on any given campus.

IMPLICATIONS

Building on data presented in the first part of this chapter, in this section I will examine implications beyond the organizational level of analysis. My point in doing so will be to tie the data to a critical framework. I will argue that embracing the research imperative creates tensions for the higher education system as a whole and for the academic profession. Within each of these levels, there are contradictions that undermine the current trajectory of institutional ambition, and leave open the question of what constitutes genuine excellence for the system and for the profession.

As more institutions have embraced the research imperative, the result is a more stratified and sponsor-driven system of higher education that moves farther away from its broad educational mandate. In the current system-wide division of academic labor in this country, different institutional sectors have assumed different and differently valued functions in the production and transmission of knowledge. This system has been highly regarded in some international arenas and by some on the domestic front, for ideally allowing access to the masses in the "lower echelons," while boasting flagship campuses as centers of excellence where the best and brightest faculty and students do research with a concentration of the nation's resources. Crane (1965, p. 713) described the rationale for the concentration by saying, "The best students are selected by the best graduate schools, the best of these are selected for training by top scientists, and from this highly selected group come the generation's most productive scientists." The incentive is for an upward drift of institutions trying to be more and more like the top ten, if not one of the top ten, which may mean that increasingly more resources go to fewer people and fewer institutions, thus widening the gulf between the very top and the bulk of the system.[4]

Asserting that the broader educational mandate for higher education has not been served by their hierarchy, Astin (1985) and Giroux and McLaren (1989) have argued that perpetuating and extending a disproportionate share of resources to a few institutions makes it difficult to move beyond the prevailing, narrow conceptions of excellence and talent. From this perspective, the costs of selectivity and stratification are indeed for the entire system, in that there are insufficient resources allocated to develop inherent talent throughout the system. In a national context that nurtures sciences over humanities, that values research training over scholarship and both of those over teaching, this view disputes that such hierarchy is a functional requirement of the system.

A related yet distinct concern raised by critics is that the system has sold its soul to external sponsors. From this perspective, the uncritical acceptance of the imperative for universities to become modern research complexes marks a blurring of lines between academic and industrial/governmental agendas. Making problematic the ways the higher education system, especially the research university sector, has functioned within the larger society, some scholars have argued that self-interested actors established and sustained a system of selectivity to serve business interests and class privilege under the myth of a meritocracy (e.g., Silva and Slaughter, 1984; Noble, 1977; Aronowitz, 1988; Bledstein, 1976).[5]

Such critiques of stratification and sponsorship reveal an important social contradiction embedded in American higher education. There are two contradictory legitimating foundations for higher education—economic power versus egalitarianism. Economically speaking, research universities have come to play a key role in national defense and economic competitiveness. Stakeholders in the present stratified arrangements see social justice as a move to mediocrity; the have-nots would "have a claim for a principle of fair share which is met by uniformity" in the system (Clark, 1983, pp. 243–244). Framed in this way, pursuing equity would be incompatible, and economically unwise, for the research university sector. Yet, demands for social justice have not been rendered invisible, as universities that embrace the research imperative are openly challenged to be socially responsible, in light of their premier status and their ties to sponsors. Thus, the apparent incompatibility of economic and egalitarian foundations for higher education leaves open the question of what constitutes genuine excellence, not only for the research university sector but for the system as a whole.

Turning next to implications for the academic profession, embracing the research imperative has both present and future consequences. The present concerns the way in which the star system diminishes faculty who are labeled deadwood. The future concerns the changing nature of doctoral education and, hence, the socialization of the next academic generation.

As current members of the academic profession are differentiated into stars and deadwood, a single criterion of research productivity becomes paramount over the quality of scholarship and teaching. This criterion becomes an axis along which faculty are judged within the entire profession, although it is most pronounced within research universities. A whole range of faculty contributions is either unnoticed or devalued, such as teaching undergraduates, spending time polishing work rather than rushing to publish it, and helping colleagues to improve their work. Moreover, productivity priorities encourage entrepreneurial and self-aggrandizing behaviors that attribute individual credit in the academic reward system rather than appropriately acknowledging the implicitly social nature of academic work, that is, the social development of ideas through collegial interaction, if not in person, then in text.

As productivity criteria are reconstituted and internalized by faculty, so is a personal sense of being good or bad. The dynamics that produce a stratified system of organizations seem to produce stratified identities (a term borrowed from Wexler, 1989, p. 101) as well. If one is labeled as deadwood, and especially if one feels dismissed without the work actually being reviewed, one may start acting like deadwood. Thus, the labeling becomes self-fulfilling.

In addition, the simple differentiation of faculty into these two classes renders a wide range of faculty as uniformly deadwood. Different kinds of active yet marginalized people actually become uniformly classified as deadwood. One such group is humanities scholars, who, although trained to think broadly and perhaps even provocatively, do not have much external sponsorship to support their work. Another group consists of scholars whose work has political overtones, such as Marxist and feminist scholars. Still a third group consists of interdisciplinary humanists and social scientists whose work does not fit neatly into "home" departments and does not command the legitimacy of the "cutting edge" interdisciplinary sciences (e.g., cognitive science or molecular biology). Thus, the star system suggests a more divisive differentiation in the academic profession than the sector-specific fragmentation that other scholars have described (e.g., Ruscio, 1987; Clark, 1987).

With regard to the future of the academic profession, the changing nature of doctoral education is of central concern, since faculty tend to reproduce the system they grew up under. Current doctoral students may see a wide range of major changes: reconstituting the criteria by which faculty productivity is measured, the erosion of departmental autonomy replaced with an increase in centralized administrative discretion and interdisciplinary units that bypass departmental authority (Rhoades, 1988), and the prominence of sponsors' agendas in directing the content and rhythm of campus research as well as in establishing new and interdisciplinary graduate programs that respond to funding opportunities. In an era of research-compulsive higher education, what is represented as their role in furthering good science entails expectations for faculty to seek and find sponsors outside their home institution, and for doctoral students to provide short-term research and development (R and D) labor. Interestingly, given the pull of the research imperative, the next generation of academics may be trained to participate in a less critical way, which would be an internal contradiction, or self-defeating element, in the current system of socialization.

CONCLUSION

Other scholars have criticized the research imperative for creating a dominance of research and research universities that imbalances the system of higher education. What loses is generally characterized as undergraduate education (see for example Astin, 1989). My point in critically examining the consequences of the research imperative has been to explore other potential losses, to understand short-term effects of changing faculty relations and the nature of doctoral education, as well as to suggest possible longer-term implications for the system and the profession.

As researchers of higher education, we need to be skeptical about prevailing norms and ask what are the organizational consequences of seeking to be upwardly mobile, seeking more funded research, more stars, more training, and a co-mingling of higher education and industrial/government sponsors' agendas. Deciding to embrace the research imperative does not only depict an organizational strategy, but it reflects economic, political, and social assumptions that need to be carefully examined for their consequences beyond the organization.

As we think about whether there can or should be a public philosophy of higher education, the research enterprise is clearly a component around which a community discourse can be mobilized, that is, to redefine higher education as within the public sphere with problems of concern to members of the wider society. Building on the work of Giroux and McLaren (1989), I suggest that the imperative for universities is not to blur the distinction between academic and industrial/governmental agendas; rather, the purpose of a university is to be critically engaged with society. The present trends may unwittingly lead to such critical engagement, as increasingly participants and interested observers challenge the trajectory of institutional ambition, along with the increased stratification and sponsorship of the system and the changes in socialization for the profession.

With regard to the study of higher education, my final point is that we need not take our research questions as givens from the perspective of urgent calls by experts in science policy and economic productivity. The next step for the study of higher education may be to develop scholarship that looks less like post-hoc functionalist explanations and moves more toward cultural criticism. Such a move would entail a genre of inquiry that is not strictly about efficient means, but also about desirable ends. This wider range of questions remains unasked—perhaps because of an incommensurability of paradigms or because of a professional self-interest in conveying the image that those of us in the field of higher education have nonpartisan expertise and technical know-how, rather than ontological and epistemological standpoints that are situated in the subject matter we seek to understand. We have only to gain from collective deliberation on these points.

NOTES

I wish to thank the following colleagues for thoughtful comments on a draft of this manuscript: Yvonna Lincoln, Alex McCormick, Gary Rhoades, Karen Sacks, Sheila Slaughter, and William Tierney.

1. This case study is drawn from a larger, cross-national product on graduate education and research in the United States, England, France, Germany, and Japan, supported by the Spencer Foundation. The four case studies I conducted in the United States in 1987–89 included 160 campus interviews with administrators, faculty, and graduate students in four disciplines (physics, history, economics, and biological sciences).

2. Even 25 years ago, observers of the American higher education system knew well the impetus for keeping one's university up-to-date and at the forefront of science; as Rudolph stated, "The institution which is not steadily advancing is constantly falling behind" (Rudolph, 1962, p. 329). Embracing the research imperative promised to be a particularly good

ticket to institutional advancement, or at least to gaining a reputation for excellence. This promise originated in the founding of U.S. research universities in the late nineteenth century, although its link to federal government funding did not emerge clearly until the post–World War II era, with the national belief in science as "the endless frontier" and the vehicle for economic competitiveness and national defense.

3. The conventional wisdom about "the 'deadwood' problem" is that administrators need to "ease out unproductive older faculty . . . in order to maintain quality" (Alpert, 1985, p. 271). This meaning of the term is evident on this campus, although some more recent interpretations, as in a critique of the University of California system for being "a forest of deadwood," are intended to criticize "people in their prime who 'haven't published anything in years,' " for doing "no research at all during time bought for them by the tax payers" (Miles, 1989, p. 3). In both cases, nonstar faculty are seen as "a drag on academic competitiveness" (Miles, 1989, p. 3). See the section of this chapter entitled Implications for a discussion of the implications of this labeling for the academic profession.

4. Evidence for upward drift in the system is the shift in Carnegie classification (Carnegie Foundation, 1987), which has the first four categories based on annual amounts of federally sponsored research and doctoral degree production. Between 1976 and 1987, the upward drift reflects more of an isomorphism, especially in this uppermost sector, where 16 institutions moved from RU II to RU I, 10 from DG I to RU II, 9 from DG II to DG I, and 23 from comprehensive I to DG II. The downward drift is not as marked in the top sector, where 0 moved from RU I to RU II, 6 from RU II to DG I, 10 from DG I to DG II, and 0 from DG II to comprehensive I.

5. While over the past 100 years, U.S. science has been mobilized under the guidance and financial backing of private elites, the historical record offers different interpretations of the extent to which universities have adapted to external sponsors or have maintained their autonomy and academic values. See Noble (1977) and Geiger (1986) as examples of critical and celebratory interpretations, respectively. Geiger even acknowledges the prominence of these elites in mobilizing science (Geiger, 1986, pp. 99–100), yet he argues that universities' "independent interests" and "pluralism prevailed" "due to diverse social linkages" (Geiger, 1986, p. 267). This view corresponds to what most observers of the university research system refer to as "a plurality of sponsors." Challenging this assessment, I have argued elsewhere (Gumport, 1989) that the presumed plurality may reflect more of a homogeneous set of interests among leaders

of foundations, government funding agencies, science agencies, and universities. Note that, as the literature on university–industrial relations grows, authors focus more attention on how to establish healthier partnerships, and address fewer concerns about whether or not such relations are appropriate in the first place or what are the consequences of more of them beyond such issues as who owns the rights on new products (e.g., Powers et al., 1988).

REFERENCES

Alpert, Daniel. (1985). Performance and paralysis: The organizational context of the American research university. *Journal of Higher Education, 56*(3), 241–281.

Aronowitz, Stanley. (1988). *Science as power: Discourse and ideology in modern society.* Minneapolis: University of Minnesota Press.

Astin, Alexander. (1985). *Achieving educational excellence.* San Francisco: Jossey-Bass.

———. (1989). Moral messages of the university. *Educational Record, 70*(2), 22–25.

Benson, J. Kenneth. (1977). Organizations: A dialectical view. *Administrative Science Quarterly, 22* (March), 1–21.

Bledstein, Burton J. (1976). *The culture of professionalism.* New York: Norton.

Carnegie Foundation for the Advancement of Teaching. (1987). *A classification of institutions of higher education.* Princeton, NJ: Carnegie Foundation.

Clark, Burton. (1983). *The higher education system: Academic organization in cross-national perspective.* Berkeley: University of California Press.

———. (1987). *The academic life.* Princeton, NJ: The Carnegie Foundation for the Advancement of Teaching.

Crane, Diana. (1965). Scientists at major and minor universities: A study of productivity and recognition. *American Sociological Review, 30*, 699–714.

Geiger, Roger. (1986). *To advance knowledge: The growth of American research universities, 1900–1940.* New York: Oxford University Press.

Giroux, Henry A., &McLaren, Peter. (1989). Introduction: Schooling, cultural politics and the struggle for democracy. In Henry A. Giroux and Peter McLaren (Eds.), *Critical pedagogy, the state and cultural struggle* (pp. xi–xxxv). Albany: State University of New York Press.

Gumport, Patricia J. (1989). *American transformations in graduate education and research: Institutional, philanthropic and federal initiatives.* Unpublished manuscript.

Miles, Jack. (1989, August 13). UC tenure: A forest of deadwood. *Los Angeles Times*, pp. 49–50.

Noble, David F. (1977). *America by design: Science, technology and the rise of corporate capitalism.* New York: Alfred Knopf.

Powers, David, Powers, Mary, Betz, Frederick, & Aslanian, Carol. (1988). *Higher education in partnership with industry.* San Francisco: Jossey-Bass.

Reed, Michael. (1985). *Redirections in organizational analysis.* London: Tavistock.

Rhoades, Gary. (1988). *Academic culture and professional mandate.* Paper presented at the Association for the Study of Higher Education, St. Louis, November.

Rudolph, Frederick. (1962). *The American college and university: A history*. New York: Vintage/Random House.

Ruscio, Kenneth. (1987). Many sectors, many professions. In Burton Clark (Ed.), *The academic profession*. Berkeley: University of California Press.

Silva, Edward T., & Slaughter, Sheila. (1984). *Serving power: The making of the academic social science expert*. Westport, CT: Greenwood Press.

Wexler, Philip. (1989). Curriculum in the closed society. In Henry A. Giroux and Peter McLaren (Eds.), *Critical pedagogy, the state and cultural struggle*. Albany: State University of New York Press.

6 A MODEL OF AGENCY FOR POSTGRADUATE EDUCATION

William Foster

A critical and nonfunctionalist model for the preparation of professionals through postgraduate education is no longer an unorthodox possibility favored by an *avant garde*. Rather, a critical yet realist conception of postgraduate education has become a serious alternative to traditional approaches. In particular, a critical-pragmatist conception, as will be developed here, is a viable alternative to both traditional, functionalist models and the more contemporary psychological accounts. A critical-pragmatist theory of educational preparation adopts parts of these models, showing how educational organizations *are* constructed entities that assume objective characteristics over time. The theory is also, however, critical, in the sense that it requires a continual assessment of the source of the theory, and of its impact on its audience. The theory must always be considered in relationship to the practices that occur in postgraduate education. By postgraduate education, I mean those professional preparation programs at postsecondary institutions that qualify students for higher degrees in such areas as educational administration, public administration, business administration, nursing administration, social welfare, and so forth.

This chapter explores the dimensions of a critical and pragmatist model of postgraduate education. I attempt to show why orthodox, psychological models of education are deficient; I then develop alternative possibilities, incorporating ideas drawn from the sociology and philosophy of science.

The intent is to demonstrate how postgraduate education is largely based in a framework that misconceives both the nature of those organizations within which students will work and the nature of knowledge itself, and to assert that a framework for such postgraduate education based in a critical but realist social science (my comments are limited to social scientific disciplines) better serves the ends for which postgraduate education is itself established.

This chapter essentially tries to establish the weakness of both functionalist and constructivist positions as the epistemological foundation of postgraduate education and to suggest that an educational model derived from a critical-pragmatist tradition makes more sense for such programs, because such a model restores the notion of agency. By *agency*, I mean that individuals with particular professional backgrounds are agents of social change, can indeed make a difference in their social networks, and are fundamentally committed to creating practices intended for social progress.

THE ORTHODOX FRAMEWORK IN POSTGRADUATE EDUCATION

Whether the social sciences operate under a particular paradigm is debatable, given the disparate collection of concepts, methodologies, and frameworks used in the many disciplines. If, however, there is a dominant paradigm, particularly one that governs research at the postsecondary level, then that paradigm is both functionalist and positivist. Functionalism asserts that social systems are real, concrete endeavors in which certain systemic regularities occur, each serving to enhance or disable system equilibrium (Burrell and Morgan, 1979, p. 123).

Positivism—used here loosely to incorporate various forms of logical positivism—was the method of choice to investigate system regularities. Positivism embraced a philosophy that held that all science could be unified under one rigorous method, that methodology is primary, and that values are emotive statements and not subject to scientific consideration.

The assumptions used in this framework are that the social sciences, supposedly immature, would become more and more like the natural sciences in degrees of rigor and predictive ability, with the ultimate goal of developing generalizable laws of human behavior. This, of course, would lead to the preoccupation by organizational theorists with the use of objective methods borrowed from the hard sciences and a corresponding repudiation of "soft" anthropological, textual, or literary approaches. The methodology used, replete with sophisticated statistical analysis, became the measure of quality. Such hard data were to replace the value-laden observations of previous social thinkers.

Positivism as a mode of thought dominated for a period both the methodology and the theoretical apparatus of the social sciences in general. Functionalism was its major carrier, and the role of the social scientist became that of charting the systemic properties, with little regard paid to the intentions or actions of the agents therein. Burrell and Morgan (1979), for example, talk about what they label "sociological positivism" and say that:

In essence this reflects the attempt to apply models and methods derived from the natural sciences to the study of human affairs. It treats the social world as if it were the natural world, adopting a "realist" approach to ontology. This is backed up by a "positivist" epistemology, relatively "deterministic" views of human nature and the use of "nomothetic" methodologies. (p. 7)

Positivism also became a received paradigm for many working in various postgraduate programs and has correspondingly affected their analyses of organizations. This view of organizations suggested a particular, functionalist vision of social reality, and most administrative programs (whether public, educational, or others) adopted this vision.

An example of this framework can readily be found in both educational and public administration programs. Waldo (1948) was one of the first to decry the impact of logical positivism on the study and practice of public administration. He says:

Students and reformers of all kinds fell to making human relations and governmental practices scientific: the students by engaging in a new and recondite branch of inquiry called Scientific Methodology, and the reformers either by applying current conceptions of scientific method or by the simpler method of putting a scientific wrapper on old nostrums. This faith in science and the efficacy of the scientific method thoroughly permeates our literature in public administration. (pp. 20–21)

This concern with science, with establishing a positivistic base for public administration, remains unabated today. Similarly, in education, the search for a "grand theory" of administrative behavior has been pursued relentlessly. A functionalist systems approach is undoubtedly the major foundation of the high majority of postgraduate programs in educational administration, and, while positivism has been labeled dead, its reign in the field of postgraduate administrative training is still unchallenged. This means that dominant viewpoints stress a "scientific" method, journals look for hypothesis-testing research, and students are expected to become experts in technical specializations. Postgraduate programs that engage in professional preparation, then, are characterized generally by an attempt to "scientize" their curriculum, to teach specific and largely technical skills, and to socialize the novice into a world of specialization. In educational administration, for example, a student would be expected to study social systems theory, role theory, techniques of supervision, and so on without ever encountering a philosophy course or a course dealing with the fundamental assumptions of administration and schooling in this society.

AN ALTERNATIVE APPROACH: CONSTRUCTIVISM

While the functionalist agenda has been dominant, a different tradition, originating out of nineteenth-century German idealism, has begun to influence the way we study organizations and their management. For a number of researchers, the constraints of the functionalist paradigm have proved unduly restrictive, largely because its ability to provide research-based, generalizable laws of behavior for social reality was never realized. This alternative approach is now a popular epistemological foundation for a number of postgraduate programs in education and other fields.

This emerging paradigm—constructivism—is characterized by the following qualities. First, there is a recognition that social science is embedded with values, and that any hard and fast distinction between facts and values is itself arbitrary. Second, reality itself is considered as socially constructed, not as historically given. Seeing social reality as constructed means that a good deal of what goes on in social collectivities involves efforts at sense-making and efforts at sustaining the current interpretation of events. Language usage thus figures prominently in such accounts; metaphor and metonymy are the means through which organizations are shaped.

The social sciences, in this way of thinking, are guided largely by a search for an understanding of different ways of being—the *verstehen* of different social lives. It is the understanding of "forms of life," "language games," "*Geisteswissenschaften*," and the everyday, normative order that become important. Methodologically, the new paradigm is not constrained by the traditional canons of science. Indeed, the range of acceptable research methods is wide, though qualitative methods—case study, ethnography, life histories, and so on—figure prominently.

For programs in postgraduate education, a constructivist paradigm means that educational institutions, and the training that they provide, are more complex and heterogeneous than a rational, goal-seeking, and functionalist approach might acknowledge. A constructivist outlook means, for example, that programs in public administration cannot simply be considered as mechanisms for preparing future administrators in the appropriate and proven ways of governance; rather, they must be considered in problematic ways, with each local program creating itself anew. Thus, preparation programs will be concerned with showing students the ways of qualitative inquiry, with showing them how different agendas pertain in different organizations, and with showing them how a leader's role in the organization consists of manipulating the symbolic context of organization. In educational administration, for example, a professional preparation program based in the constructivist position would suggest that school principals and superintendents must take seriously the way social realities are developed within their institutions, and must further pay particular attention to the ways in which these realities are developed—through symbols, myths, rituals, and so on. Courses in such a program would deal with the psychology of participation, with the creation of organizational structures where meaning is clearly available, and with the social nature of organizations.

THE PROBLEM OF METHODOLOGY

Both the structuralist–functionalist position and the constructivist alternative have basic methodological problems, rooted in the epistemological claims that each makes. The methodological problems of the structuralist–functionalist paradigm have been clearly discussed elsewhere (see, e.g., Burrell and Morgan, 1979). Essentially, they have to do with conceiving of social reality as a concrete entity about which researchers can make truth-statements. The structural–functionalist position would adopt a methodology reminiscent of Comte's positivism: That social laws can be discovered and that these will mimic in many ways the laws of nature. This position, given the insights that constructivism provides, must be rejected. Human action is too diverse, too historical, and too unique to allow general and universalizable laws of behavior to be discovered.

The more interesting work now has to do with those research questions engendered by constructivist conceptions: How does sense-making occur in organizations? How is social reality constructed? A number of theorists (Weick, 1976, 1979, 1985; March and Olsen, 1979; Lincoln, 1985) have endeavored to sketch out competing versions of organizational life and, consequently, professional preparation programs; ultimately, they fail, or at least are incomplete, as I intend to show. Nevertheless, they bear examination for the ways in which they push us to re-examine familiar terrain.

Weick (1976, 1979, 1985), coming out of a Meadian social psychology, has been among the leaders in thinking of organizations as being psychological enactments of the members. The organizational "reality" is created by members of the organization, and it is to this mutual creation that they then respond. This process largely involves a model of organizing whereby there is a relevant environment of information that is ambiguous and uncertain. Organizational members select from this environment and retain those parts of it that lead to unambiguous organizational routines.

Weick (1976, 1985) explains his analysis of the process of organizing and of enactment with the metaphor of a (skewed) soccer game. In this game, all the conventional rules—shape of the field, scoring rules, number of balls—are flouted, yet the game is played by the participants as if it made sense. This metaphor serves to suggest that organizations are much like the soccer game: In the abstract, there are rules of rationality and performance, but in the actual playing out of day-to-day relationships, the governing rules are spontaneously created. A large part of organizational performance, then, consists of figuring out how to make sense of *this* particular combination of events.

Cohen and March's (1974) analysis of leadership in the university supports the essential nonrationality thesis embedded in Weick's example. They suggest that the traditional model of university governance—setting goals and developing long-range plans that strategic initiatives by the president will accomplish—is a convenient fiction. Reality suggests that both goal-setting and planning are ambiguous events, that the role the president can play is limited, and that often the university administration is simply carried onward by the flow of events. Similarly, Weiner (1979) found that a rational model was only a weak explanation for the way a school district handled a desegregation order. Rather, the implementation of the decree depended upon who was where at particular times, whether the actors had any interest in the issue and were willing to spend time on it, and who set the agenda the organization used to address the issues.

In this sense, the organization is very much like Cohen, March, and Olsen's (1979) "garbage can" model of decision-making. No one individual, such as the university president, has the degree of control often ascribed to such a role; the horizon of problems and solutions is ambiguous, and chance plays as great a part as planning. However, regularity and order are not completely lacking; there are, Weick (1985) maintains, in fact several sources of order in the organization. However, these are tenuous and fleeting, applicable only under constrained circumstances, and often a source of ill-advised action by members ("leap before you look," Weick advises managers: 1985, p. 133).

The implicit methodology contained in Weick's organizational arguments then largely have to do with the development of an understanding of the social–psychological dimensions of individuals in organizations. The implications of this, in his work, are quite clear. On the one hand, it is clearly the enacting processes and the meaning-creating properties of individuals that are important; on the other hand, the residue of the idea of "organization" is very much there. The organization and the embedded idea of system is both the foil of the argument he mounts as well as its very justification. Clegg and Dunkerley (1980) have observed:

Weick's originally promising model of organizing seems to lead only to either an empty formalism or a content which cannot meaningfully be compared. The environment, from being an objective determinant in earlier theories of organization, has become the enacted consequence of the decision of the organization. As such it takes on a fantastic quality. It has no objective existence: it does not exist in laws, institutions, or material reality—except in as much information which constitutes it as such is enacted. The environment loses all determination and becomes the ideal conditions of the organization's existence. (p. 272)

Thus, in Weick's view, social reality presents a paradox of sorts; it has a material existence, but this existence is continually created through members' cognitive processes. This attempt to combine an "objective" systems perspective with a more idealistic, "subjective," and phenomenological perspective creates a number of problems for the organizational observer.

Weick's advice in this regard—to look for instances of, or the absence of, "loose coupling," to look for examples of sense-making, and so on—is not particularly helpful. The organizational researcher has to be aware of the absence of routinized performances as well as their presence; yet the absence of phenomena is certainly much harder to document than their presence. Indeed, one wonders how in fact to document the absence of organizational data.

This short foray into some of the major ideas dealing with constructivism was designed to illustrate a number of common philosophical traditions and assumptions. Methodology is neither prior to philosophy nor epistemology, and it is important that before being able to talk about the success and/or failure of methods in studying constructivism, one looks at the world view such methods impute. A postgraduate education that relies on constructivism as its informing paradigm is one that relies on the social construction of realities and that assumes that organizations are by nature ambiguous creations. Each venue for such graduates is by definition one where no certain knowledge accrues, and one in which the graduate must negotiate his or her role.

In general, then, the sense one has of what social realities *are* is that they are, first, composed of individuals, each sharing a common language used to create and maintain cognitions about the organization. The concept of "reality" is itself, then, a creation, a shared common sense. Second, many explanations of social reality are rationalizations often done post hoc, yet necessary for maintaining a facade of instrumental activity. One needs, as it were, to get behind the linear, textual accounts to see and understand how members relate.

Third, the process of sense-making in such realities is a cognitive one; individual actors are meaning creators and agents who impute cause and effect to their actions. Thus, a behaviorist psychology, in which events are the result of stimuli, or a functionalist sociology, in which events are the result of system imperatives, is rejected. Much more apropos to this outlook would be a cognitive psychology where intuition, feelings, and mind itself are the conceptual underpinnings.

There are certain limitations, however, which bear on a discussion of how social reality is constructed and discussed in organizations. Methodological avenues to discovering patterns of constructivism are implicated somewhat directly by other, more overriding issues of an epistemological and even ontological nature. These issues have to do with the concept of "constructivism" itself and its adequacy given the current emphasis on methods.

In much of the literature concerning constructivism, especially in the case of psychological enactment, there is a strong sense of methodological individualism; here, the social life can ultimately be reduced to the cognitions of individual actors. Social structures, organizations, groups, and so on become reduced to (simply) the aggregation of individual actors, created out of their common-sense attitudes but with no "reality" of their own. The major methodological problem, then, becomes one of how such structures are created; what do those individuals *do* that results in their objectification of structure?

The assumption of methodological individualism, however, poses the problem in the wrong terms. Its reductionist argument, as Giddens (1984) has noted, creates a false polarity between "subjective" and "objective." To see all structures as ultimately reducible to individual aggregations is as false as to see organizations and institutions as objectively concrete. It is a mistake, for example, to see social structures, such as nursing or public administration programs, as simply a collection of individual intentions brought to them by the participants in such programs; this view has no place for history and structure. It is also a mistake to see such programs as purely history and structure, with no regard for how the individuals modify, change, and even disrupt these programs; this view has no place for individual agency.

Weick (1985) provides an illustration of the subjectivism of methodological individualism in the following:

Thus, the trappings of rationality such as strategic plans are important largely as binding mechanisms. They hold events together long enough and tight enough in people's heads so that they do something in the belief that their actions will be influential. The importance of presumptions, expectations, justifications, and commitments is that they span the breaks in a loosely coupled system and encourage confident interactions that tighten settings. *The conditions of order and tightness in organizations exist as much in the mind as they do in the field of action.* (pp. 127–128; emphasis in original)

Weick's view is probably unobjectionable as far as it goes; however, it seems to carry an implication that social creations are solely dependent on their maintenance through individual cognitions, and do not, in some degree, structure what those cognitions are in fact able to conceive.

What a radical methodological individualism (as is, I believe, embraced by Weick and other social psychologists) fails to note, in reducing all action to individual cognitions, is the purposive and active dialectic that occurs between individual and structure—what Giddens (1984, p. 25) labels the "duality of structure." This means that a "society" or a "social system" consists of individuals in interaction governed by rules and resources. This interaction produces *and reproduces* structure, and structure in turn "governs" to some degree how future interactions are developed. As Giddens (1984) has it:

According to the notion of the duality of structure, the structural properties of social systems are both medium and outcome of the practices they recursively organize.

Structure is not "external" to individuals: as memory traces, and as instantiated in social practices, it is in a certain sense more "internal" than exterior to their activities in a Durkheimian sense. Structure is not to be equated with constraint but is always both constraining and enabling. (p. 2)

In this way of conceptualizing structure, structure is the active outcome of individual agents, which has both a constraining and an enabling effect over them. It is not wholly "out there" nor "in there"; rather, structure is continually re-created in the practices of agents who conform, more or less, to social rules and who use, more or less, material and social resources. This is substantially different from a methodologically individualist stance that seems to see social structures as individually constructed and, as such, capable of an infinite number of constructions.

IMPLICATIONS FOR POSTGRADUATE EDUCATION

So far, I have discussed three of the possible ontological and methodological foundations for postgraduate education in the professions. First, a functionalist approach, which assumes certain knowledge is possible and postgraduate education should be engaged in the dissemination of such knowledge, has been considered. Second, I have discussed a constructivist approach, which assumes that social knowledge is socially created and that postgraduate programs should demonstrate the importance of sense-making within the organizational context. Third, a realist position, which states that social knowledge is both historically determined and transformed, and that postgraduate programs should be engaged in the critical and pragmatic development of social agents, has been outlined.

It is this last that I will now make an argument for, by suggesting that, first, if society is to succeed according to democratic ideals, then it must prepare individuals with a sense of these ideals and that this is a fundamental rationale for postgraduate education. Second, this requires reconceiving of postgraduate education as a moral context, which neither functionalism nor constructivism can adequately do. Third, the two points above require the adoption of a critical, realist, and pragmatic stance toward the education of professionals.

THE POSTGRADUATE AS AGENT

This argument maintains simply that social ideals are ones that are only achieved by actively working toward them. This means that ideals such as equality and freedom are only important to the extent that both institutions and individuals are actively striving for them. One role, then, of postgraduate education is to engage in the active development of *agents*, individuals working within a moral context to achieve those goals valued by their particular programs.

This, then, relates to the purpose of a postgraduate education. One can ask whether the purpose of postgraduate education lies in the technical training of individuals or in their overall education in a social agenda? Ultimately, it is both, of course. However, I suggest that the technical dimension of training has come to be detached and free of the social or moral dimension of education. Postgraduate programs see themselves as sites for skill development regardless of the moral context within which they find themselves.

Education, per se, is always of a moral nature. It is moral not in a moralistic sense of right and wrong, but in the sense of developing an ethics of participation and of inquiry. The basic achievement of an education is the achievement of participation in an educated community and the achievement of a more sophisticated moral agenda. This stands true for the elementary teacher, the secondary teacher, and the tertiary teacher: Each strives to bring his or her pupils up to the level of participation in a more complex moral agenda. Certainly, the teaching and applications of technical skills stands in respect in this picture; yet, these skills remain secondary to the ultimate purpose of education. This is the message that Dewey (1926) brought us: "When the acquiring of information and of technical intellectual skill do not influence the formation of a social disposition, ordinary vital experience fails to gain in meaning, while schooling, in so far, creates only 'sharps' in learning—that is, egoistic specialists" (p. 10).

However, the moral agenda engaged does not stand context-free, like a set of universal principles that have never seen their realization in actual practices. Rather, the context is always the set of social conditions that itself informs both higher education and social life in general. The context is that of individuals working to achieve a system of governance that promotes self-satisfaction, not in the sense of narcissistic achievement, but in the sense of communal development oriented toward the actualization of the social ideal. Thus education, and particularly postgraduate education, is ultimately tied to the ends of the just community (which may not be the ends of the modern state). Education, in this sense, means the formulation of attitudes and strategies designed to work toward the achievement of democracy, equality, and emancipation. If these are not concerns addressed in educational programs, then where will they be addressed sufficiently? Educational administration, public administration, and social welfare programs, for example, are ultimately tied to the idea of social change and more emancipatory conditions for their clients. This means adopting structures and strategies that allow free discourse on contentious issues, which empower those without voice and which problematize the role of postgraduate education. Reflective dialogue, critical analysis of social and economic realities, and participative class-room environments are all ways by which postgraduate programs could set out to attain an emancipatory ideal. This does not mean relinquishing the authoritative voice of the instructor; it does mean the assertion of the value of free communication without the domination that institutional bureaucracies seem to impose.

Unlike functionalist and constructivist positions, this model of post-graduate education provides power to the notion of agency; that, indeed, individuals acting within a social organization can create change, though, as will be developed, not through scientific paradigms. Rather, the agent here is a moral actor whose preparation allows her or him to exert leadership actively in a social setting. Agency, then, is a construct that suggests the active, engaged efforts of individuals to effect changes in social structures. It assumes a "real" world, historically informed, yet one that can be altered through the interventions of actors. Reality, in this view, is not a system that operates regardless of the individual actors within it, as functionalism would seem to claim, nor it is an ahistorical construction of social actors, as constructivism would have it. Rather, in this view, it is an on-going accomplishment of the particular agents who act within the constraints imposed by history and circumstance. The notion of agency further supposes that a fundamental drive for change that leads to further emancipation is a feature of human history.

The claim that postgraduate programs are ultimately tied to emancipatory practices is sustainable only if we reject a technical model of administration as a value-free activity designed for goal achievement. While this model has been the dominant one at least since Simon's (1965) *Administrative Behavior*, it conceives of the administrator as an individual decision-maker free of context. Yet the context is inescapable. This argument suggests that the technical model of administrator–bureaucrat is a cultural fiction based in a positivistic mindset whose ultimate triumph was scientific management, and that a more fruitful approach is to conceive of postgraduate education as education for *practice*. This, in turn, carries weighty implications for how postgraduate education should be conceived.

MacIntyre (1984) has argued convincingly that a "science" of management is a moral fiction. His argument is based in an analysis of the shift to logical positivism at the beginning of the century, where the only valid and true knowledge was either analytically true or empirically demonstrable. This meant that science could not be concerned with values or morals, and therefore management science must itself be an empirical and value-free endeavor. However, management science, as a branch of the social sciences, has so far failed to discover any universal laws of administrative or organizational behavior. Yet a belief in managerial expertise remains, and "it follows . . . that the realm of managerial expertise is one in which what purports to be objectively-grounded claims function in fact as expressions of arbitrary, but disguised, will and preference" (MacIntyre, 1984, p. 107).

The conclusion, then, is this: There is no systematic law-like knowledge base for training social welfare, public, or educational administrators in professional, postgraduate education programs, but this is not to dismiss the significance of such programs. Their significance lies largely in raising the consciousness of professionals about the nature of what it is that they do and to develop within this community of practice the concept of agency. An agent is what Fay (1987) calls an active being, a person with "four fundamental dispositions: *intelligence, curiosity, reflectiveness*, and *willfulness*" (p. 48).

How might this be accomplished? MacIntyre's argument regarding the development of a practice makes a good deal of sense for such preparation programs. This argument is founded in the proposition that the development of meaningful communities is an accomplishment and that this accomplishment depends on the commitment of individuals linked together in ways designed to achieve excellence. Excellence is achieved through practices. A practice is a set of activities that are coherent, purposive, and rewarding because of their nature, and that, moreover, allow a profession to extend the boundaries that have constrained it.

This essentially is what I mean by agency, with, however, a critical and emancipatory dimension attached. The various forms of administration, for example, could be practices, but only if they are performed in contextually specific situations that attempt to advance the profession to new heights.

This conception of a practice is also a pragmatic one, in the sense that it is a working definition of what a profession is. This definition rejects any concept of finding the truth about a profession and substitutes for this the idea of a community working toward ways of perfecting their activities together. As Howe (1988) observes:

For pragmatists, "truth" is a normative concept, like "good," and "truth is what works" is best seen not as a theory or definition, but as the pragmatists' attempt to say *something* interesting about the nature of truth and to suggest, in particular, that knowledge claims cannot be totally abstracted from contingent beliefs, interests, and projects. (pp. 14–15)

For postgraduate programs, this line of reasoning contains a number of implications. The first is that such programs should orient themselves more to the development of competent practitioners than to technical specialists, for it is the competent practitioner that will make a difference. A competent practitioner is one who maintains a sense of the issues and problems facing the field, who develops a practice designed to address these, and who has control over the technical demands of his or her career. Of course, I am talking here about a practitioner in the above sense: An individual who engages others in attempts to achieve excellence in a profession. Another goal is that such programs need to rethink their mission in terms of establishing community rather than in terms of individualistic decision-making, for it is really within the community that social problems are addressed. Questions of participation and of voice are not "problems" that the administrator finds solutions for; rather, they are issues of relevance to the various communities involved, who need to participate mutually in discovering structures wherein such issues can receive attention. Thus, postgraduate education might well examine the local communities within which their practices will be developed, discover the issues where changes may occur, and provide leadership in exposing those areas where progress needs to be made. Finally, such programs need to see themselves as developers of excellence, and that they do so through developing practitioners committed to a moral agenda valuing excellence.

TOWARD A CRITICAL MODEL

However, the achievement of excellence is dependent upon a critique of the present situation. Excellence in a professional sense is not just reaching the pinnacle of orthodox knowledge but lies in pushing such knowledge to new possibilities, and to do this requires critical awareness. Ultimately, postgraduate programs must be considered as efforts to develop critical practices. Graduates of such programs, in other words, should become the leaders in their fields, and leadership means "raising consciousness on a wide scale" (Burns, 1978, p. 43). Raising consciousness requires engaging individuals in the critical assessment of their own situations, and this is what a critical practice means.

Fay (1987) provides a cogent analysis of what a critical practice might mean, through his analysis of a critical social science. Fay defines a critical social science as "an endeavor to explain social life in general or some particular instance of it in a way that is scientific, critical, practical, and nonidealistic" (p. 26). A critical practice, by extension, can also be taken with these dimensions. It is (socially) scientific in the sense that it is making publicly arguable claims about the social world and presenting evidence for those claims. It is critical in the sense that it refuses to accept given social structures and conditions as nonproblematic. It is practical in the sense that its goal lies in showing the possibility of the transformation of current practices. It is nonidealistic because it "is not committed to the claims either that ideas are the sole determinant of behavior (idealism I), or that emancipation simply involves a certain sort of enlightenment (idealism II), or that people are able and willing to change their self-understandings simply on the basis of rational argument (idealism III)" (Fay, 1987, p. 26).

For Fay (1987, pp. 31–32), a critical theory embodies a set of related theoretical constructs (his "basic scheme," which he later adds to). First, there is a "theory of false consciousness," which addresses those understandings a society shares that are patently in error but nevertheless retain a certain power over social reasoning. As a term, "false consciousness" carries perhaps too much baggage with it. However, if used, as I use it here, to indicate a general acceptance of orthodox theories and models, of normal ways of performing, and of unchallenged beliefs, then it can be useful to understanding why tradition remains such a controlling force. In terms of postgraduate programs, the idea of false consciousness means essentially an unsupported belief in the veracity of the orthodox social science paradigm; that such a paradigm, for example, will in fact lead to greater and more specific knowledge regarding human behavior, whether that behavior occurs in educational, public, or welfare settings. False consciousness, in this regard, simply means that a number of social actors are simply unaware of the conditions of their formation, and that one thing postgraduate programs could do is to problematize the formation of consciousness regarding their profession. This means to make problematic the epistemological, axiological, and ontological foundations of their professions: To ask, in essence, what is it that we do and why.

Second, there is a "theory of crisis," which attempts to document a sense of ill-being for certain or even all social institutions. The theory of crisis is a set of explanations (many oppositional in nature) of why the educational system is not meeting the expectations put on it. Such explanations vary from a blaming-the-victim pose to economic and structural analyses, but essentially—and whether one reflects conservative, liberal, or radical views—suggest that the various educational systems in this country are failing their obligations.

There are, of course, a number of explanations of root causes for a theory of crisis. Habermas (1975), for example, has discussed the idea of "legitimation crisis." By this, he means that social institutions are under an attack on their legitimacy, largely because the scientific and technical promises that such institutions make are unattainable, and thus, they are unable to meet the raised expectations of the population at large. The legitimation crisis, he argues, depends on crises in motivation and rationality. A motivation crisis results when the work ethic becomes eroded and people look to the State to meet their needs. A rationality crisis results when what is promised by the State (such as an increasing standard of living, eradication of poverty, and so forth) cannot be achieved, therefore calling into question the rational basis of State activity. Both such crises lead eventually to questions about the legitimacy of the State. More economically motivated theories of crisis are also available, such as the national concerns about the inability to meet worldwide economic competition with the resulting decline in standards of living.

The theory of crisis is, for Fay, balanced by a theory of education that offers a view of possibilities and of the future. A theory of education asks in what ways consciousness can be raised and what the alternatives are for achieving a more just social order. This is where postgraduate programs can find their place: by offering not only a presentation of critique, but also a presentation of possibility. Such an agenda may well examine the social, cultural, and linguistic foundations of social and educational institutions, question the nature of structures in our society, and engage the professional in an intellectual journey of self-emancipation.

Finally, there is a "theory of transformative action," which details the type of activities that would provide progress toward such a different future. Transformative action means developing intellectual leadership within a critical practice. It means, further, conceiving of one's profession as a moral quest for the good life and the just life. A theory of transformative action asks what particular strategies, viewpoints, and perspectives are important to achieving the kind of social reality that lends itself to more equitable relationships within communities. Such transformative action may well involve the critique of current structures—whether social or economic—and the development of arguments for structures that are more inclusive and that model our democratic traditions within postgraduate education itself.

The combination of these constructs into some kind of coherent accounting of preparation programs offers the possibility of a different discourse about postgraduate education and administration. This discourse would include by necessity the idea of the professional graduate as a moral agent, and such agency would incorporate the four dimensions of critique addressed above. It would also include the idea of a moral agent as one who engages in a practice, the outcome of which is related to the achievement of valued social goals. A preparation program that takes seriously Fay's theories of social action, MacIntyre's notion of a practice, and its own model of educative preparation must then incorporate the idea of individuals as agents oriented toward change and emancipation.

CONCLUSION

I have argued in this chapter that there are three major epistemological foundations for postgraduate work in the social sciences. The dominant one is by far a structural–functionalist account of social reality supported by a positivistic approach to social inquiry. An alternative foundation is based in a constructivist position supported by a psychological research agenda. Both, I have argued, are inadequate to the task that postgraduate programs face—essentially to make a difference

Social science must itself reject its positivistic background and explore different ways of "being in the world." Bhaskar (1986) has made these observations about social science:

On the thesis advocated here, social science is non-neutral in a double respect: it always consists in a *practical intervention* in social life and it sometimes *logically entails* value and practical judgements. In particular the possibility of a scientific *critique* of lay (and proto-scientific) ideas, grounded in explanatory practices based on recognition of the epistemic significance of these ideas, affords to the human sciences an essential emancipatory impulse. . . . Appreciation of the emancipatory dynamic of explanatory theory dissolves the rigid dichotomies—between fact and value, theory and practice, explanation and emancipation, science and critique—structuring traditional normative discourse. (p. 169; emphasis in original)

This, then, is what postgraduate education could be all about: Dissolving the false hierarchy that exists between the academic and the practitioner, and making social science knowledge an emancipatory knowledge that finds its application in the improvement of practice.

What might this then require? Some of the issues that I think will, or, at least, should, come to the fore in the discussion of the role of postgraduate education in the future include the following.

Voice: Are the voices of the constituencies being heard, and those of the students? Are alternative voices allowed expression?

Power: Can the Academy empower students, practitioners, researchers themselves? What are the issues of power that underlie the relationship of postgraduate education to the rest of its community?

Purpose: What, indeed, is the fundamental purpose behind postgraduate education, and what is the relationship of this purpose to the kind of society we would wish to live in?

Pragmatics: How can postgraduate programs avoid becoming anachronisms? What models for education can provide relevance to a way of life that has become increasingly individualistic and hedonistic?

Community: The achievement of the just society is a community's search for the just society. In what ways can postgraduate programs participate in the building and sustenance of community?

Critique: Finally, without critique, the Academy lapses into orthodoxy and dogma. How can critique—both internal and external—come to form the basic core of beliefs that both social scientists and postgraduates have?

Emancipation is the end result of the postgraduate experience. This does not mean that struggle ceases, nor that some kind of perfect union exists. Rather, it means that men and women are simply more aware of the conditions that disempower them, and that they are more free in determining the directions in which their collective lives should go. This may well be a worthy vision for postgraduate education.

REFERENCES

Bhaskar, R. (1986). *Scientific realism & human emancipation*. London: Verso Press.

Burns, J. M. (1978). *Leadership*. New York: Harper.

Burrell, G., & Morgan, G. (1979). *Sociological paradigms and organisational analysis*. Exeter, NH: Heinemann.

Clegg, S., & Dunkerley, D. (1980). *Organization, class and control*. London: Routledge & Kegan Paul.

Cohen, M. D., & March, J. G. (1974). *Leadership and ambiguity: The American college president*. New York: McGraw-Hill.

Cohen, M. D., March, J. G., & Olsen, J. P. (1979). People, problems, solutions and ambiguity of relevance. In J. G. March & J. P. Cohen (Eds.), *Ambiguity and choice in organizations* (2nd ed.) (pp. 24–37). Bergen, Norway: Universitetsforlaget.

Dewey, J. (1926). *Democracy and education*. New York: Macmillan.

Fay, B. (1987). *Critical social science: Liberation and its limits*. Ithaca, NY: Cornell University Press.

Giddens, A. (1984). *The constitution of society: Outline of the theory of structuration*. Berkeley: University of California Press.

Habermas, J. (1975). *Legitimation crisis*. Boston: Beacon Press.

Howe, K. R. (1988). Against the quantitative–qualitative incompatibility thesis or dogmas die hard. *Educational Researcher, 17*(8), 10–16.

Lincoln, Y. S. (Ed.). (1985). *Organizational theory and inquiry: The paradigm revolution*. Newbury Park, CA: Sage.

MacIntyre, A. (1984). *After virtue: A study in moral theory* (2nd ed.). Notre Dame, IN: University of Notre Dame Press.

March, J. G., & Olsen, J. P. (1979). *Ambiguity and choice in organizations* (2nd ed.). Bergen, Norway: Universitetsforlaget.

Simon, H. (1965). *Administrative behavior: A study of decision-making processes in administrative organizations* (2nd ed.). New York: The Free Press. Originally published 1945.

Waldo, D. (1948). *The administrative state: A study of the political theory of American public administration*. New York: The Ronald Press.

Weick, K. E. (1976). Educational organizations as loosely coupled systems. *Administrative Science Quarterly, 21*, 1–19.

————. (1979). *The social psychology of organizing* (rev. ed.). Reading, MA: Addison-Wesley.

————. (1985). Sources of order in underorganized systems: Themes in recent organizational theory. In Y. S. Lincoln (Ed.), *Organizational theory and inquiry: The paradigm revolution* (pp. 106–136). Newbury Park, CA: Sage.

Weiner, S. S. (1979). Participation, deadlines, and choice. In J. G. March & J. P. Olsen (Eds.), *Ambiguity and choice in organizations* (2nd ed.) (pp. 225–250). Bergen, Norway: Universitetsforlaget.

Part III   PEOPLE ON
           THE BORDERS

7 UNDERSTANDING CULTURAL CONFLICT

Ken Kempner

Although schools are not always at the center of political contention, they are a site where individuals with differing values and beliefs meet each other, often for the first time. The beliefs and values that individuals hold form the culture or "webs of significance" humans spin about themselves (Geertz, 1973, p. 5) that define how members of a cultural group think and behave. Because public schools introduce children to the webs of significance that are meaningful for cultures different from their own, parents have to compete with the schools to determine what their children see and hear. Shor (1986) calls this inherent conflict over whose cultural beliefs should dominate a "culture war." He explains that foremost in this struggle over whose webs of significance are most important are advocates of the "conservative restoration," those individuals whose goal for the schools is to preserve the predominant beliefs and values of white, Anglo-Saxon, Protestant America. Opposing those who favor the cultural status quo are individuals whose goal is to create schools that are transformative institutions for social and economic equality. Whereas in the 1960s proponents of social justice focused national attention upon the schools as the place to bring about social equality, Wexler (1987, p. 64) observes: "Education is now the site of another social movement. The present crusade is a fight against the public school as a central means of national integration and social development." This balance between the role of the schools as institutions for conservation or as institutions for transformation swings from one side of the scale to the other depending upon the dominant political ideology (Carnoy and Levin, 1985).

Conflict between those who wish to conserve or restore the dominant reality and those who wish to transform schools into agents of social change occurs not only in elementary and secondary schools, but in higher education as well. This conflict at the postsecondary level is especially apparent at community colleges, which have generally been "open-door" institutions. By keeping their doors open to all individuals, community colleges need to respond to the variety of cultural attributes students bring to the colleges. This potential variety in the cultural values and beliefs of its students and the different character of the local community lead to "considerable variation" (Clark, 1980, p. 29) in these institutions, and diversity in the perspectives of its students, faculty, administrators, and staff.

Although over one-third of all students in American higher education are enrolled in community colleges, the effect of these institutions on the students and on society is not yet well understood. With a nation-wide enrollment of over 5½ million students among approximately 1,300 colleges (Reinhard, 1989), community colleges profoundly affect the nature of higher education in American society. What this effect actually is, how it operates, and the role of community colleges in American higher education is less clear. Even though community college proponents believe their institutions to be the most democratic of postsecondary institutions (Deegan, Tillery, et al., 1985), a number of authors criticize community colleges for contributing to class stratification (see, for example, Karabel, 1972; Zwerling, 1976; Pincus, 1980; Grubb, 1984).

To further complicate the situation, few studies offer in-depth analyses of the meaning of the community college in the lives of its students, faculty, and community. Clark's (1960) pioneering study and the works of London (1978) and Weis (1985) are notable exceptions to the atheoretical nature of much community college research. Other than these studies, we know relatively little about how the culture of community colleges defines what they are today or the meaning the participants make of their daily reality within these institutions. More recently, Brint and Karabel (1989) added to the scant literature on the theory of community colleges, but the social and educational functions of these institutions are still not well understood.

In this chapter, first, I will indicate how a cultural approach helps us understand the process of education and the function of community colleges in particular. Second, I will illustrate through a case study how a cultural analysis informs the meaning of a particular college. I then will address how community colleges are dependent upon the larger, external culture, and are sites of cultural conflict between advocates of the conservative restoration and proponents of social and educational equality. Finally, I will identify the areas or battlegrounds in which these tensions between competing political ideologies for change are played out within a particular college.

Understanding the Social Context of Education

To understand the significance and meaning of formal education, Wexler (1987, p. 15) proposes a social analysis that accounts for the historical and social context of an educational movement. By focusing on this context, investigators are more capable of understanding the social and political tensions of education that provide its shape and form. Likewise, to understand community colleges, we need to employ investigative approaches capable of discerning the effects of this conflict. Similar to the other authors in this book, I use a critical perspective that assumes the culture of an institution to be central to understanding its reality. Guided by Fay's (1987, p. 66) aim for critical theory, my goal also is to encourage "people to subject their lives and social arrangements to rational scrutiny so that they can re-order their collective existence." My approach enables me to isolate, as Fay explains, the aspects of a society's or institution's culture that must be changed if the present "crisis" is to be resolved.

My intent here is to understand the collective reality of a community college's participants, rather than to convince anyone of the truth of my interpretation. "I am trying to understand rather than convince," as Wolcott (forthcoming) explains. I am guided in this inquiry by a critical framework that attempts to discover "a coherent pattern at work in the affairs of people, albeit a pattern which lies beneath the surface of social interaction, hidden from the social actors themselves" (Fay, 1987, p. 69).

Community Colleges and the External Culture

Organizational culture, as a metaphor, is a frequently but loosely used concept in educational research. We can define more clearly the webs of significance that form organizational culture by understanding that they are composed of the norms, values, beliefs, symbols, and myths members bring to the organization to help form its character. In this manner, the culture of an educational institution interacts with the larger culture in which it resides. I agree with Grieco, (1988, p. 85) that the definition of organizational culture used by many authors, "is too absolute and does not give sufficient credence to the interactive and political aspects, either within or between cultures, be they societal or organizational." Because individual participants in any organization are previously and concurrently enmeshed in webs of significance of the external culture, the internal culture of an organization does not develop purely of its own accord.

An organization's culture has no absolute boundaries. Individuals always bring the attributes of their external culture to their organizations. At the end of the workday, they return home to be transfused anew by the external culture through television, religion, politics, and friends. In this manner, the culture of an organization is constructed from the interaction of its members with each other and with the external environment. This interaction is not without some conflict, because the culture of the external world is not always consonant with the internal culture of an organization. The degree of this conflict depends upon how different the organization is in character from the external culture; that is, the more cultural attributes the organization shares with the external culture, potentially, the lower the degree of conflict. I define cultural conflict as the opposition or antagonism among individuals over the beliefs and values they hold. When beliefs, values, and symbols of one group clash with what is significant for another group, we find cultural conflict.

The community college is embedded, likewise, in this larger cultural conflict that helps define its role and function in society. All community colleges are linked to a larger social movement, yet, they differ from each other because of the character of the local community and the internal culture of each particular college. Differing pressures are exerted on each individual community college from its local constituency and from its role as an educational institution in the larger society. Brint and Karabel (1989, p. vii) note the "powerful external constraints" on community colleges and the often contradictory nature of the messages from the larger society.

As public institutions, community colleges are sites where proponents of opposing economic and social ideologies compete for dominance of their beliefs and values upon the goals and character of the colleges. Such conflict is evident at specific locations within colleges, most notably vocational education, transfer, basic skills, and continuing education programs. These locations are battlegrounds in which students, faculty, administrators, and members of the community contest the goals, purposes, functions, and outcomes of these programs.

Although various assumptions abound concerning what the goals of community colleges should be and how the institutions actually operate, much of what we understand about community colleges and higher education in general is based upon anecdotal and descriptive studies that fail to address how internal and external cultures interact and conflict to shape what these institutions are to their participants and external society. My goal in studying one community college is to search, as Fay (1987, p. 69) proposes, for "a coherent pattern" that will enhance our understanding of how this inherent cultural conflict defines the meaning of these colleges to their participants and community.

THE CASE STUDY

The presentation of the case study is organized around two key informant groups: students, and faculty and administrators. Faculty and administrators are grouped together, because so many of them had teaching and administrative duties and most administrators had once been faculty members. Staff members are not ignored in the study, but my focus was intentionally upon the academic participants of the college.

For over a year and a half, I studied Hill Community College (a pseudonym) and its participants by attending meetings and interviewing (formally and informally) students, faculty, and administrators. I also joined individuals in social outings, and otherwise observed and participated, as an outsider, in the interaction of all these players with each other and with the external community in the daily life of Hill College. I returned to many of the same "informants" for subsequent interviews or observations from them on events that transpired throughout the year. Since I live within easy commuting distance of the college, I dropped in frequently. Also, because of my proximity to the campus, I was able to interview individuals where they were most comfortable (i.e., office, home, restaurant, bar), and catch them at various times and in various moods throughout the year.

Hill Community College is located in the Northwest United States in a mid-sized, urban area known for its attractive environment. The community college was founded 25 years ago, and enrolls approximately 12,500 students in credit classes and 20,400 students in noncredit classes. Hill College is financed from local property taxes (about 52 percent), tuition (20 percent), and state support (28 percent). During the past few years, the college has had a decline in full-time enrollment with subsequent reduction of revenue. Enrollment has recently started to rise, but the college continues to face budget reductions. The students at Hill are primarily white and represent a diverse social strata. The "average" student is 38 years old, but the actual distribution of students is bimodal, reflecting the group of post–high school aged students (18–21) and the older, retraining students who are in their thirties and forties.

Students

Age. One of the most visible aspects of this community college was the range in age of its students. Students of all ages were found throughout the college in day and evening classes and in liberal arts and vocational courses. The goals, experiences, and educational preferences of the younger and older students were not always the same, however. As one student explained:

Day classes are geared more to the younger students—they don't have the life experiences of the older students, but at night it is different. In night classes the instructors assume too much about the [younger] student's knowledge—especially when they mention something that happened 20 years ago. The older students have a better sense of history.

The older students seemed to have their educational goals defined better than many younger students who focused more on social relations than academics. This difference in goals between the younger and older students was expressed well by a student in his late thirties who felt some urgency to start a "career." He was annoyed by younger students in his classes who did not share his concern: "They don't have the life experiences of the older students." Whereas this older student thought 18-year-old students could be less serious in their class attendance and homework, he came to school because, "I can get a computer degree in a couple of years . . . [and] if I get a good job at night then I could pick up a BA during the day." He was at Hill College because it "fit his needs" to be trained as quickly and as inexpensively as possible. Another older student in his forties explained he needed to complete his education and get out in the job market because time was running out. Although he would have liked to sample different courses, he believed he had forfeited his chance for a more liberal education, because his age no longer allowed him the time and freedom for intellectual exploration. He felt he had little choice now other than to seek an education that would make him competitive in the job market. For this reason, Hill College was best for him; he explained: "Hill teachers teach reality—there is a greater focus on current issues, it is more relevant to real life . . . this is the way it really works in the real world."

As a group, the older students appeared especially motivated to complete a degree. Most did not outwardly resent the younger students, but preferred taking classes at night. One older student liked being with his peers, because he felt they were more "serious" in their studies. Similarly, many of the older students expressed the goals they had in mind and felt they had little time to waste. There was a feeling of urgency among many of them to get on with their lives, and they resented anything or anyone at the college who appeared to hinder their goals. As one student explained:

We're not into the A's and B's; we're not interested in grades; we're here to learn. The point is to know the material not to get a grade. They need to focus on the student and worry less about the grade and more about content. . . . I need to keep motivated because it is so hard when you have other responsibilities of the family and work. I've been real close to bagging it. We need to be encouraged.

Because many of the older students were so goal-directed, they experienced a certain amount of conflict not only with younger students, but with the college as well: "[Hill] needs more weekend and night courses for those of us who are working. They should gear education to people in the work force. It is like since there is a surplus of college graduates they make it harder for those of us who can't afford it." Some of the older students were frustrated as well with the scheduling at the college. One student complained: "There needs to be better coordination. . . . It takes four years to finish an AA in Business. I get funding from work, but I don't know how long they'll keep paying me to go to school."

Motivation. Categorically, younger students appeared no less motivated than older students. With the wide range in ages of students at Hill College, I found 28-year-old students who were adrift and much less motivated than some 18-year-old students who had an educational goal. For many of the younger students, however, the college served as a holding station; they sensed few options other than to continue school and to work part-time. Because of the uncertain economy in the area and these students' lack of skills, full-time employment for many was not an option. For some, there was a vague feeling that continuing in school might be of help. School offered a break from the drudgery of a menial, part-time job, and being a college student justified dead-end employment. Many of these younger students focused more on the social aspects of the college than the academic ones. Indeed, many of them had no specific educational goals, and were willing to just wait and see what would happen in the coming year in terms of employment and social relations.

Certainly, it was not only the younger or less "mature" students who lacked educational goals and motivation. Many students of all ages used Hill College as a way to pass time or simply as a place to get financial aid to help with their living expenses. Yet, when high school graduates are uncertain of their vocational future, further education can delay entry into the work force and can buy individuals time to shop for an occupation, career, or even a mate. Being younger places students in a cultural group whose concept of time and motivation is different from that of older students.

Among the students at this college, there was no pride in resisting the messages of the dominant culture, in contrast to what Weis (1985) observed among minorities in her study. Weis noted that minority students who wanted to succeed at the community college were considered outsiders by their peers. To be academically motivated was to reject the minority culture and one's friends in the urban college Weis studied. It was quite the opposite situation for the students at Hill College. Because Hill has a homogeneous, white student body, conflicts in motivation were more apparent by age than by race. Even though class differences existed, the predominant student ethic was to embrace the dominant white culture of success. In fact, the motto of Hill College, "Go for Success," was readily championed by most students, even though many of the younger students had little understanding of the commitment in time and energy it would take to achieve such "success."

Financial and Social Support. Regardless of their level of motivation, many students (young and old) had difficulties balancing the competing demands of school, family, and money. Because of these burdens, they felt it was the college's and faculty's responsibility to provide a climate that further encouraged them. Most students were quite positive about the support the college provided: "You need to keep a positive attitude out here. Attitude isn't everything, but with support you can go a long way." This student saw "support" coming not only from faculty, but from other students as well. The atmosphere of the classroom was very important for this student, who believed the college's climate depended upon motivated students and effective teaching. Another student praised one of the college's liberal arts faculty members for his encouragement and devotion to all levels of students: "No one was insignificant [in this class] . . . it is real easy to sneer at someone, but he worked real well with beginning students. He had a good way of letting people know how to improve." Many students remained at Hill College because of such positive experiences or because individuals encouraged them to stay. One student was particularly impressed with how the college helped new students: "[Hill College] gets them on the right footing. It lets people know who don't have any academic bent that they can do OK in college. . . . If a kid has trouble in high school, the community college shows you you can do it."

Not all students had such positive experiences, nor did they receive encouragement from all faculty. One student from a working-class background carefully chose instructors because he could not afford to take a class from a teacher who tried to "weed us out." Because this student was working full-time and going to school, he felt he could not risk his time or money on a "bad class or teacher." Generally, students were positive about the level of teaching at Hill: "Almost every instructor gives a lot of information on what the school provides. They are all trying to turn it into a good experience. Most teachers are interested in promoting their teaching."

Status. Although differences in age provided an easy way to identify students, a student's major or future educational goals were not so evident. Within all institutions of higher education, a student's declared major upon entering school is not necessarily a valid indication of the person's educational goals. For example, at Hill College students enrolled in a transfer program have priority in registration for some classes. Obviously, it did not take long for students to figure out how to gain this advantage. The distinction then between "true" transfer students, who really intended to go to a four-year institution, and the "undecideds," who may simply give a socially acceptable response, was not clear. Similarly, the courses in which students enrolled did not always accurately reflect the student's intentions. Distinguishing between a vocational class and a transfer class was easy in some instances (e.g., machine shop or welding), but not so simple in others (e.g., freshman math).

Students and even faculty were not always certain who was a transfer student and who was a vocational student. This distinction was important for some students who found themselves enrolled in classes that served both transfer and vocational students. For example, one student complained that, in her computer classes, she was not "sure if instructors ever knew students were there for anything other than vocational purposes." Since vocational programs relied more on computers and advanced technical skills, both vocational and transfer majors found themselves in the same classes. I did not find open resentment of one group to the other, but one student thought vocational students were "pampered." Her feelings were that vocational students were not as academically challenged and instructors did not expect as much academically from them as they did from transfer students.

Status differences between transfer and vocational students were an inherent part of the community college's culture. By status I mean the level, type of participation, and eventual goal of the students in the college. Students could attend the college on a full-time or part-time basis, for credit or noncredit courses, and enroll in transfer, vocational, or community service classes. However, even though Hill College had an open-enrollment policy, students were not free to enter any program they wished. Enrollment in some specific vocational programs, such as computers, nursing education, and electronics, was competitive and largely gender specific. Furthermore, all students, whether transfer or vocational, who enrolled in credit classes were tested on their reading and mathematics levels, and then placed in appropriate level courses. Because of this situation, some students found themselves unable to enroll in a vocational program of their choosing, succeeding marginally in remedial classes or basic-level transfer courses, or counseled into programs for which they had little interest. Although half of all the students at Hill College initially indicated they intended to transfer to a four-year institution, only 15 percent eventually transferred. This apparently large failure rate was somewhat deceptive, since many of those who initially enrolled in the transfer program did so for lack of a definitive educational plan. One such student commented: "I didn't know what I was going to do. I had no expectations whatsoever when I got in the program." Another student in the transfer program said: "I didn't really know what I wanted for a major . . . . I was lost from day one."

A student's status was composed not only of the program in which he or she enrolled, but where and when the student was found on campus: transfer or vocational courses, part-time or full-time, day or evening classes, on-campus or off-campus courses. Students were able to discuss these status differences by program and enrollment level, but they were not as able or they were less willing to reflect on the differentiation by social class at the college. Several faculty members and administrators did comment, however, on differences in class status of students at the college. They explained that students from the middle class, who had college preparatory training in high school, were the ones most likely to be enrolled in transfer programs, and those from the working classes, who were enrolled in the general or vocational track in high school, were more likely to be found in vocational programs. This differentiation by social class was further evident within the upper and lower tracks of the programs. For example, vocational students who had the poorest math and science abilities (most often those from the lowest social classes who did not take college preparatory courses in high school) were found in the least skilled vocational programs, while more able working- and middle-class students were in the high-tech vocational programs (e.g., computer, electronics). Similarly, more academically talented middle-class students were enrolled in the higher track of the college transfer programs (e.g., sciences, business), while less able middle-class students were found in the lower track, "general humanities" programs. For this reason, the transfer or vocational label no longer distinguished accurately between students' abilities. Because admission was competitive in the high-technology vocational programs, transfer students, especially those in the lower track, were not the top performers in math or science courses where both vocational and transfer students were enrolled.

Only a few students commented on differences in academic ability among their peers, but a number of faculty members noted the inadequate academic preparation of many of the students and the subsequent uneven levels of academic rigor throughout the college. Several faculty members explained they lowered their standards to accommodate certain students in their classes. One instructor described the wide variety of students at the college, and noted they had some "pretty rough students" who needed extra care and attention because of their poor academic and social skills. A different faculty member explained: "We have lots of kids with different backgrounds, more and more people who are 35 to 50 who can't keep doing what they have been doing because of jobs, economy, injury, family, high school, whatever." Another instructor observed that a teacher at the community college was perhaps like a "nurse or missionary" for many students.

Although class issues helped explain who would be admitted to what programs, the meanings associated with gender were equally important in explaining the cultural issues that defined Hill College. Male students predominate in the high-tech vocational programs, while female students were more likely to be found in "nurturing" vocational programs, such as nursing, child care, and social service. Men are also more often found in the prerequisite courses to the high-tech vocational programs than were women. One administrator explained, however: "It is changing slowly. We have more women who are single heads of households and they are catching on to the higher pay in male occupations and enrolling in those programs." He elaborated: "We do have some token examples of men in nursing programs and women in mechanic courses, but women lack role models and don't usually enroll in technical classes. We do see more women in computer programming courses though, and they are taking more math and sciences classes, too."

Gender alone was a significant factor in determining program enrollment at this college, but it also interacted with an individual's age, class, and race. At Hill College, there were slightly more younger men (approximately 55 percent) enrolled than younger women, but more older women (approximately 60 percent) than older men. Women accounted for about 60 percent of the college's total enrollment, but they were least likely to be found in the higher track of the transfer or vocational programs, regardless of age, class, or race. Although only a small percentage of minority students enrolled at the college, like women, they were more likely to be found in the lower track of the transfer and vocational programs.

The students at Hill College represented a broad spectrum of class, ability, and age. Certainly for some students, the college could be a transforming influence by offering a path to upward mobility. This potential outcome was influenced by the interaction of the students' attributes with the cultural climate of the college and community. One faculty member observed that "we offer them [students] an opportunity—not a lot of guidance." She felt that the college was "passive" in its encouragement of students; the model of support being more conserving than transforming.

For students at Hill College, the webs they spun about themselves that defined their culture were based to a large extent on their age, level of motivation and understanding of the educational process, the financial and social support they received, and their status as students. Their cultural beliefs and values interacted to affect how students perceived themselves, each other, the faculty, and their experience at the college. Moreover, the differences in these cultural values and beliefs define the areas of conflict at the college between younger and older, transfer and vocational, and middle-class and lower-class students and the faculty, counselors, and administrators.

Faculty and Administrators

Part-Time versus Full-Time Status. Hill College had a hierarchy of status for faculty members similar to that for students. Faculty members were employed full-time or part-time, and taught in transfer, vocational, and community service programs for credit and noncredit. Unlike students, however, faculty were further differentiated by their degrees and their

status as "contracted" or "noncontracted" employees (i.e., hired or contracted on a continuing basis with a full benefits package vs. hired term
by term without a contract and partial benefits coverage). Noncontracted,
part-time faculty constituted a substantial part of all faculty members
(30 percent to 35 percent of total faculty) and were vital to the operation
of Hill College. One administrator observed: "The truth is, it is the
noncontracted people who carry the college." Part-time, noncontracted
faculty allowed the college the flexibility to change programs rapidly, to
bring teachers on campus from the community, and to save money.
Conversely, as one faculty member explained, "Many people who are
part-time are not really involved in the mission of the college." In order
for the college to meet its goals and mission, this particular faculty member
believed a strong, unified faculty was needed who shared the goals of Hill
College.

Because such a high proportion of part-time employees were women,
comparable worth and pay equity was a concern. The concern over gender
issues was noted by one male administrator who explained: "The faculty
are predominantly female, but not administration. At the policy level it is
predominantly males who determine what students need, but they [admin-
istrators] are not in as direct contact with the students." A faculty member
observed there was "not really a concerted effort to support women" at
Hill College. She believed there was "some level of individual support for
women—even though they are the majority [of students] at the college.
Attracting women is not seen as a major issue."

Credit versus Noncredit Status. Status differences were also apparent
at Hill College between the faculty who taught credit and noncredit
courses. For example, an instructor in the Adult Basic Education program
(ABE) explained that the location in which their program was housed was
like a "campus ghetto." She believed their facilities to be among the "worst
on campus" and that such treatment reflected the value the administration
placed on ABE and other noncredit programs. She explained that not only
was the program relegated to a campus ghetto, but that instructors of
noncredit courses generally earned less money and were required to work
longer hours with more students than instructors in the college credit
program: "It is real frustrating." For this instructor, there was a "great deal
of shame and embarrassment if [someone] is connected with our program
. . . but I'm not buying that anymore; we are not less valuable." Although
this instructor was adamant in her defense of noncredit instructors and the
students she serves, the faculty union representative at the college was not
so supportive. To my question about the equity of salary and work

differences between credit and noncredit faculty, the union representative explained: "ABE instructors are overworked but they are not necessarily underpaid."

Part-time instructors also had second-class status at Hill College. For example, the bottom of the full-time instructors' pay scale was the top of the scale for the part-time instructors. Because of the growing number of part-time faculty and the college's increasing reliance on them, their lower pay and marginal status was an increasing source of conflict. This conflict was also apparent between the part-time faculty and the union, which, according to several part-time instructors, had only recently begun to bargain for equitable salaries and benefits for them.

Transfer versus Vocational Status. The status hierarchy at Hill College extended as well to differences between the transfer and vocational faculty. Faculty who taught in the collegiate transfer programs were more likely to have higher degrees, to be engaged in scholarly activities, and to have higher administrative positions in the college. The vocational faculty constantly battled the negative image of "vo-tech," both within the college and within the community. This conflict increased in intensity because of successive budget cuts over the past three years at the college. How best to allocate scarce resources and whether to cut transfer or vocational programs were the source of constant debate among the faculty and administration. One administrator believed community colleges should "throw out the whole notion of vocational education." Training people for one particular job is a "conservative mind-set," he explained. "The market changes rapidly and people will have many different jobs—vocational education should prepare them for the market out there, not only one specific job."

With the increasing diversity of the college's mission, the debate over resources was no longer only over transfer and vocational programs, but also among the noncredit adult education, at-risk youth, small business support, and community education programs. This competition over re-sources escalated the conflict over the status of programs and their students and faculty. Whose beliefs and values should dominate and who the college should serve were unresolved issues of cultural conflict at the college.

Mission. A number of faculty expressed their concerns over which students should be the focus for Hill College. As one faculty member explained: "Some students are so petrified they only complete one credit a term. Our goal is to see these people succeed." Similarly, an administrator explained the objective of the community college to be to "take someone where they are and move them up as many notches as we can." For this administrator and many faculty members at Hill College, there was a particular concern about those students who were not well served by the traditional institutions of education. This attention to students with academic, financial, or social needs, according to one administrator, was the original purpose of the college. She explained that the college was supposed to serve "those people who are not served by anybody else," and to do whatever the college could to get students where they "want to go." For one faculty member, such a goal was not enough. She wondered if:

[Hill College] is really changing the way people think about the world—we don't really talk about it. I don't think we worry about it—we just want them to get a job doing what they were trained for. We think we are successful. This is a pretty limited vision of what we should be doing—making them fit into the slots out there.

Regardless of a student's declared major or vocational destination "out there," many faculty members found it difficult to serve the diverse needs of students. Several instructors noted the conflict between students and some faculty whose expectations were perhaps too high for the typical community college student. One faculty member explained that there were a few of her colleagues who were "preparing students for the big time—the university," and ignored the needs of the majority. She did not see that as a common problem, but one teacher, in particular, was an "authoritarian ass," because he was only teaching to the top students.

Faculty who taught courses that served both vocational and transfer students recognized the difficulty in teaching to the disparate levels of students in the same class. One teacher gave grades for the vocational students as a form of "encouragement," while grades for the transfer students were based more on academic ability. This faculty member thought his double standard would not work as well in a more objectively measured subject area (math, for example), but he saw his role as encouraging all students to succeed.

The focus of the faculty on the top students who would transfer to a university appeared to be less pervasive at Hill College than at the community college Weis (1985) studied. Weis found that a majority of the faculty focused on the top students and had a certain antipathy toward the less motivated, marginal ones. Faculty at Hill College were more supportive of the diversity of students and their abilities, but conflict among the faculty existed over the importance of serving the university-bound, transfer students compared to vocational, remedial, or adult education students. However, not all faculty shared a common sense of purpose.

Some faculty reported that there was considerable disagreement over what was the "true" mission of their college. For example, after an in-service at the college, a faculty member complained that she could not understand why the college "did not do what it was supposed to do [vocational education]."

Pedagogy. Several faculty members believed the most significant area for concern at Hill College was not over contention between vocational and transfer programs, but the larger, philosophical debate between individualized, open-entry and open-exit instruction and the traditional, contained classroom approach. According to one faculty member: "The conflict in philosophy shows up more in the difference between a traditional program and individualized instruction. Teachers are for individualized instruction or against it and very traditional."

The same faculty member noted further the conflict among her colleagues over the philosophy of teaching at the college and over the "capability and direction the students can go and want to go." Individualized instruction was more in keeping with this particular faculty member's philosophy of the role of the community college. For her, individualized instruction offered an alternative way to teach alternative students. She saw individualized instruction as helping to build morale: "It is opposed to the attitude of traditional instructors who are isolated in their classroom versus a team approach to working together. . . . Students are on their own when they get to the next teacher under the traditional format."

Her perception was supported by several students who complained they could not study with friends enrolled in the same course but with a different instructor, because the course content was so different. One student commented: "You're looking at something that's basically independent . . . faculty don't seem to coordinate." Within individualized instruction programs, another faculty member explained that instructors had to coordinate their efforts and focus upon the needs of the student, rather than engage in behaviors that merely facilitated the teacher's instructional task. A number of faculty members and administrators believed that individualized instruction was the pedagogical tool most appropriate for the diverse needs of students at Hill College. Instead of assuming all students gained the same from a typical classroom setting, several faculty members explained that individualized instruction fit better with the goals of the community college, because it served the varied needs of each student. Since many students were at Hill College because they did not do well in traditional academic settings, the goal of the college, according to a number of faculty members, should have been to offer an educational alternative to these students: "Individualized instruction doesn't match the traditional structure; it is a different way of thinking and of being funded." Not only did individualized instruction require a different method of teaching, but also a different mechanism to pay teachers and fund the college. Traditional methods of instruction in a contained classroom operated on a term basis and were FTE-driven models (Full-Time Equivalent). One administrator explained that individualized instruction did not fit the traditional FTE structure, "since teachers don't do the usual five classes, thirty students per class. They may teach seven or ten classes with three or four students in a class."

For an institution that prided itself on innovation, the structure of Hill appeared to hinder such innovation. One administrator explained: "No one is going back and taking a look at the answer to how we got this way. We are so busy balancing budgets no one thinks that there are other ways. We keep driving the car when maybe we should take a bus—does it still make sense?" This administrator continued: "The formulas for funding favor one philosophy. . . . We have an FTE model, based on a traditional classroom approach that makes sense only for a traditional classroom. It all goes back to a traditional mode of academic credit."

Other faculty members and administrators noted the incompatibility of the two approaches to teaching and funding. One administrator explained: "The academic folks were traditional and more conserving in their view . . . the more liberal is the noncredit, individualized instruction." For this individual, there were "huge differences" in philosophy between the credit and noncredit parts of the campus: "If you look at conservative as traditional, they are in how they organize classes, office hours, time of the day classes are offered—it is a conservative approach to education." Another administrator explained that the transfer faculty "feel better with the lock step" way of teaching; "they are not so used to attending to the needs of the students." This administrator noted the reluctance of some faculty to rethink their philosophy of teaching: "It is a change and change brings about conflict."

Certainly, at least two disparate cultures were present at Hill College with regard to teaching and approaches to funding the college. Proponents of a nontraditional model for teaching at the college were almost zealous in defense of their position. Alternatively, I found advocates of the more traditional teaching approach to be unsure why anyone would criticize the existing model. They typically defended the status quo as an organizational necessity due to funding restrictions, union agreements, or state regulation. Fay (1987, p. 27) termed the lack of these individuals' awareness of the drama around them and their weak justification of the role they played a "false consciousness" or "systematic ignorance" individuals "have about themselves and their society." Perhaps this is one of the ultimate anomalies of the community college—the false consciousness of its professed philosophy regarding innovation and change, and the reality of its traditional structure.

One faculty member summarized her concern about the faculty at Hill College and the college's ability to change its present reality:

The faculty lack awareness of themselves as educators. They can teach but they don't understand their role. We need to be more introspective. These issues need to be raised—it has to be the administration who think about philosophy. They need to set the guidelines and designate the spare time to do this.

This faculty member's perception of the need for critical thinking among her colleagues was similar to Fay's (1987, p. 66) goal for critical science to "stimulate" individuals to a "rational scrutiny" of their existence. An administrator also expressed this concern for critical thinking and self-reflection by asking: "Have community colleges really addressed the issue of what business are we in?" Because he believed "community colleges are microcosms of society, much more so than universities," he felt it was time to question how well community colleges were fulfilling their role in society. "Maybe the whole way we are set up doesn't make sense. . . . Maybe it is time to change all this."

DISCUSSION

Initially, I proposed that the complexity of education requires a form of analysis that addresses the social and cultural processes of education that provide meaning to the participants of a community college. Guided by Fay's (1987) components of critical theory, I used a case study to help identify the cultural dynamics of the students, faculty, and administrators at Hill College. I sought to explicate the meaning of this college to students, faculty, and administrators through a phenomenological approach that was sensitive to the cultural dynamics of the college.

Even though Hill College may be transformative by concept, a basic component of its culture is a conservative tradition of curriculum and pedagogy. Internal tension in the college exists between advocates of the conservative traditions and proponents of curricular and pedagogical innovation. Such conflict between the conserving and transforming roles of education is not always negative, so long as the nature and consequences of this conflict are understood both by community college participants and by external change agents. My goal in this case study was not to resolve this cultural conflict, but to identify it and understand how it was perceived by the students, faculty, and administration of Hill College.

Age, academic program, motivation, social class, and gender help define in what programs, what time of the day, and how often a student will be at Hill College. Each of these attributes affects a student's likelihood for success. The interaction of these and other undetected factors defines the webs of significance the students, the faculty, and the administration spin about themselves, which are the culture of Hill College. For example, that students are generally very practical in their goals at Hill College is not surprising given the attributes they bring to the college, their interactions with each other and the faculty, and the pressures from the external society. Although counselors may influence the direction certain students take, the attributes students already possess define to the greatest extent why they are at the college in the first place and where they might eventually go. The college is not helpless in overcoming the attributes the students bring with them, but, as one faculty member noted, the college is typically "passive" in its response to students. Who the students are prior to their enrollment helps define what the college will be for them.

Although the community college is naturally a site for contestation between conserving and transforming elements of society, the students generally are not aware of this struggle. Again, herein lies the false consciousness Fay (1987) considers central to the development of critical theory. Students unwittingly support the conserving functions of education when they feel they have neither time, motivation, nor freedom to explore educational options. This conserving aspect of the students' culture is not the fault of the students alone. That time appears to be running out on many of them and that domestic responsibilities overshadow their educational future are problems counselors, financial aid officers, and administrators should help mediate. Postsecondary education need not be a "single elimination" tournament (Rosenbaum, 1976), where individuals who leave education can never return. Unfortunately, the external culture does not readily support restarting players who may need child care, sufficient income to support a family, or time to devote to rigorous academic study.

Few students seemed aware of their roles in the culture of the college, but many faculty members understood the inherent cultural tensions present at Hill College. One faculty member in particular expressed the need for "self-awareness" among her peers concerning their roles and obligations to students. Foremost for her was the need for the faculty to be aware of their choice of pedagogy—individualized versus traditional instructional methods. Although status differences existed among faculty, the concern that crossed all status boundaries was pedagogy. Stereotypes about vocational faculty being inherently conservative in their pedagogical techniques and transfer faculty being liberal no longer hold. Not all vocational education teachers are conservative in their pedagogy, just as not all liberal arts faculty are transformative. In fact, some of the most innovative and equitable approaches to teaching at Hill College were in the vocational, community education, and study skills programs, while some of the most conservative and elitist approaches to teaching were in the liberal arts areas.

This conflict between proponents of the status quo and those of innovation was the coherent pattern that gave definition to Hill College for its participants and community. The false consciousness of the faculty over the effectiveness of traditional pedagogy for the nontraditional students of the community college and the false consciousness of the students over their educational options in this drama indicate how culture shapes collective behavior.

CONCLUSION

The community college is a natural site of cultural conflict between the conserving and transformative forces of education, but this conflict is not only imposed externally; the students and the faculty also participate in this conflict over whose values and ideas should predominate. This inherent cultural tension for students, faculty, and administrators at Hill College is based upon the cultural attributes these individuals bring to the college, and how their cultural beliefs and values converge and conflict. Predominant in this conflict is the coherent pattern of contention between advocates of the conservative restoration and proponents of social and educational equality. Whereas proponents of one group see transformation as the way to meet best the needs of Hill's diverse students, the other group believes students should fit into the existing structure that is currently sufficient to meet any of their needs. For faculty, one of the principal battlegrounds for this competition or conflict is over pedagogy and the appropriateness of the dominant teaching model for the nontraditional needs of students. Additional sources of conflict among the faculty themselves and between the faculty and administration is over employment status (part-time, full-time, credit, noncredit), program (transfer or vocational), and pedagogical philosophy. For students, their ages, motivation, financial and social support, and status (including class and gender) provide major areas of conflict over whose values are dominant.

That there is continual conflict among the students themselves, between the students and faculty, and among the faculty is inherent in the reality of community colleges and their multiple functions. As we have seen, some of the battlegrounds for this conflict are in the classrooms over the appropriateness of the dominant pedagogical methods and in the counselors' offices over the appropriateness of a student's goals. Because the traditional system of education has been inappropriate for so many of the community college's students, merely reproducing the structure in which they have failed previously offers merely a further dose of inappropriate education.

If a more equitable distribution of education and knowledge is a role community colleges profess to play in American society, community college participants should understand how their institutions filter people and knowledge, and how such filtering favors conservation of the educational and economic status quo. A greater awareness of the role students, faculty, and administrators play in supporting an educational culture at the community college that employs sexist and racist methods of pedagogy, support, and expectations is needed to facilitate change. The conflict between the conserving and transformative processes of education at the community college is a confrontation over who should be allowed access to the paths of upward mobility. The college doors may be open, but the paths to upward mobility are accessible only to those who possess the appropriate attributes. Proponents of educational equality both inside and outside the community college first need to be aware of their contribution to the college's culture, and then understand how the college controls access to knowledge and mobility. Even though a capitalist society does not allow everyone to be upwardly mobile, access to the paths of mobility can be distributed more equitably. Only by understanding first the culture of an educational institution can the process of transformation begin—the goal of critical theory.

REFERENCES

Brint, S., & Karabel, J. (1989). *The diverted dream: Community colleges and the promise of educational opportunity in America, 1900–1985*. New York: Oxford.

Carnoy, M., & Levin, H. M. (1985). *Schooling and work in the democratic state*. Palo Alto, CA: Stanford University Press.

Clark, B. R. (1960). *The open door college: A case study*. New York: McGraw-Hill.

————. (1980). The "cooling out" function revisited. *New Directions for Community Colleges, 8*(4), 15–32.

Deegan, W. L., Tillery, D., & Associates. (1985). *Renewing the American community college.* San Francisco: Jossey-Bass.

Fay, B. (1987). *Critical social science: Liberation and its limits.* Ithaca, NY: Cornell University Press.

Geertz, C. (1973). *The interpretation of cultures.* New York: Basic Books.

Grieco, M. S. (1988). Birth-marked? A critical view on analyzing organizational culture. *Human Organization, 47,* 84–87.

Grubb, W. N. (1984). The bandwagon once more: Vocational preparation for high-tech occupations. *Harvard Educational Review, 54*(4), 429–451.

Karabel, J. (1972). Community colleges and social stratification. *Harvard Educational Review, 42,* 521–562.

London, H. (1978). *The culture of a community college.* New York: Praeger.

Pincus, F. (1980). The false promises of community colleges. *Harvard Educational Review, 50,* 332–361.

Reinhard, B. (1989, October 24). Enrollment up dramatically. *The Community, Technical, and Junior College Times, 1,* 8.

Rosenbaum, J. (1976). *Making inequality: The hidden curriculum of high school teaching.* New York: Wiley.

Shor, I. (1986). *Culture wars: School and society in the conservative restoration, 1969–1984.* Boston: Routledge & Kegan Paul.

Weis, L. (1985). *Between two worlds: Black students in an urban community college.* Boston: Routledge & Kegan Paul.

Wexler, P. (1987). *Social analysis of education: After the new sociology.* New York: Routledge & Kegan Paul.

Wolcott, H. (forthcoming). On seeking—and rejecting—validity in qualitative research. In E. Eisner & A. Peshkin (Eds.), *Qualitative inquiry in education: The continuing debate.* New York: Teachers College.

Zwerling, L. S. (1976). *Second best.* New York: McGraw-Hill.

8 BRINGING SOME CLASS TO TEACHING: FOLLOWING THE PIED PIPERS OF TEACHER EDUCATION REFORM

James T. Sears, Amy K. Otis-Wilborn, and J. Dan Marshall

Into the street the Piper stept . . .

Robert Browning (1970:404)
The Pied Piper of Hamelin

During the decade of the eighties, educational institutions were under increased pressure to produce a more competitive work force in the United States (e.g., Carnegie Forum on Education and the Economy, 1986).[1] This drive resulted in calls for renewed educational excellence and the restructuring of postsecondary education. Perhaps nowhere has the drive for refurbishment in postsecondary education been discussed more than in teacher education (e.g., National Education Association, 1982; Holmes Group, Inc., 1986).[2] Two prominent teacher educators, captivated with the reform spirit, wrote:

We believe that the most effective way for schools to develop and maintain quality is to examine the way many high technology organizations (e.g., IBM) train, lead, manage, and evaluate their workforces. Schools are not factories, but they are organizations. Furthermore, the purpose of these organizations is to direct the activities of children in ways that make them effective and efficient knowledge workers. Thus, organizations that have experience in managing knowledge workers may provide instructive models for those who would reform schools to meet the conditions of the twenty-first century. (Schlechty and Joslin, 1984, p. 60)

The metaphor of students as "knowledge workers" and teachers as "managers" corresponds to concerns and priorities of Corporate America. This momentum for a higher GNP and a larger share of the world market has been thoughtlessly translated into higher education reform; reforms in which little attention is given to expanding economic democracy and enhancing social justice. Thundering ideological cattle calls, such as the National Education Association's *Excellence in Our Schools* (1982) have produced a seemingly melodious harmony of the corporate will with the commonweal.

One commonly cited reform strategy is the recruitment, preparation, and retention of high-ability persons into the profession of teaching. Programs that operationalize this strategy are proponents of a corporate, not a critical, agenda. The Bridenthal Internship in Teaching Program (BIT),[3] which has been described as an "innovative," reform-oriented teacher education program, is illustrative of the underlying corporate agenda upon which such a strategy is based. Rooted in Calvinist principles of industry and discipline, and relying upon axiomatic educational tenets, Wright, the program's innovator and director, took full advantage of the ever-shifting political winds of educational reform to further professional and institutional interests. Wright reformulated the role and structure of a professional school in higher education to conform to an emerging corporate agenda in which schools produce "effective and efficient knowledge workers" in an information age of global corporate economies. Wright, like his contemporaries, did not challenge the social and economic relations that undergird this agenda; he is a proponent of this agenda, as interviews over the years reveal:

I was in Capitol City last week talking with the Tandy Corporation. They had had an overture from the superintendent of schools. He didn't have a project in mind but said that the recruitment of high ability people is a problem and we've got to do something about this. (circa 1984)

I was in California three or four weeks ago talking to the Hewlett Foundation. They're really interested in networks, supportive networks. I think I have a good shot at joining that with half a million dollars and that will take us down a different road but, again, in the right direction. (circa 1987)

The hidden curriculum of Wright's reform-based model evidences how corporate power and state control are maintained within an apparent whirlwind of educational reform.

This chapter examines the BIT program, whose proposed solution to the perceived lack of "quality" education in the nation's schools was to target the recruitment and preparation of high-ability individuals into classroom teaching. In the process, we explore three common-sensical axioms associated with recruiting the best and brightest, creating educational reform, and transmitting knowledge. Each axiom is revealed and supported through the examination of (1) relevant educational literature, (2) curricular and programmatic BIT activities, and (3) the expressed beliefs and attitudes of those individuals directly involved in the program, including its director, Dr. Wright, the 17 students recruited into the program, and higher education faculty. We argue that these axioms are not merely idiosyncratic features of this teacher education program but reflections of the hegemony of ideology in a corporate culture that corresponds to a misplaced conception of what constitutes the commonweal.

CASE SITE AND METHODOLOGY

Calvin College is a liberal arts college in a major metropolitan area in the southwestern United States. Formerly a church-controlled school, Calvin became a nonsecular institution in the late fifties. For many years, it was a sleepy undergraduate school principally serving a well-heeled, female student body. Since the late seventies, fueled from oil-based stock revenues, it has sought to establish itself as a premier co-educational undergraduate establishment. During the past decade, it has moved successfully along the path: faculty have been lured away from prestigious colleges; each entering freshmen group has been accompanied by an increase in SAT/ACT scores; and prominent public figures routinely visit and lecture. Recently, Calvin was named as one of the country's "best buys" for a college education and cited as one of the top small, liberal arts colleges in the South. In 1984, the year these 17 interns entered Calvin, their freshmen class averaged 1,120 on the collegiate test scores, and its undergraduate student body numbered approximately 2,400 with a student/faculty ratio of 10.5 to 1. By 1988, the year the interns graduated from Calvin, the entering freshmen average SAT test score was 1,220, with about the same number of students attending the college. The Bridenthal Internship in Teaching Program is one example of Calvin's quest for excellence in undergraduate education.

Calvin College's Department of Education was one of the first in the country to implement reform efforts to meet the challenges of recruiting, preparing, and retaining high-ability persons into teaching.[4] Under the leadership of John Wright, 17 top high school graduates were recruited into a specially designed, six-year teacher preparation program. Among the 14 women and three men, selected from more than 100 qualified applicants, were five in *Who's Who Among American High School Students*, a national merit scholar, two valedictorians, and ten National Honor Society members. All earned SAT scores exceeding 1,000, and all graduated in the top ten percent of their high school class. All but four had seriously considered nonteaching careers, such as law, medicine, psychology, and engineering. During the next four years, this cadre of the "brightest and the best" progressed through the academic curriculum at Calvin and, in addition, benefited from a BIT-specific curriculum. In effect, their teacher education began with their first day of classes and continued through their first two years of teaching.

A three-member independent research team conducted this six-year study, which employed a multi-stage design and a complementary combination of qualitative and quantitative methods.[5] These methods included: individual, audio-taped *structured interviews* of the interns, their parents, and the BIT program principals; standardized as well as site-specific *paper-and-pencil instruments*; structured video-taped *classroom teaching observations*; and *personal journals* as well as *informal interviews* and *portfolios*.[6]

IDENTIFYING THE RIGHT PEOPLE

During their four years at Calvin, the interns participated in three unique phases of BIT: initial recruitment, extended recruitment, and professional socialization. The initial recruitment period began with Wright's announcement of the Bridenthal Internship in Teaching Program and ended with his selection of the 17 BIT Interns. The extended recruitment phase witnessed these interns meeting frequently as a group, attending special seminars and education-related functions, and participating in practicum experiences as they weighed their decisions regarding certification programs and content areas. The professional socialization phase commenced in their junior year when the interns were integrated into Calvin's regular teacher education curricula and progressed into their induction as classroom teachers. These three phases represented the surface curriculum of the BIT program.

There was also a hidden curriculum. During their four years at Calvin, the interns made career-shaping decisions, tested their degree of commitment to teaching, and struggled with their role as student teachers. In the process, these interns were exposed to a variety of hidden ideologically rooted messages embedded in axioms of conventional educational discourse.

Recruiting the Brightest and the Best

Education needs students with more intellectual power. How will future students learn if they have incompetent teachers? Businesses will be affected as they receive students who are less capable of handling business duties. Better teachers must be recruited!

Donna

Funding and Recruitment. Touting a scholarship package of $26,000 in forgivable loans, Professor John Wright began scouting for high-ability high school seniors in the fall of 1983: "We recruit halfbacks. We recruit oboe players. But we don't recruit teachers. We sit back in our colleges and universities and wait for them to appear." In the midst of the first wave of educational reform, Wright had no such patience. His search for the "brightest and the best" was thus premised on the axiom: *The brightest students make the best teachers.*

An imaginative educational entrepreneur, Wright set out to produce a "new breed" of teacher: one that would transform the classroom into an efficient knowledge production factory, restore the status of a much maligned profession, catalyze educational change, and in the process, firmly establish Calvin College as the region's premier teacher preparation institution:

What we want to do is to become one of the places in the country where bright people who want to teach would want to go. We simply want that reputation. A few weeks ago, I was sitting at that table with two parents. The daughter wasn't here yet but was coming the next day. I asked them where she was looking. They said, "Rice, Calvin, and Yale." The mother interrupted and said, "Where would you send her?" I said, "Well, if she's interested in pure math, science, and engineering—Rice. If she wants to get a first-class general education—Yale. If she wants to teach—Calvin."

In order to accomplish these goals, Wright sought funding from the Bridenthal Foundation, a charitable trust established from monies generated from corporate ventures. In his formal proposal, he penned:

While overall our system of public education is the best of its kind in the world, there continue to be problems that beg solution. . . . The critical problem is our inability to recruit sufficient numbers of highly-qualified persons for the teaching profession, to provide quality, effective preparation programs in our best colleges and universities for these young people, and to retain these persons in the teaching profession. (Calvin College, 1983, pp. 4–5)

After funding was secured, Professor Wright launched an intensive media campaign in the metropolitan market. He personally telephoned each principal of the 35 area high schools asking them to help with recruitment, and tirelessly roamed area high schools speaking with guidance counselors, conferring with Calvin alumni, and speaking before student assemblies in his search for the "brightest and best." As a result, more than 100 high school seniors who ranked in the top ten percent of their graduating class applied for the (original) ten internships.

The selection process was equally rigorous: recommendations, essays, and interviews were required. At this stage, Wright was concerned with personal qualities: "You've got to look for tenacity, commitment. Some bright kids don't do well in college. They don't have 'the bottom,' like they say with horses, to see it through." In the end, Wright could not winnow his list down to a mere ten. With his formidable persuasive skills and graceful style, he quickly received funds for six additional internships.[7]

The Problematics of Recruitment. The importance of recruiting the "brightest and best" students into teaching fits Calvin's Ivy-League image, where the number of freshmen who are national merit scholars is slightly less than the number of Mercedes Benz convertibles and Jaguars that crowd the student parking lot. Embedded in this goal was a meritocratic ideology, in which the academic playing fields of schools become social tournaments in which all compete for status, power, and money within a society stratified by social class and fractured with racial and gender divisions (Turner, 1960). Participants in the BIT program were disproportionately drawn from the Anglo middle class. Like children of other middle-class parents, these interns could not have reasonably expected to attend Calvin without such a scholarship program. The class-based composition of the Ivy League curriculum and its student body is well documented in a recent study of the enrollment patterns at elite institutions during the late 1980s:

Those who make it through the highly competitive admissions process of the prestigious universities are considered "the best and the brightest," those qualified, perhaps even destined, to have the most prized careers. Often overlooked, however, is the fact that the student bodies of these institutions are drawn heavily from affluent families . . . the elite private institutions appear to remain linked to an upper-class constituency within this putative meritocratic order. (Lewis and Kingston, 1989, p. 28)

Noting that, while increasing financial support for middle- and low-income, high-ability students might result in a more diverse student body, these researchers observe that, without concomitant changes in institutional definitions of "high ability," the "two-tier" system in higher education will continue:

If the very selective private institutions remain committed to the conventional measures of "merit"—high scores on standardized tests, well-balanced interests, special skills—in their admissions decisions, any increase in aid is likely to have only a slight impact on the social background of their students. Most students who are meritorious in the conventional sense come from high-income families where they have enjoyed special opportunities; children from lower-income families acquire relatively fewer linguistic and cultural skills—a decided disadvantage in their school work. (Lewis and Kingston, 1989, p. 32)

The importance of recruiting "high-ability" students who had "the bottom" to become Bridenthal Interns and classroom teachers reflects a corporate agendum: knowledge managers who can efficiently educate the work force of the twenty-first century. Wright's program to recruit the brightest and best into the teaching profession quickened the heart of the most downtrodden teacher, the mind of the most concerned policy-maker, and the roughened hands of the most menial laborer. All knew that the brightest people are the crown jewels of schooling and that the best people should be educating our youth, just as all know of the poor quality of our present teacher crop.

According to pollsters (e.g., Gallup and Clark, 1987), the public shares Wright's assessment of "our inability to recruit sufficient numbers of highly-qualified persons for the teaching profession and to provide quality, effective preparation programs in our best colleges and universities for these young people." According to researchers, teacher education graduates of the early 1980s, particularly those most interested in teaching as a career, are generally less academically talented than those who graduated a decade earlier (Pigge, 1985).[8]

Equating Academic Ability with Teaching Performance

If all the people at the upper end of the bell curve—as far as grades and SAT *scores go—enter into professional things like medicine and business, who is left to teach the children? Do you want somebody who made C's all the way through high school to teach your child how to make A's? Is that even possible? A person who made C's will settle for C's from his students, but a person who made A's is going to push the students to make A's. What kind of teacher do you want for your children? I want the best for my children.*

Mary

While academic ability and performance are not the only factors in the formula for an "effective teacher," most teacher educators, as far back as Boyce's (1912) early studies, consider such factors necessary preconditions or, at minimum, characteristics that do not place teachers at a disadvantage in the classroom (Vance and Schlechty, 1982). Summarizing research on effective teachers, Brophy echoes this commonplace belief when he concludes, "Effective teachers . . . are *probably* brighter and more dedicated than average" (Brophy, 1982, p. 529; emphasis added).

Data supporting Brophy's contention are ambivalent, at best, and meager, at worst.[9] This lack of consensus among research studies is, in part, a conceptual problem: What does one mean by "quality students," and how does one define "success in teaching"? There is also the methodological problem of how to measure these two concepts. Little research data support Brophy's statement. Even Brophy's proponents, such as Schlechty and Vance (1983, p. 101) admit: "We are aware that no convincing evidence links measures of academic ability to teacher effectiveness" (Schlechty and Vance, 1983, p. 101)—a conclusion reached by others who have systematically reviewed the literature.[10]

For Wright, however, the inconclusiveness of research studies and the lack of ongoing research into reform programs were of little importance.

It's going to be a criticism where the SAT for most teachers is 300 or 400 points below. Some kids who are not as bright will also make outstanding teachers, but I don't think that this means that we should not try to recruit bright people for teaching. I think that it is ludicrous to get into a debate about whether or not you have to be smart to be a good teacher. If the other qualities are present—such as the ability to work with children—then it's *got* to be a plus for the person to be bright and to be well educated.

In his recent text *America's Teacher Quality Problem*, Weaver, like Wright, simplifies the discussion of teacher quality by reducing it to academic ability (Weaver, 1983, p. 270). He then curiously offers the following remarks: "Academic ability is one measure of teacher quality, but it is not the only one and perhaps not even the most important measure" (Weaver, 1983, p. 1). The suspect axiom and its associated corollaries (that "bright" means academically able and "best" means the production of high student test scores) do not, in Weaver's view, represent "a definition that educators will agree on but one that is unarguably important and of self-interest to educators for other reasons having to do with legitimating claims for support of public schooling" (Weaver, 1983, p. 4).

Similarly, Victor Vance and Phillip Schlechty (1982, p. 25) advance this axiom by employing an argument echoed by Wright. They state,

"Whereas the ability to score high on measures of academic ability may not assure competence, scoring low on such measures does not give one an advantage over the competition." Like Wright, they neither argue that students with high academic ability will be better teachers nor that those with low academic ability will make poor teachers; they simply believe that "all things being equal, demonstrated intellectual ability is an advantage in the classroom. It is certainly not a disadvantage" (Vance and Schlechty, 1982, p. 25).

Of no minor importance, of course, is that those "things" Vance and Schlechty allude to (family income, community resources, race/gender, and so forth) are never equal. In fact, these other "things" are the principal contributors that differentiate among students (and teachers) on alleged measures of "high ability"[11] and form the basis for legitimizing their eventual socio-economic role in the postindustrial machine. "High ability," a supposed combination of the forces of nature and nurture, is defined by standardized test scores and class rank. The racial, gender, and social class biases of such indicators as well as the hegemony of social forces over those of nature and nurture are downplayed.

Further, despite protestations of persons such as Wright, there are disadvantages to recruiting high-ability students. For example, providing scholarship funds to students who already have amassed a significant amount of "cultural capital" (i.e., the knowledge base, values, and language of the controlling cultural group) and who will likely do well without any such support depletes resources for others who lack such capital and further reinforces the "brightest students make the best teachers" axiom.[12] As these resources are depleted and these assumptions reified, no scholarship programs for "low-ability" students who evidence qualities of a "good teacher" are developed.

The brightest and best axiom, then, is not about securing the "best" classroom teachers who are committed to working in schools *over the long haul*: it is about recruiting persons who fit an image. Just as we elect an actor to play the role imagined of a president, so, too, can we select "bright" persons to portray an image of good teachers. Even advocates like Vance and Schlechty acknowledge the imagery of such reforms: "Although some educational theoreticians and researchers may regard the link between measured academic ability, technical and instructional competence, and effective teaching as tenuous, politicians and policy makers have demonstrated their strong belief in the existence of such a relationship" (Vance and Schlechty, 1982, p. 25). Public perception delimits intellectual parameters; public language dominates educational discourse; public images translate into programmatic reform.

These public beliefs, of course, rooted in culture and ideology, eventually become an expression of faith reified into a law-like formula:

high ability (i.e., academically superior) students = quality teachers = quality (composite test scores) education = quality (high scoring) students = a more productive (GNP) and competitive (trade balance) work force

The opaque certainty expressed in this simple-minded statement reveals a corporate ideology of power and control veiled in a "ritual of technical rationality" (Cornbleth, 1986) and meritocracy that legitimates and depoliticizes the very inequities of advanced monopoly capitalism. In the words of Bourdieu:

By making social hierarchies and the reproduction of these hierarchies appear to be based upon the hierarchy of "gifts," merits, or skills established and ratified by its sanctions, or in a word, by converting social hierarchies into academic hierarchies, the educational system fulfills a function of legitimation which is more and more necessary to the perpetuation of the "social order" as the evolution of the power relationship between classes tends more completely to exclude the imposition of a hierarchy based upon the crude and ruthless affirmation of the power relationship. (Bourdieu, 1977, p. 496)

The process whereby this ideology is constructed, reproduced, and reified is aptly demonstrated in the interns' socialization process as educational reformers, described in the next section. Interests in control, certainty, and measurement—elements of this techno-rational ideology—dominate contemporary discourse on educational reform.[13] These elements pervade the interns' perspectives on classroom knowledge and management described in the final sections of this chapter.

Creating the Context for Educational Reform

There hopefully is going to be a major movement in the United States to revamp the education system. We are at the forefront.

Carl

Wright's recruitment efforts did not end when the brightest and best became Bridenthal Interns; he devoted two years to developing them into informed, eager educational change agents. How five of these interns—Vince, Rachel, Mary, Carl, and Donna—experienced this process reflects the extended recruitment phase of the Bridenthal curriculum; the messages regarding the process of change in education and their role as reformers are the hidden curriculum that was fostered by private seminars and public appearances. This curriculum is premised on another axiom: *Our best teachers will reform America's schools.*

These five interns, like the other dozen, described themselves as "high achievers" who were "privileged" to be part of this unique program. Most, like Carl, Vince, and Donna, saw their school success in academics and extracurricular activities as the key to their acceptance into the Bridenthal program. Several, like Mary and Rachel, added that their commitment to teaching was an important factor in their selection to be an intern. Mary recalls, "In my interviews, I tried to talk about education and all the state legislature's dealing. I read the paper every day so when I went into my interview I could ask questions about education."

Factors Influencing the Decision to Become an Intern. By far, the primary influence in their decision to enter the BIT program and to consider teaching as a career was Professor John Wright. Donna remembers, "He grabbed us and pulled us into education." Interestingly, more than half the interns disclosed that one or both parents were less than enthusiastic upon first learning of their child's interest in the BIT program. Carl's father, a veteran teacher, questioned the wisdom of his son's career choice: "I told him at supper that I had applied. He stopped chewing his food and looked at me. 'Carl,' he said, 'Are you feeling alright?'" Donna's parents were leery of the instant financial burden their daughter (and they) would incur should she later decide to leave the program before her six-year commitment, but "they're impressed by Dr. Wright."

Why, then, did they accept the internship? Donna had the same question in mind: "I wonder why some of the other interns really took this program; I wonder whether they really wanted to go into teaching. I *wanted* to go into teaching as a career. Although I considered engineering seriously, I felt that I wouldn't be happy in it. Teaching is a strenuous job, but I figured that engineering would just blow me away."

Carl was one of the persons Donna had in mind. Adopting an intellectual image, this entering freshman boasted, "I see myself as having touched just about every area of knowledge in some way, shape or form." His reason for accepting the internship was pragmatic: "I wouldn't have been able to go to Calvin; it is just too expensive. I would have gone into political science or philosophy at State University."

Mary describes herself as "dedicated, committed, hard-working, concerned, kind, and thoughtful." She lived at home with her parents until they separated. She has since moved in with her boyfriend's parents. Though she loves her boyfriend, they have no plans to marry.

He is dominating and often abusive; he never listens to me. The only reason I put up with [him] is because I'd rather live at his house than move back home. There, pandemonium and filth are commonplace; my mom has just remarried to a man I can't stand. My life sounds terrible and sometimes I think it is, but it's really not that bad. Calvin is a bright spot. This year I'm receiving $10,000 to go to Calvin, plus my dad sends me $200 a month and I have free room and board.

Rachel viewed herself as more socially oriented than many of the other interns and less concerned about grades. Living with her grandparents, she was grateful for the opportunity to attend Calvin, which, without the BIT program, would not have been financially possible. However, she was quick to point out that, "We're not in it for the money; we're in it for the fact that it's going to help us become good teachers."

Vince, a young man quiet of demeanor, stated: "I had never looked into being a teacher. I didn't know really what I wanted to do. I had to sit down and take a good look at myself. I decided to apply and to see what happened."

Developing Commitment. Each intern, then, entered the program for different reasons, but what was the degree of teaching commitment for each of these entering freshmen? Rachel, like seven other interns, had seriously considered teaching prior to the BIT program. She stated early on, "I like helping people work out their problems, so I think that has a lot to do with why I want to be a teacher—to help people get through school and to talk with them on a one-to-one basis." Carl, on the other hand, "had not considered teaching as a prime option" before applying to the program and had a rather weak commitment to classroom teaching for any length of time. Vince, like Carl, had not considered teaching a legitimate career choice in high school. Unlike Carl, however, he expressed a long-term commitment to classroom teaching during his first-year interview. "The more I read," Vince said, "the more I wanted to be a teacher." Though Mary had seriously examined teaching as a career option prior to the Bridenthal program, she remained uncertain about the wisdom of her career choice at the beginning of her freshman year. "It's hard," Mary explains, "when you're growing up and your parents and your teachers and everyone tell you, 'Oh, you're so smart you can do anything you want.' I have so many choices. What do I choose?"

Wright's challenge was to enhance these interns' commitment to teaching if they were to meet his reformist goals. However, commitment, according to research, is generally absent among high-ability students. Only five percent of college freshmen in the 1980s expressed an interest in becoming teachers (Astin, 1983), and those individuals who demonstrated the greatest academic talent were the least likely to choose teaching as a career (Roberson, Keith, and Page, 1983; Sykes, 1983; Empey, 1984). Nevertheless, a recent survey of a sample of academically talented high school seniors from schools throughout the southeastern United States revealed that eight times as many students (25 percent) would seriously consider teaching as a career if certain preconditions, such as money, prestige, and positive community attitudes, were met (Brogdon and Tincher, 1986).[14]

Wright skillfully manipulated these variables in the BIT curriculum. A $26,000 forgivable loan coupled with the prestige of attending Calvin College and the publicity associated with the BIT program attracted many students. The 17 selected echoed these themes during their first interviews. When asked for the first thing that came to mind when hearing the phrase "Bridenthal Program," Mary candidly replied: "Prestige, honor, and meeting lots of neat people—high achievers." Vince humbly remarked, "We're the hope for education," and Carl categorically asserted that the program "is a valuable starting point for reform of teacher education in the United States." Rachel, on the other hand, spoke about its importance in her quest to become a teacher, and Donna uttered two words: "John Wright."

Once the 17 interns were "in the harness," Wright routinely reinforced these themes. In the process, the interns acquired a particular vision of educational reform and their role as reformers—a glamorized version of the "top down" reform model. On the surface, the Bridenthal Program appears to be a grass-roots strategy: changing schools via classroom teachers. In reality, it is the opposite. Through the hidden and not-so-hidden BIT curriculum, the interns learned that reform begins with the impetus and agenda of those on top (e.g., policy-makers and molders of public opinion). From their seminars, discussions with educational leaders, and their public presentations, the interns came to view themselves as different and detached from those currently working in the classroom. These self-proclaimed "saviors of the profession" and "super teachers" found little in common with veteran classroom teachers: they expected to teach, cajole, and inspire—not to collaborate with them or learn from them. In short, the interns brandished a corporate, not a teacher-inspired agendum, where the identification of problems and the formation of decisions for resolving them were typically made by leaders far removed from the organizational grass roots. While such an agendum may succeed in serving the overall corporation and its leaders, it simultaneously breeds cynicism and polarization among mid-level managers and workers. Ultimately, under such a model, reform efforts serve the corporation first and best; diminishing benefits may be accrued by the corporate work force and clientele.

CREATING THE RIGHT PROGRAM

Developing Informed Change Agents

> *I was talking with Dennis [a local high school principal] the other day about the problem of staff morale. We [some of the interns] may visit his school soon to talk to his teachers.*
>
> Mary

Wright cultivated the image of the interns as the vanguard of educational reform through his weekly seminars attended exclusively by the interns and his individual, "fatherly" chats. The early seminars focused on criticism of public schooling and praise for current reform efforts. The interns read, reported, and discussed every major publication on educational reform, including *The Paidea Proposal*, *A Nation at Risk*, *Horace's Compromise*, and *A Place Called School*.

As the interns' first semester progressed, well-known speakers (not everyday classroom teachers) addressed them on issues ranging from pending state legislation to qualities of a good teacher. They listened to community leaders and local administrators discuss career ladders, curriculum revision, and teacher evaluation. During the last meeting of the semester, Wright asked the interns if they thought they could hold their own with anybody in the community when discussing educational reform. The college freshmen replied in a unanimous voice of certainty: "We know the issues!"

The second semester seminar focused on community issues and educational reform. Interns read about and analyzed the city's diverse communities and the schools that served them. Midway into the semester, the interns journeyed into the city, amassing data about a specific community, school, and student. Mary recalls:

I went to the school district to interview the associate superintendent and then to the school to talk with the principal. I talked to the principal twice and also to the guidance counselor. She was really helpful. She gave me a whole class schedule which had the enrollment in every class. I took the enrollments and added up how many people, for example, took electives. I added up how many people took enriched, basic, regular classes. I made little pie graphs. Then, I made little charts with the parents' occupations and educational levels.

The interns prepared student case studies that focused on their "emotional, social, and intellectual development." In their papers, some discussed obstacles confronting "disadvantaged" students, while others examined how academically able students were being served by the school. However, neither the interns nor Dr. Wright examined structural reasons for these successes or failures; the emphasis was on the individual student, his or her family, and their efforts (or lack thereof) in school. Lacking a theoretical framework to explore alternate hypotheses or conceptions of student "success" or "failure," these interns relied upon the conceptual framework at hand. Of course, such explorations not only require a bracketing of one's world view, but demand a journey into "theory," a journey that few preservice teachers, even the "brightest and the best," view as important or integral to their professional studies.

Furthermore, during their field assignments, there was little indication that the interns were encouraged to embark upon a phenomenological journey into the domain of the other: the family living on a fixed income in the barrio, the child struggling in class with little physical, emotional, or intellectual nourishment, the teacher overwhelmed by paperwork and overcrowding yet not too busy to provide individual attention to some of her 150 students. In short, these interns did not immerse themselves in the community, the child, or the classroom; their "case study," largely based on school data, minimal observations, and brief interviews, was devoid of critical interpretations or personal meanings.

Nevertheless, even these limited safaris into the "chalkboard jungles" of inner-city schools challenged the interns' sheltered existence. Donna, anticipating the journey, wrote in her journal: "It's going to be a really new experience. I'm scared. I've heard all these stories about inner-city schools and the minority groups." Carl, following his inner-city school experience, stated: "The teachers seemed to have the attitude, 'Don't bother me, I won't bother you. You be quiet in class, stay off my case, and I won't assign you a lot of work.' Those kids are victims of a self-fulfilling prophecy." Asked if he would be willing to apply his insights and talents to work in such a school, Carl replied:

I can't say I would go to that type of high school. I'd feel very uncomfortable in it. . . . I felt like I was teaching elementary school. I just can't see myself teaching there. It would be admirable and virtuous of me to want to go there and contribute my teaching skills to those who are less advantaged. Maybe I'm an elitist, but I just cannot do that. I cannot teach students who have absolutely no respect for learning.

No efforts were made in the seminars, however, to bridge Donna's construction of stereotypes to an understanding of the social dynamics that foster such divisions. Also, Wright did not examine with Carl how these lower-class students' partial penetration of the contradictions of schooling ("lack of respect for learning") resulted in the reproduction of existing class divisions. As students of *The Paidea Proposal* and *A Place Called School*, the interns were unaware of the more sophisticated arguments and research represented in parallel texts like *Learning to Labor*, *Education and Power*, and *Power and Ideology*.

Interacting with the Public

It's neat that we get a chance to talk to the mayor and to talk to people in the community. We get to tell them what we're doing and what our goals are.

Donna

Like the seminars, dialogue with "important people" was another component fostering a hidden agendum for creating educational reform. The interns discussed current issues with the city's mayor, Carnegie Foundation president Ernest Boyer, and the Chair of the State Board of Education. Through such dialogues, the interns gained insight into the dynamics of educational reform while establishing contact with educational leaders about whom most preservice teachers only study.

The program director, Dr. Wright, projected a similar power broker/reformer image. A fellow professor remarked:

The man knows what to say, what to do and how to carry himself so that he comes across as right, and right for the right reasons. . . . He is a thinker. In order to get things done, you first have to envision it. Then you have to set up a plan of action and carry it through. You just don't let things ride by. He definitely doesn't let things roll over. When he wants something to happen he does what is needed to get things done. He looks at little things that may seem enormous as no big deal.

From the interns' perspective, Wright was a man who cultivated personal relationships with those holding power, exuded the confidence to influence important decision-makers, bypassed bureaucratic constraints, and translated ideas into reality. Accustomed to frank discussions of educational problems with school superintendents and free-wheeling debates with prominent persons, as a sophomore, Mary wrote in her journal:

Dr. Wright is in Washington DC on business. Rumor has it that he's going to ask President Reagan to speak at our lecture in April. Christa McAuliffe was supposed to speak. . . . It will be exciting if the President can come. I hope the Bridenthal Interns will have special privileges like we did last year when Dr. Boyer spoke. We got to sit in the front and go to a special party afterwards at the house of Calvin's vice-president. To meet with President Reagan and to talk with him about education would be a highlight of my life. If Reagan asked me what we could do to improve education in the United States, I would say "Recruit and retain high-ability young people to become teachers."

The interns' entry into the public arena in which their vocational choice and role in the reform effort were positively valued was an important dimension of Wright's two-year extended recruitment strategy. Mary states, "Dr. Wright was really intent on what he wanted to do. It was obvious that he had certain goals. One of them was to promote the Bridenthal Program. He wanted us to be visible. He was always finding somewhere for us to speak or somewhere for us to be written up." Wright acknowledged the importance of these experiences:

They've had opportunities to have exchanges with people from all over the country. I took four [interns] to Florida after the Chicago trip. We started at eight in the morning and finished about 3:30 in the afternoon. . . . Women were there from the League of Women Voters, the Junior League and the American Association of University Women. The kids had two hours of exchange after their presentations. That is very unusual. How many sophomores have had that opportunity?

Most of the interns spoke publicly at conferences and public forums ranging from the state teachers' association to the American Association of Colleges of Teacher Education. Mary remembers speaking before the state teachers' association. "It made me feel good. It was almost like they knew what they used to be like: excited and enthusiastic, but now they're older and a lot of the enthusiasm is gone. I think we helped them. I don't know if we brought [their enthusiasm] back, but we sure displayed a lot of our own."

Frequently featured in the local media, the interns were no strangers to national reporters representing *Newsweek*, *The Christian Science Monitor*, *Business Week*, ABC's *Good Morning America*, and *The Chronicle of Higher Education*. Though the coverage was routinely positive, the interns were sensitive to any message at variance with that projected by John Wright. In his first interview with the research team, Carl lambasted the media:

I was interviewed by the woman who wrote the [*Newsweek*] article. She was trying to trap me into saying something I didn't want to say. She kept asking me if Dr. Wright was in the room. She said, "Oh, I wish I could get an unbiased answer from you." In the article, she mentioned about our money—our endowment, but she implied that it was going to run out and that the program will be ineffective.

About that same time, Carl wrote in his journal:

We are learning how the media operates. We are learning that it specifically focuses on propaganda, sensationalism, and the creation of issues. The media can form issues and set the agenda for the solving of problems. Ted Koppel, in his address at Calvin, said that good news is no news. . . . The media is a bit prone to be overly negative about everything. I am worried that the Internship Program will be a victim of negativity.

While their surface curriculum prepared the interns academically, the hidden curriculum readied them for their ministerial mission in public education. For these interns, the BIT program would produce, in Carl's words, a "race of super teachers." These competent, dedicated, skilled, caring, and enthusiastic young people would be "the pacesetters for the new generation of teachers."

Their particular view of reform is captured well in Donna's account of a panel discussion for teachers at a school district that she and several other interns attended. The topic was the forthcoming state bill mandating teacher competency examinations and more careful monitoring of classroom teachers. Reacting to one of the few times she had heard classroom teachers formally speak about the profession, Donna wrote in her journal:

The teachers in the audience were out to kill. Dissension and sarcasm were in their voices as they chattered with others during the presentation. At the question and answer period, fire broke loose. The teachers voiced their complaints and questions in a rude manner and tone. The teachers at the forum seemed to be objecting to the proposed reform before even considering its benefits in the long run. With teachers who cannot accept change with its hardship and who cannot go through this change with a professional and rational attitude, the reform will have *no* chance! Grow up teachers and use your sense!

Donna, of course, does not represent every intern. Some, like Carl, are more ambivalent about the bill. "Teaching is not viewed as a profession anymore. You cut down on what the teacher has to decide for himself. That's part of your profession; you get to decide for yourself." On the other hand, Carl noted, "Teachers who have seen better, simpler times and less paperwork are the most discontented—and that is understandable. . . . But loads of paperwork is a sign of the times. All occupations have more paperwork. It's called progress."

Meanwhile, the outstretched hand of Professor Wright moved behind the scenes: "They know they are pacesetters in certain ways. They know there is a terrible problem in recruitment of high-ability people. All of them can look back and see they can be helpful." As he talked about the program and the interns, Wright uttered certain words and phrases that the interns themselves had used in describing their visions: catalyst, pacesetters, educational revolution, first class.

The BIT program clearly succeeded in creating the belief among its participants that they were indeed the kinds of leaders needed in the classrooms of reform-starved schools. It neglected, however, to facilitate an understanding among the interns of the problems inherent in leaders who are not able to recognize the complexity of surrounding phenomena and who perceive their understanding of the world from comparatively simple, taken-for-granted frameworks. What happened when these students completed this internship, and the novelty of their program vanished from the educational spotlight? What happened to these interns when the cheering ballroom audiences of 500 were traded for classes of 35 unattentive sophomores? What happened when these interns, who had fought on the rhetorical front lines of an educational revolution, traded newspaper headlines for lesson outlines and their swords for chalk? In the following section, we address these questions by following the interns through their professional studies and into their first year as beginning teachers.

HEADING IN THE RIGHT DIRECTION

Acquiring Knowledge

My ideal job would be to have really hungry kids. Kids that are just thirsting for knowledge and they just want to soak it up. You can lead them and give them direction and they'll go ahead and find out the answer before you tell them.

Donna

At the end of their sophomore year, 16 of the interns[15] entered Calvin's regular preservice education sequence, at which point the program's structure changed. During the next two years, the special seminars disappeared, academic programs became more idiosyncratic, and the interns were integrated with other education majors pursuing specialized certification requirements. The emphasis of the professional curriculum shifted from discussion about broad educational issues to the task of pedagogical preparation, with few opportunities to speak at conferences, meet with prominent individuals, or to be in the media spotlight.

As the interns completed their professional studies and entered the classroom as novice teachers, they adopted a teaching philosophy not dissimilar from that experienced at Calvin and echoed by John Wright. Having acquired a specialized knowledge base, they asserted the primacy of a content-based curriculum. As students, these interns were absorbed with the process of learning and the acquisition of knowledge; as teachers, they assumed the corporate agendum of producing a more competitive work force by transmitting skills and knowledge.

The program's success at Calvin, like the interns' effectiveness in the classroom, is captured by a simple educational equation: teachers transmitting knowledge + students acquiring knowledge = schools producing good test scores. In short, the hidden curriculum reflects the uncontested axiom: *improving the nation's report card reflects successful school reform.*

This axiom is evident in the interns' conception of the quality of their educations, their image of a competent teacher, and their views regarding the transmission of knowledge. In each of these areas, they articulate a curriculum-as-content perspective, in which "what knowledge is of most worth" is unasked, who has access to what type of knowledge is uncontested, and how that knowledge gets transmitted in the classroom is unexamined.

What Knowledge Is of Most Worth? Discussing their effectiveness as future classroom teachers, the interns returned again and again to the knowledge they had acquired as Calvin undergraduates and the knowledge they were to transmit as Bridenthal teachers. Carl stated: "One of the most prominent criticisms of teachers today is that they barely know the material they teach—and nothing else. I don't think that could ever be said about a Calvin graduate because our General Education Curriculum prepares us well." Carl further proclaimed the BIT program a success: "Just look at our placement ratings! Look at how well we do on standardized tests [teacher exit examination]!"

The centrality of knowledge was echoed by Calvin education faculty. In comparing the interns' preparation as teachers to other Calvin education students, John Wright stated: "I don't think the interns would be any different. They might have had an extra practicum or two. Again, the quality depends on *what they know*."

Mastery of subject-matter content—what teachers know—was the barometer of educational excellence and teaching effectiveness in the reform movement of the eighties. Teachers with dunce caps and students unable to compete with their foreign counterparts were the icons of the decade.

Within this context emerged Wright's plan: recruit high-ability persons, prepare them through a first-class education, and retain them in schools to transmit knowledge and skills to the future workers of a new corporate age, thus transforming the image of teaching and improving schools.

The choice of teaching roles reflects the interns' pursuit for high-status knowledge. Nearly one-half of the group chose to enter into the special education program, and all but one of the remaining interns sought secondary certification, primarily in the fields of mathematics and science. Mary chose science: "I couldn't decide at the very beginning whether to go to elementary or secondary, but I picked secondary because I wanted people in college to respect me." No intern chose to pursue a general elementary certificate. Since that time, the "Humanitas" curriculum replaced Calvin's traditional elementary education program, and education courses, particularly those in methods, have dwindled. Wright's position reflected support for these changes:

I've had students tell me over the years, "I'm damn sick and tired of going home to my dorm room with my roommate writing a paper and I'm cutting and pasting on the floor for elementary education." I know there is some methodology necessary, but good kids can pick that up reasonably fast. You don't have to have five methods courses in an elementary education program for them to get the point. . . . I mean, how many damn times can you talk about the discovery technique?

Content knowledge, the currency of the academic marketplace, was the focal point of the Bridenthal curriculum and at the apex of the interns' image of a competent teacher. As a beginning teacher, Carl made extensive use of mimeographed materials in lieu of the textbook. "My students like to joke that I have murdered a few trees for their class. They had two or three notebooks about eight inches each. At the end of the semester we stacked them up and they were taller than I am." Carl's demanding teaching made enrollments in even his gifted classes low. "It's not really fair," Carl objected, "when the guy down the hall shows *Top Gun* and *Platoon* instead of teaching and I require papers. I started with thirty-two kids and I'm down to twenty." "Being prepared" was also important for Rachel, who found a lack of correspondence between the knowledge she acquired as a Calvin student and what she was expected to transmit as a Bridenthal teacher: "In college we would spend the whole semester on the French Revolution; in the classroom it was one or two days. Then, there was a lot of stuff that I didn't know anything about. When I first started teaching world history (almost all of my credits are in U.S. History) I was teaching ancient Egypt and that was really hard for me."

Transmitting their love for knowledge acquisition was an important goal for many interns. Donna, excited about teaching, noted, "I picked teaching because I wanted to be somewhere I could influence other people's lives. I just got so caught up in learning." Similarly, Carl spoke of "an ability to communicate not only the information but that drive to learn."

However, nowhere during their preparation were the interns encouraged to "engage in the prior examination of what is considered valuable knowledge both overtly and covertly in school settings, why this is considered valuable knowledge, and how this conception of valuable knowledge is linked to institutions in the larger society" (Apple, 1974, p. 13). Had such questions been posed, the interns may have realized that what knowledge is of most worth is a question of ideology, not epistemology. As Pierre Bourdieu forcefully argues, schooling has a distinctive political function by legitimating and transmitting particular forms of cultural capital distributed unequally to students. Schools reproduce "the structure of the distribution of cultural capital among classes in that the culture which it transmits is closed to the dominant culture" (Bourdieu, 1977, p. 493).

This cultural capital corresponds to the *Paidea* curriculum at James Madison High School developed recently to eradicate "cultural illiteracy."[16] However, we must not lose sight of the essence of such seemingly innocuous proposals. In his study of nineteenth century educational reform in Massachusetts, Katz concluded: "The fable that the high school serves the entire community was naturally attractive to middle-class parents because it justified having the entire community support an institution most useful to the middle-class" (Katz, 1968, p. 92). The rise of modern public schooling, therefore, represents a convergence of middle- and upper-class interests. Universal public schooling was established in order to satisfy the labor demands of American industry, to provide preliminary training for children of middle-class parents entering professions in which apprenticeships were no longer available, to permit the continuance of private education, to enable the middle class to transform their cultural capital into an economic advantage, and to depoliticize socio-economic disparities.[17]

Those who reside in the upper portion of the socio-economic pyramid complete secondary school with higher grades, attend more prestigious colleges, and generate greater earnings than equally talented students from the lowest economic strata.[18] In the most recent study, nearly one-quarter of freshmen entering elite undergraduate institutions reported family income exceeding $100,000, yet this income bracket accounts for less than five percent of the general population. Further, the probability of a family member who is in this income bracket enrolling at a selective private institution is *ten* times greater than it is for a young man or woman whose family net income is less than $20,000 (Lewis and Kingston, 1989). In short, good students are those who have the cultural capital—the knowledge base, values, and language—most compatible with schooling. Good teachers are those who efficiently transmit this cultural capital and effectively manage the classroom; good schools are those that evidence this transmission via above average test scores.

Who Has Access to What Type of Knowledge? In higher education, different types of institutions distribute different forms of knowledge. Among the interns, there was little doubt about which form of knowledge they were exposed to. Donna once noted: "When I first came to Calvin, I was impressed with the quality of the courses, but I was more impressed after I started talking to Ben over at the Barnard Community College. In English he was learning nouns and verbs; in our language class we were studying thesis statements. It's much deeper. It's such a higher level; it's the right level for me."

Of course, who has access to what type of knowledge is largely a function of social class. In his analysis of higher education, Karabel reported that community colleges were lowest in terms of social class, highest in attrition, and the least selective. "The community college, as the bottom track, is likely to absorb the vast majority of students who are the first generation in their families to enter higher education." Karabel goes on to state, "Community colleges exist in part to reconcile students' culturally induced hopes for mobility with their eventual destinations, transforming structurally induced failure into individual failure" (Halsey, 1977, p. 249).

The attribution of school success to individual talent, merit, and ability veils pervasive structural, economic, and social relations that reproduce and reify this hierarchical differentiation. Reconciled to her position within this hierarchy, Donna believed she had earned matriculation to Calvin and deserved the benefits that graduation from Calvin would provide. Why she had access to a Calvin education and Ben did not or why a degree from Barnard Community College was worth less than one from Calvin were questions easily explained through a meritocratic ideology; why low-status groups had little access to high-status knowledge and the validity of such knowledge, itself, were not questioned.

In choosing highly specialized content programs like special education and secondary education, the interns further distanced themselves from the perception of "plain teachers." This, however, created problems in the interns' professional preparation. As early as her junior year, Donna expressed the need for more methods courses. "We don't have methods courses; it's one thing that we lack that I was hoping we would have." At that time, she was told that "the reason why we don't have a math methods course is because we would take it as a math credit and then we wouldn't know the subject matter well enough to teach it."

The hierarchical similarities between schools and corporate America promote similar kinds of thinking among their participants: Certain roles are inherently more valuable than others; those in higher roles have earned, and thus deserve, those roles as well as the status, power, and money accompanying them. Such assumptions not only mask structural questions pertaining to who gets (and does not get) such rewards, but perpetuate myths about those at the bottom of these structures. One such myth is that "these people" are unwilling or unable to work as hard as others and, therefore, do not merit greater rewards. Less obvious and usually ignored is the extent to which schools and corporations create, perpetuate, and legitimate such circumstances.

SHOWING THE RIGHT STUFF

Problems

A lot of these kids are below the fortieth percentile in skills, actually below the thirtieth as far as the national test scores. . . . They're a different type of student; they're not motivated. That sort of gets you down. You've got to give them a chance, but I'm still frustrated. I can't get them to think faster. I'm more used to students that will behave and listen to you.

Donna

The basic view in the administration is don't cause waves. I was told by my cooperating teachers not to write up any students. They hadn't written up anybody for years and they didn't see any reason why I'd have to—despite the fact that I had a student threaten me and I've been called names.

Carl

What happened when these interns entered the public schools as transmitters of knowledge? From their student teaching experience through their first year of teaching, the interns consistently spoke of two fundamental problems: poor-quality students and discipline. Additionally, their eminent preparation in content proved problematic in particular classroom contexts.

Remembering her student teaching, Donna remarked, "Student teaching can be kind of fun. If I had a problem, I could always talk with my cooperating teacher, but it's not the same the first year." The loneliness of being a first-year teacher was particularly stressful in managing the classroom and matching content with student abilities. "The greatest challenges have been learning how to deal with the kids and learning how they are going to respond to the subject material. Just knowing how high I can set my expectations and how to be an authority figure have been the challenging parts of being a first-year teacher." Donna faced routine resistance from the "weaker students," such as "smarting off," sharpening pencils, or throwing away paper during her lectures. During the year, she described her most difficult class: "After the first three weeks, they [the administration] folded one of my geometry classes and gave me twenty-eight new kids from various math teachers. It seems to me that they picked the kids that the other teachers didn't want. That's the worst class I have. I don't have control over them. A lot of the kids are the weaker students and they're very loud."

Rachel also spoke of control problems in the spring of her first year of teaching: "It's pretty late in the year for me to finally be getting it under control. They always tell you that you don't smile until Christmas, but I just couldn't do it. I was really having problems with them. Now they call me 'Grumpy' because I walk in and I'm not as friendly as I once was, but it was the only way I could get them to start behaving." As she prepared for her second year of teaching, Rachel pledged:

I'm really going to work a lot harder on discipline this year, especially with the students in my fundamental classes. It's gonna be a lot more difficult to control them than it was to control my regular students. I've never worked with the fundamental students. When I was originally hired, they told me I was on too high a level [to teach fundamental students]. Now I have two classes of them. Maybe the administration decided I'm low level now.

In the midst of his student teaching experience, Carl spoke angrily:

All the classes are overcrowded. The class size is between thirty-five and forty. It's a jungle. Of course, with the overcrowding, we have discipline problems. I've already faced some of those. I had no idea that the students would be as belligerent as they are. . . . I anticipated traumas, but I didn't anticipate the total lack of support from the administration and from the teachers. . . . They feel it can be dealt with in the classroom. I've done everything in the book for classroom management.

There are, of course, some aspects of beginning teaching that are difficult to acquire through book knowledge. Noteworthy among the interns, however, was their ability to begin to reflect critically upon their preparation program and their changing views about teaching. Given his previous claim of knowing the issues, his high scores on the teacher exit examination, and his disdain for classroom teachers who resisted additional paperwork in the wake of "progress," Carl's concern with classroom management was ironic. Donna's concern with discipline recalls her earlier concern with the lack of pedagogical knowledge provided in her professional preparation. She eventually came to believe that "nothing can really prepare you for teaching. Some of the education courses were useless. The examples of discipline and classroom management were more for elementary or more related to English and history."

Rachel's transformation moved from the ideal of "relating to students" to the reality of a teacher battered by classroom turmoil: "Maybe I was naive when I was in public school. I've had 15 kids expelled for serious things like possession of a weapon. I never had thought of teaching as dangerous before. It just really took me for a loop. They don't tell you how to handle being threatened by a child with this knife or a kid who is just totally spaced out on drugs in a methods course."

The interns' cognitive orientation and professional preparation placed them at a further disadvantage in working with low-ability, working-class students. Many of these students, like the "lads" in Willis' classic ethnography (Willis, 1977), resisted school-based knowledge. This resistance reflects a partial penetration of the dynamics of schooling within a class-based society. Just as the accumulation of capital in the hands of management demands that the workers produce material that in itself is intrinsically valueless, so, too, does the cultural capital of a cultivated minority demand that those with different cultural knowledge, language, and values learn this school-defined knowledge, which is devoid of any deep personal meaning.

When confronted with students' resistance, these interns lacked the critical perspective to understand the structural dynamics at work. In Donna's words, "I've never worked with these kinds of kids before. They have no skills and I don't understand why they can't understand." She, like many of the interns, fell back on explanations rooted in teacher folklore: "Teachers said it was one of the worst years that they had. . . . At the end of the year, it seemed like I didn't end with a very good rapport with my ideas. Except for sixth and third periods, the other classes really couldn't care less. By the time the kids get into high school a teacher is just something you stay away from."

Transmitting Knowledge in the Classroom

I hated, at first, having them do worksheets in class, but it's the only way to keep our sanity. It's what they want to do; it keeps them quiet.

Rachel

A lot of my kids are Special Ed. I just feel so sorry for them. I feel frustrated because I can't get them to think faster or understand the material any better. I'm more used to students who will behave and listen to you.

Donna

We're changing our math from ability groups to self-contained. I was just getting used to teaching the high kids. Now, I'll have them all.

Vince

The division of knowledge, like the division of labor, reflects the realities of social class, privilege, and power. The legitimization of these divisions is a function of schooling; the commodification of knowledge is a function of teaching. Both functions have their origins at the turn of the century.

Adopting the practices of business, educational architects, such as Frederick Taylor, Franklin Bobbitt, Elwood Cubberley, and Edward Thorndike, introduced intelligence testing, scientific management, and a product orientation to evaluation (Kliebard, 1971). Practical efficiency and productivity were central to Taylorism. The grandfather of intelligence testing, Edward Thorndike viewed "education as one form of human engineering which will profit by measurement of human nature and achievement" (Thorndike, 1922, p. 1). One of the first exponents of modern-day curriculum development, Franklin Bobbitt reminded teachers that "no amount of educational labor will develop large ability on the part of those possessing low natural capacity" (Bobbitt, 1924, p. 41). Furthermore, a major spokesperson for the emerging science of educational administration, Elwood Cubberley categorically stated, "Industrial and company training is especially significant of the changing conception of the school and the classes in society which the school is in the future expected to serve" (Cohen and Lazerson, 1977, p. 377). Control, efficiency, and measurement—components of a techno-rational ideology—remain important staples in contemporary American schooling. The widespread use of tracking, the primacy of a subject matter, the use of a systems management approach to curriculum development, and the evaluation of teachers and students through standardized instruments are notable examples.

As Calvin undergraduates, the interns held conventional views regarding the transmission of knowledge. According to Mary, "Teaching is telling somebody something or showing them how to do something that you know." Carl understood teaching as "the ability to convey thoughts and ideas to individuals or groups of individuals."

There is a difference, however, between imparting specific skills and content as a means toward improving the school report card or ultimately producing skilled laborers for the corporate work force (also known as the philosophy of *Nation at Risk*) and using classroom knowledge to stimulate intellectual inquiry or develop analytical thinking (also known as *A Place Called School* and *High School*). Competency testing of teachers, exit examinations for high school seniors, and basic skills and achievement tests for students at every grade level coupled with progress reports, worksheets, and multiple-choice tests constitute the nation's report card. Improving that report card is the measure for effective teaching and evidence of successful school reform. Also, while teaching working-class students to think and reflect is not necessary, their acquisition of fundamental work-related skills and values is essential.

Educational reform, however, also is designed to provide specialized training for a new middle class who "perform an important role in an increasingly knowledge-intensive reindustrialization process" (Carlson, 1987, p. 174). Preparing middle-class, high-ability teachers for the corporate information work place was a primary objective of the Bridenthal Program toward this end. Nevertheless, once in schools, some interns were assigned fundamental courses with low-ability students, and had to deal with the bureaucratic requirements and mundane routines of schooling. Can the brightest and the best effectively work within these circumstances?

Asked if the interns' professional studies prepared them adequately for their first year, Wright paused for an uncharacteristically long time. Finally, he replied "Yes." Hesitatingly, he offered a reservation. "You know a lot depends on one's ability to adjust to the demands of the job." As they entered their second year of teaching, few of the interns, however, evidenced an ability to make such adjustments. They were overwhelmed by the amount of time teaching demanded, the constraints of grading and standardized testing, and bureaucratic insensitivity.

During her first year of teaching, Donna announced, "I'm at school by 6:45. I teach. I don't leave school until five o'clock. I spend an hour watching television, and then I work until midnight grading papers." Carl elaborated:

I expected to be very busy, but I had no idea that I had to do as much paperwork as I do—noncurricular, nonpertinent paperwork. . . . I didn't take into account that the school district had a strict policy on the minimum number of grades that each student can have. . . . You have to have a certain number of grades for each student or the parent calls and says, "Why did my child flunk? You only gave him ten grades." I spend five or six hours a night grading. The off-periods I spend filling out progress reports, which have to go out every three weeks. Then, of course, three weeks later, you have a report card.

Trying to cope with state- and district-mandated standardized tests was another difficulty that none of the interns overcame. Rachel noted:

The district gives a test. I have to make sure that everything is covered. Now, they're not going to have the test I want them to have. It's what the district wants, not what I want. So, I have to see if we're behind others or where we should be. Maybe we speed up or combine a whole lot of things. Maybe we can take time and talk more about it, or we just have to do "these are the facts" and shove it down their throats.

Vince also confronted this dilemma:

I felt like we were teaching to the test. I never liked that idea but I had to do it. I asked myself, "How can I fit this into all the rest of the stuff that I am doing?" I couldn't. There wasn't enough time and it just wasn't the kind of teaching that I wanted to be doing. I lost my confidence. I was being told what to do and what to use, but all they were telling us was, "Well, you know people are gonna look at this and they're going to look at your classroom and what you did. They'll be able to see how you're teaching them."

Teaching performance evaluations accompanied student tests. Every intern was evaluated on a standardized evaluation form several times during his or her first year by two observers, and every intern expressed serious reservations about this practice. Donna declared, "It's all a staged game. You learn what they're looking for. I make sure I do those things." Carl recalled: "In the fall evaluation I think I got zero merit points, and in the one right after that I got three. But that spring I got nine! But, they have virtually no meaning. The evaluators come and I get the evaluations two weeks later after I've all but forgotten what the lesson was. If they write anything it's usually nothing positive." Mary was more blunt: "The appraisal system has nothing to do with excellent teachers. It just tests if you can teach a certain way—and most people can, with practice."

Finally, most interns faced problems with the school administration. Rachel complained, "This school has done a lot of cutbacks on employees.

So, they're adding to what the teachers already did last year. For example, last year we had three weeks on bus duty; this year we are going to have eight." "The morale stinks at our school," Donna noted simply. "A lot of teachers quit at the end of the summer." Carl lamented about his district's budget crisis. "I requested a classroom set of textbooks. I'm getting one textbook. At the same time, I have a paper ration. What am I supposed to do?" Carl was also concerned about the raising of his insurance deductible to $1,000. "When you make $12,000 after taxes, that's not an insurance policy." All were skeptical about the concern administrators had for teachers. Carl observed, "Administrators focus on efficiency. They don't worry about educating the kids; they just worry about numbers." Rachel noted, "It's not like they're not friendly; it's just that they're not people I would turn to for much advice or to ask them to back me on anything."

CONCLUSION

This reform program failed to serve the interests of the interns adequately, the metro schools where they taught (and will probably not remain), or the "low-ability" students who are viewed as reformers' greatest "cause" and challenge. At best, a handful of successful, middle-class high school students got a rare opportunity to attend an elite college inexpensively and an opportunity to experience life as a teacher quickly. Ironically, the very conditions that these interns railed against in their college speeches to dispirited teachers are those from which they now suffer.

Few of these interns will continue teaching past their two-year commitments. Carl, for example, suffers from the Rodney Dangerfield syndrome, "If I am not going to get a lot of respect in the community for what I am doing, I can't see myself staying with it very long. . . . I can't see myself doing something for people and them having contempt of me doing it." Rachel, one of the interns who always wanted to teach, also has serious reservations: "I can't handle worrying about being threatened by one of my students, being shot or knifed to death by a student. I've started thinking about some things that really interest me: interior design, archaeology." Other interns are considering similar moves. Donna, who is most disenchanted with America's system of public schools, may teach overseas. Both Mary and Vince have committed themselves to enter Calvin's graduate program in school administration.

The reform thoughts of those interns, if any, who remain in teaching will dissolve into youthful reminiscences of college days when the present seemed so immediate and the future so certain. The reform proposals of the 1980s, too, will enter educational folklore as yet another failed reform effort. The problem, of course, is that neither the interns nor their mentor acknowledges that educational reform requires a critical, not a corporate agenda. Like the children of Hamelin, the interns lured by the pied pipers of teacher education reform find the magic of the pipers' melody fading. We fear, though, that unlike the story, there will be few adults who resist the pipers' hypnotic sounds to rescue their children or themselves from the failed ideology.

NOTES

1. For a critical analysis of the responsibility of educational institutions to meet the nation's economic needs, see Feinberg, 1987.

2. For a review of the efforts of postsecondary institutions to implement many of these reforms, see Sears, Marshall, and Otis-Wilborn, 1988, and Marshall, Otis-Wilborn, and Sears, in press. For a critical assessment of these reforms, see Apple, 1987; Giroux and McLaren, 1986; and Sears, Marshall, and Otis-Wilborn, 1989.

3. The name of the program, as well as the institution and participants, have been altered.

4. Few teacher education institutions have an active recruitment program to attract academically talented persons into the teaching profession (Laman and Reeves, 1983; Sears, Marshall, and Otis-Wilborn, 1988). These include the Lyndhurst Fellowships at Memphis State and the University of Tennessee at Knoxville (Boser, Wiley, and Pettibone, 1986; Wiley, 1986; Wisniewski, 1986), and the Honors Scholars at Wright State University (Evans, King, and Landers, 1986).

5. For a discussion of the meta-theoretical assumptions guiding this type of inquiry, see Sears, Marshall, and Otis-Wilborn, 1986.

6. For a detailed discussion of the methods and techniques used during the first four years of this study as well as a complete set of research instruments, see Sears, Moyer, and Marshall, 1986; Marshall, Sears, and Otis-Wilborn, 1987; Otis-Wilborn, Marshall, and Sears, 1989; and Sears, Otis-Wilborn, and Marshall, 1990.

7. An additional intern position was available when one of the original ten interns chose to use his National Merit Scholarship award rather than the Bridenthal award. Thus, 17 persons comprised the Bridenthal Interns.

8. For elaboration, see Borkow and Jordan, 1983; Feistritzer, 1983; Laman and Reeves, 1983; Weaver, 1979; and Weaver, 1981.

9. Brophy's assertion is not supported even within his own paper. Among the eight teacher characteristics/benefits associated with producing student learning gains, which he contends are supported by research, are teacher expectations, classroom management, mastery teaching, and curriculum pacing. Characteristics commonly associated with "bright persons" are *not* discussed.

10. Getzels and Jackson, 1963; Pugach and Raths, 1983; Marshall, Sears, and Otis-Wilborn, 1988; Morsh and Wilder, 1954; Sears, Marshall, and Otis-Wilborn, 1988; Sykes, 1983.

11. For studies supporting this position, see Oakes, 1985; Rist, 1973; and Rosenbaum, 1976.

12. Cultural capital is the "symbolic property . . . which the schools preserve and distribute . . . . In its very production and dissemination as a public and economic commodity—as book, films, materials, and so forth—it is repeatedly filtered through ideological and economic commitments . . . . Cultural capital ('good taste,' certain kinds of prior knowledge, abilities, and language forms) is unequally distributed throughout society and this is dependent in large part on the division of labor and power in that society" (Apple, 1979, pp. 3, 8, 33). For a further discussion of the concept of cultural capital, see Apple, 1974; Bourdieu, 1977; and Giroux, 1988.

13. For an elaboration, see Apple, 1987; Carlson, 1987; Ginsberg, 1987; Popkewitz, 1989; Shapiro, 1985; and Shor, 1986.

14. See also Kemper and Mangieri, 1987.

15. The lone intern who did not continue with the program was also the only person not under its financial obligations. As a National Merit Scholar, this intern abandoned the Bridenthal Program (without incurring two years of debts) to pursue a prelaw degree.

16. See, for example, Adler, 1982; Bennett, 1987; and Hirsch, 1987.

17. For further elaboration, see Greer, 1972; Karier, 1975; Katz, 1968; Katz, 1971; Swift, 1980; and Tyack, 1974.

18. See, for example, Bowles and Gintis, 1976; Folger, Astin, and Bayer, 1970; Kolko, 1962; Lewis and Kingston, 1989; and Sewell, 1971.

REFERENCES

Adler, M. (1982). *The Paidea proposal: An educational manifesto.* New York: Macmillan.

Apple, M. (1974). The process and ideology of valuing in educational settings. In M. Apple et al. (Eds.), *Education evaluation: Analysis and responsibility* (pp. 3–34). Berkeley, CA: McCutchan.

————. (1979). *Ideology and curriculum*. Boston: Routledge & Kegan Paul.

————. (1987). Will the social context allow a tomorrow for "tomorrow's teachers"? *Teachers College Record*, *88*(3), 330–337.

Astin, A. (1983). *The American freshmen*. Los Angeles: American Council on Education/University of California at Los Angeles.

Bennett, W. (1987). *James Madison High School: A curriculum for American students*. Washington, DC: United States Department of Education.

Bobbitt, J. (1924). *How to make a curriculum*. Boston: Houghton-Mifflin.

Borkow, N., & Jordan, K. (1983). *The teacher workforce*. Washington, DC: Congressional Research Service, Library of Congress.

Boser, J., Wiley, P., & Pettibone, T. (1986). *A comparison of participants in traditional and alternative teacher preparation programs*. (ERIC Document Reproduction Service No. ED 278 648).

Bourdieu, P. (1977). Cultural reproduction and social reproduction. In J. Karabel & A. Halsey (Eds.), *Power and ideology in education* (pp. 487–510). New York: Oxford University Press.

Bowles, S., & Gintis, H. (1976). *Schooling in capitalist America*. New York: Basic.

Boyce, A. (1912). Qualities of merit in secondary school teachers. *Journal of Educational Psychology*, *3*(3), 144–157.

Brogdon, R., & Tincher, W. (1986). *Higher aptitude high school student's opinion of career choice*. (ERIC Document Reproduction Service No. ED 279 632).

Brophy, J. (1982). Successful teaching strategies for the inner-city child. *Phi Delta Kappan*, *63*(8), 527–530.

Browning, R. (1970). *Browning: Poetical works, 1833–1864*. I. Jack (Ed.). London: Oxford University Press.

Calvin College (1983). *A demonstration project related to the recruitment, preparation and retention of highly qualified persons for the teaching profession*. Unpublished manuscript.

Carlson, D. (1987). Teachers as political actors. *Harvard Educational Review*, *57*(3), 283–307.

Cohen, D., & Lazerson, M. (1977). Education and the corporate order. In J. Karabel and A. Halsey (Eds.), *Power and ideology in education* (pp. 373–386). New York: Oxford University Press.

Cornbleth, C. (1986). Ritual and rationality in teacher education reform. *Educational Researcher*, *15*(4), 5–14.

Empey, D. (1984). The greatest risk: Who will teach? *The Elementary School Journal*, *85*(2), 167–176.

Evans, S., King, R., & Landers, M. (1986). *A comprehensive plan for attracting able students to teacher education*. (ERIC Document Reproduction Service No. ED 267 042).

Feinberg, W. (1987). The Holmes Group Report and the professionalization of teaching. *Teachers College Record*, *88*(3), 366–377.

Feistritzer, C. (1983). *The condition of teaching. A state-by-state analysis*. (ERIC Document Reproduction Service No. ED 238 869)

Folger, J., Astin, H., & Bayer, A. (1970). *Human resources and higher education*. New York: Sage.

Gallup, A., & Clark, D. (1987). The 19th annual Gallup poll of the public's attitudes toward the public schools. *Phi Delta Kappan*, *69*(1), 17–30.

Getzels, J., & Jackson, P. (1963). The teacher's personality and characteristics. In N. Gage (Ed.), *Handbook of research on teaching* (1st ed.), (pp. 506–582). Chicago: Rand McNally.

Ginsberg, M. (1987). Teacher education and class and gender relations. *Educational Foundations, 2*(3), 4–36.

Giroux, H. (1988). *Teachers as intellectuals: Toward a critical pedagogy of learning.* South Hadley, MA: Bergin and Garvey.

Giroux, H., & McLaren, P. (1986). Teacher education and the politics of engagement: The case for democratic schooling. *Harvard Educational Review, 56*(3), 213–238.

Greer, C. (1972). *The great school legend.* New York: Basic.

Halsey, A. (1977). Community colleges and social stratification: Submerged class conflict in American higher education. In J. Karabel & A. Halsey (Eds.), *Power and ideology in education* (pp. 232–254). New York: Oxford University Press.

Hirsch, E. (1987). *Cultural literacy: What every American needs to know.* Boston: Houghton Mifflin.

Holmes Group, Inc. (1986). *Tomorrow's teachers: A report of the Holmes Group.* East Lansing, MI: Author.

Karier, C. (1975). *Shaping the American educational state.* New York: The Free Press.

Katz, M. (1968). *The irony of early school reform: Educational innovation in mid-nineteenth century Massachusetts.* Boston: Beacon Press.

———. (1971). *Class, bureaucracy, and schools.* New York: Praeger.

Kemper, R., & Mangieri, J. (1987). America's future teaching force: Predictions and recommendations. *Phi Delta Kappan, 68*(5), 393–395.

Kliebard, H. (1971). Bureaucracy and curriculum theory. In V. Haubrich (Ed.), *Freedom, bureaucracy and schooling*, (pp. 74–93). Washington, DC: Association for Supervision and Curriculum Development.

Kolko, G. (1962). *Wealth and power in America.* New York: Praeger.

Laman, A., & Reeves, D. (1983). Admission to teacher education programs: The status and trends. *Journal of Teacher Education, 34*(1), 2–4.

Lewis, L., & Kingston, W. (1989). The best, the brightest, and the most affluent: Undergraduates at elite institutions. *Academe, 75*(6), 28–33.

Marshall, J., Otis-Wilborn, A., & Sears, J. (in press). Programmatic responses toward contemporary teacher education reform [Special issue]. *Peabody Journal of Education.*

Marshall, J., Sears, J., & Otis-Wilborn, A. (1987). *A longitudinal study of a demonstration project related to the recruitment, preparation, and retention of highly qualified persons for the teaching profession: The [Bridenthal] interns—The second year.* (ERIC Document Reproduction Service No. 282 842).

———. (1988). *The recruitment and induction of "quality" students into teacher education: A case study.* Paper presented at the annual meeting of the American Educational Research Association, New Orleans.

Morsh, J., & Wilder, E. (1954). *Identifying the effective instructor: A review of the quantitative studies, 1900–1952.* USAF Personnel Training Research Center, Research Bulletin.

National Education Association. (1982). *Excellence in our schools. Teacher education: An action plan.* (ERIC Document Reproduction Service No. ED 246 046).

Oakes, J. (1985). *Keeping track: How schools structure inequality*. New Haven, CT: Yale University Press.

Otis-Wilborn, A., Marshall, J., & Sears, J. (1989). *A longitudinal study of a demonstration project related to the recruitment, preparation, and retention of highly qualified persons for the teaching profession: The [Bridenthal] interns—The third year*. Unpublished manuscript.

Pigge, F. (1985). Teacher education graduates: Comparisons of those who teach and do not teach. *Journal of Teacher Education, 36*(4), 27–28.

Popkewitz, T. (1989). *A political sociology of educational reform and change: Power, knowledge and the state*. Paper presented at the American Educational Research Association, San Francisco.

Pugach, M., & Raths, J. (1983). Testing teachers: Analysis and recommendations. *Journal of Teacher Education, 34*(1), 37–43.

Rist, R. (1973). *The urban school*. Cambridge, MA: MIT Press.

Roberson, S., Keith, T., & Page, E. (1983). Now who aspires to teach? *Educational Researcher, 12*(6), 13–21.

Rosenbaum, J. (1976). *Making inequality: The hidden curriculum of high school tracking*. New York: Wiley.

Schlechty, P., & Joslin, A. (1984). Recruiting teachers: Future prospects. *Journal of Children in Contemporary Society, 12*(3–4), 51–60.

Schlechty, P., & Vance, C. (1983). Recruitment, selection, and retention: The shape of the teaching force. *The Elementary School Journal, 83*(4), 469–487.

Sears, J., Marshall, J., & Otis-Wilborn, A. (1986). *Conducting qualitative research in higher education*. (ERIC Document Reproduction Service No. ED 272 454).

———. (1988). *Teacher education policies and programs: Implementing reform proposals of the 1980s*. Chapel Hill, NC: Southeastern Educational Improvement Laboratory. (ERIC Document Reproduction Service No. ED 296 985).

———. (1989). The political economy of teacher training: Attracting high-ability persons into teaching, a critique. *Teacher Education Quarterly, 16*(4), 5–72.

Sears, J., Moyer, P., & Marshall, J. (1986). *A longitudinal study of a demonstration project related to the recruitment, preparation, and retention of highly qualified persons for the teaching profession: The [Bridenthal] interns—The first year*. (ERIC Document Reproduction Service No. 272 454).

Sears, J., Otis-Wilborn, A., & Marshall, J. (1990). A longitudinal study of a demonstration project related to the recruitment, preparation, and retention of highly qualified persons for the teaching profession: The [Bridenthal] interns—The fourth year. Unpublished manuscript.

Sewell, W. (1971). Inequality of opportunity in higher education. *American Sociological Review, 36*(5), 793–809.

Shapiro, H. (1985). Capitalism at risk: The political economy of the educational reports of 1983. *Educational Theory, 35*(1), 57–72.

Shor, I. (1986). Equality is excellence: Transforming teacher education and the learning process. *Harvard Educational Review, 56*(4), 406–426.

Swift, D. (1980). The problem of control. In E. Steiner, R. Arnove, & B. McClellan (Eds.), *Education and American culture* (pp. 319–344). New York: Macmillan.

Sykes, G. (1983). Teacher preparation and the teacher workforce: Problems and prospects for the 80s. *American Education, 19*(2), 23–30.

Thorndike, E. (1922). Measurement in education. In G. Whipple (Ed.), *Intelligence tests and their use: The twenty-first yearbook of the National Society for the Study of Education* (pp. 1–9). Bloomington, IL: Public School Publishing.

Turner, R. (1960). Sponsored and contest mobility and the school system. *American Sociological Review, 25*(5), 855–867.

Tyack, D. (1974). *The one best system.* Cambridge, MA: Harvard University Press.

Vance, V., & Schlechty, P. (1982). The distribution of academic ability in the teaching force: Policy implications. *Phi Delta Kappan, 64*(1), 22–27.

Weaver, W. (1979). In search of quality: The need for talent in teaching. *Phi Delta Kappan, 61*(1), 29–32.

———. (1981). The talent pool in teacher education. *Journal of Teacher Education, 32*(2), 32–36.

———. (1983). *America's teacher quality problem: Alternatives for reform.* New York: Praeger.

Wiley, P. (1986). The Lyndhurst Fellowship Program: An alternative preparation/certification program. *Tennessee Education, 15*(2), 18–22.

Willis, P. (1977). *Learning to labour: How working class kids get working class jobs.* Farnborough, England: Saxon House.

Wisniewski, R. (1986). Alternative programs and the reform of teacher education. *Action in Teacher Education, 8*(2), 37–44.

9 THE PUBLIC INTEREST AND PROFESSIONAL LABOR: RESEARCH UNIVERSITIES

Gary Rhoades and Sheila Slaughter

The notion of the public interest, expressed in ideals of service and disinterestedness, is central to professional ideology. In recent decades, professionals' claims to be working in the public's best interests have been challenged in the academic literature and the mass media. At the same time, the conditions of professional labor in the large organizations in which most professionals work are being renegotiated by the managers of these organizations, who themselves invoke the public interest in justifying their actions. For example, medical doctors increasingly work in large organizations, such as hospitals and health maintenance organizations, that are managed by administrators who have increased control over physicians' work while claiming to keep health costs in check.

In this chapter, we present an exploratory study of struggle over the term of professional labor in higher education. At a single public research university, we examine the discourse of academics and administrators about intellectual property rights. In the 1980s, federal legislation allowed universities to patent and license inventions made in faculty laboratories, causing research universities to establish policies and organizational structures for coordinating and managing technology transfer that have implications for ownership and control of intellectual property, broadly construed.[1] The negotiations surrounding the development of a range of policies concerning faculty work—in our case, appropriate faculty activity and intellectual property rights—represent an excellent case of the struggle surrounding the definition and control of academic work.

In approaching the problem of the control of professional work in universities, we consider the insights that mainstream organization theory offers. In that body of work, the relationship between bureaucrats and professionals is a classic topic. When the literature on higher education draws on such work, it generally contrasts administrators' and professionals' different bases of authority (position versus expertise) and aims of control (accountability versus autonomy) (Etzioni, 1964; Kornhauser, 1962). However, these analyses do not address professionals' claims to altruism, disinterestedness, and high standards of ethical practice. Nor does organizational theory connect internal organizational groups to external structures of power, status groups, and classes. Yet administrators cope daily, and interact constantly, with state, regional, and even national elites in developing strategies for attaining and deploying resources. With regard to technology transfer, university presidents are working openly with corporate and political elites to generate research that meets economic development and marketplace demands. Organization theory, then, accepts professionals' altruism uncritically and deals with the relationship between professionals and managers primarily in an intraorganizational context, excluding the many extraorganizational players involved in technology transfer.

In contrast to organization theory, the critical professionalization literature concentrates on the relationships of professionals to external groups. Professions are defined as corporate entities that establish and monopolize marketplaces of work (Larson, 1977). Critical professionalization scholars see characteristics—codes of ethics, certification, technical knowledge, and altruistic ideals of service—identified by functionalist scholars as being at the heart of the professions as facets of professional ideology that mediate relations with external groups, conferring legitimacy and consolidating control over domains of work. As critical scholars suggest, professional groups are connected to other social structures of power, such as class, acquiring power by serving power (Larson, 1984; Silva and Slaughter, 1984). Academics are active organizational agents with external ties that represent potential resources on which they can draw in internal organizational struggles. However, most scholars of professionalization, whether mainstream or critical, concentrate on negotiation between professionals and external lay groups for their license and mandate (Hughes, 1958). They do not focus on higher education as a contested site in which professionals have to struggle for control over their work. Instead, higher education figures in their analysis as an arena for professional certification. Nor has the critical literature thoroughly analyzed or theorized the relationships among different groups of professionals in hierarchical structures, in which one group has some authority over another. For example, it does not take the insight that the ideology of service, which advances the claim that professionals are working in the public interest, is in part a stratagem that advances the occupation's private, self- or special interest, and apply that insight, as we propose not only to professionals, but also to the administrators who manage them. In dealing with our research problem, the struggle to define and control professional work in the area of technology transfer, located at the interstices between the academic and commercial world, and at universities, the institutions that prepare professionals, rather than at professional organizations or learned societies, we have to move beyond organization and professionalization theory.

Utilizing Giddens's (1982, 1984) notion of structuration as a conceptual heuristic, we try to redress the shortcomings of organization and professionalization theory noted above by empirically studying the process by which peoples' actions in an organization are structured and, in turn, lead to the generation of new structures. We look at the ways in which academics and administrators utilize the language of public and private interest in advancing their claims as caretakers, controllers, and beneficiaries of certain areas of work. We see the discourse of faculty and administrators involved in technology transfer as providing the ground for examining the organizational struggle to define and control professional work. Without casting administrators as villains, we explore the implications of their discourse for the control of professional labor, whether areas of work (type and focus of research, consulting), the time faculty spend on different parts of their work, or the products of their work (intellectual property).[2] We examine faculty discourse to see what they say about similar issues of control.

We specify three exploratory research questions, which are derived from categories found in Giddens's framework. In each case, we attempt to combine elements of a constructionist approach, which attends to the contingent and continuous reconstitution of social relations, with elements of a critical approach, which attends to patterns of power within and external to the organization. We employ elements of Giddens's approach as guidelines for framing and conceptualizing our empirical analysis, and developing our own framework of critical constructionism.[3]

Research question #1: *How do the public statements of central administrators compare to the private dialogues of academics in their "accounts," with regard to involvement of the university and its inventor–scientists in technology transfer?*

In proposing a "hermeneutically informed social theory" Giddens (1982, 1984) is concerned with understanding meaningful action. People are "knowledgeable" agents, acting on the basis of a wide range of beliefs and information about society. Researchers must plumb the subjectivity of those they are studying. We probed accounts of university and faculty involvement in technology transfer, particularly the motivations that are attributed to different parties in explaining their involvement.

Research question #2: *How do the public statements of central administrators compare to the private dialogues of academics in the "normative rules" or systems of belief that they invoke?*

Giddens's notion of structuration suggests that the influence of structure on action is contingent, as is the structural product of action. People are "capable" agents standing in an indeterminate relationship to structure. They "could have acted otherwise." Giddens conceptualizes social structure as rules and resources that influence the constitution of social relations and practices.

Research question #3: *How do the public statements of central administrators compare to the private dialogues of academics in their perceptions of "power" in their discussions of the realities of and necessity for coordinating and controlling high technology?*

Power is central to Giddens's social theory. It refers not just to the actors' capacities to influence decisions, but to structures that mediate social relations. Giddens emphasizes the "dialectic of control," maintaining that all social relations are reciprocal and contingent. Our concern is with the ways in which the introduction of technology transfer to policy discussions prompts academics and administrators to renegotiate definitions of professional labor in the university. Central to this renegotiation is the differential power of these parties (and their sense of these differences).

METHODS

We conducted a case study of a public research university, "Nouveau University," a Research I institution that has recently moved into the top 20 institutions in terms of federal research funding. Nouveau University has an aggressive technology transfer policy. For example, it recently established Nouveau Technology, a wholly owned subsidiary of the university's foundation, a for-profit corporation designed to facilitate the commercialization of university technology.

Our data collection focused on the Technology Transfer Committee (T2C), which was created in 1986 as an advisory committee to the vice-president for research on a range of technology transfer issues. Its major role is to draft provisional policy documents. The T2C is the only committee at Nouveau University that regularly brings together administrators and faculty to deal with technology transfer and related issues of professional labor. It was, therefore, the logical unit on which to center our study.

We looked at the public statements of central administrators connected to the T2C—the president, vice-presidents, and officials related to various technology transfer units—because they represented themselves as the public voice of the university, and dominated official organs of internal and external communication. Their statements in continuous and official Nouveau University publications provided our data on administrators. We looked at the private discourse of faculty, because they did not control any public media in the organization and therefore did not have a distinctive public voice. We think that the use of administrators' public statements and faculty interviews (private discourse) captures an important disparity of power between the two groups.

There were 19 T2C members, and we interviewed the 16 who were faculty. Faculty interview data was gathered in structured, one-hour interviews with each of the T2C members, organized around our three research questions. Most of them were actively involved in technology transfer. Of the 16, 14 had industrial contracts and consultancies. Of the 14, ten held patents or had disclosed. These faculty were inventor–scientists, engaged in technology transfer. Five of these faculty were also academic unit heads.[4] Of the 16, only two were affiliated with basic science units. The rest were located in professional schools (agriculture, business, engineering, library, medicine, pharmacy). All were white men.

ACCOUNTS OF INVOLVEMENT IN TECHNOLOGY TRANSFER

Central Administrators

In talking about university involvement in technology transfer, central administrators emphasized public service and public benefit. In contrast to themselves, administrators saw most faculty as committed to a culture of research that precluded a strong interest in technology transfer. However, administrators saw some faculty, most of whom were involved in the discovery of patentable devices or processes, as inventor–scientists who were driven by and would respond to material motivations. Overall, administrators saw institutional involvement in technology transfer as a desirable and natural development, continuing the land-grant tradition. Although administrators identified possible problems stemming from commercialization and profit-oriented activities, these problems were presented as belonging to individual inventor–scientists rather than to the institution.

In describing the involvement of universities in technology transfer, Nouveau University central administrators drew on rationales that addressed the public interest, very often through economic development.

[Technology transfer] is an opportunity to translate research into reality in a way that affects people and has a positive economic impact on the community.

Ursula Chasteney, vice-president for research

If someone doesn't get these technologies into the marketplace, no one benefits.

Gerald Meronick, Nouveau University's patent organization representative

Administrators saw technology transfer as closing the gap between scientific discovery and commercialization.

Central administrators also emphasized the contributions that technology transfer would make to the welfare of the university.

If licensed to a company, patents can end up being of tremendous value both to the inventor and to the university in terms of money, prestige, and new research.

Wally Walton, head, Office of Technology Transfer

Their public discourse was marked by a sense of financial constraint. They continually talked about budgetary problems and the need for additional revenues to remain competitive in Research I circles. University involvement in technology transfer was presented as a natural response to the slow growth of research funding; technology transfer was an organizational effort to diversify university sources of support.

Central administrators presented university involvement in technology transfer as the most recent evolution of land-grant universities' public service mission, continuous with past practice.

The mission of the land grant has emphasized technology transfer as part of its basic mission for over 100 years in agriculture and in cooperative extension. Nouveau Technology Corporation is one of our youngest efforts. . . . Profit is not first on the list of the objectives; in fact, it is closer to last. In fact, it is last. First is to have an economic development impact.

Rebecca Eaton, vice-president for administrative affairs

There are also indirect benefits [of research]. Part of our mission and heritage as a land-grant university is to provide new knowledge for the benefit of citizens and taxpayers of this country and this state. True to this mission, the College of Agriculture continues to provide practical and applicable new knowledge to enhance the productivity of [the state citizenry].

Ursula Chasteney

Yet in order to deal with the new profit-oriented practices of faculty, which were represented as a break with the past, new organizations structures, such as Nouveau Technology, were required, as were changes in state conflict-of-interest laws.

We have gotten the state legislature to change some rather archaic laws concerning conflict of interest. Before, faculty had to transfer technology in secret. The university was not benefiting from the relation [between faculty and companies]. Sometimes we lost faculty who left to start companies. Revising the conflict-of-interest law is the biggest thing the state has done for economic development in the past ten years.

Daniel Eisenbarth, vice-president for university relations

However, administrators saw faculty as interested primarily in scientific research, not in the commercialization of their ideas. For example, at a public meeting of the university's Economic Development Council, there was considerable discussion of the faculty's culture of research, which was seen as mitigating against scientists' interest and involvement in technology transfer.

People do not come to the university for economic development. There is a faculty philosophy that knowledge seeking should not be tampered with.

Rebecca Eaton

Although administrators thought most faculty were uninterested in technology transfer, they believed some faculty were entrepreneurial inventor–scientists. Administrators suggested that these inventor–scientists needed some material incentives to stay in the university.

The inventor particularly has to have substantial equity. Monetary interest helps maintain his or her motivations.

Charles Murdock, head, Nouveau Technology

Nouveau Technology was created to do technology transfer and to return financial reward to the inventor. . . . One objective is to retain faculty, to not lose them. We want to keep our quality faculty.

Rebecca Eaton

Administrators also saw material incentives as a means of drawing faculty into entrepreneurial activity. Through the university patent–royalty split, administrators wanted to provide enough material incentives to induce faculty to participate in technology transfer and to retain faculty who made marketable discoveries, and at the same time, to keep as large a share for the university as possible to reinvest in promising commercial research (Rhoades and Slaughter, forthcoming). Although they did not emphasize inventor–scientists' material motivations, the public record of changes in patent–royalty formulas reveals a pattern indicating that administrators did believe inventor–scientists demanded too much for themselves.

On the surface, the public discourse of administrators was by and large promotional. Commercialization of knowledge was presented as a win–win situation. Everyone benefited—faculty, the institution, industry, and the public. However, administrators had a rather ambivalent attitude with regard to faculty. On the one hand, they thought faculty were too committed to traditional norms of science that valued research over commercialization; on the other, they saw inventor–scientists who transferred technology as wanting too much in the way of material rewards.

Faculty Members of the Technology Transfer Committee

Although many faculty were skeptical about administrators' accounts of the university's short-term motivations, they were convinced that technology transfer would serve the university and public interest in the long term. Faculty presented a more complicated view than did administrators of inventor–scientists' motivations, but they acknowledged the significance of material concerns. When speaking of their own motivations, faculty expressed delight in discovery; when they spoke about other faculty's motivations, inventor–scientists placed greater emphasis on material gain.

T2C committee members saw the university protecting and promoting its own economic interests, rather than serving the public interest, at least in the short term. For virtually all the committee members, money was a principal explanation for university involvement in technology transfer.[5]

The university wants money right away.
> Frank Krupnick, professor, basic science department

The university expects faculty to bring in money.
> Leo Zazworski, professor, health sciences professional school

If most faculty offered explanations that centered on simple institutional venality, some, like the central administrators, suggested that university efforts to generate revenues through technology transfer were a response to inadequate and/or declining public support for research. They saw administrators trying to strengthen the university's ability to do science.

A few faculty were quite skeptical about the university's ability to reap economic benefits from involvement in technology transfer, particularly in the short run.

This idea that [President Grossman] has that patents are going to support more research is nonsense. No way, that's a dream.

Michael O'Reilly, professor and head, interdisciplinary science unit

I'd like to see the books. Get the [Nouveau Technology] books and show me income and outgo over X number of years. My feeling is that it is a net cost.

Milton Klotz, associate professor, information and policy sciences professional school

At the same time, most faculty believed that university involvement in technology transfer would strengthen the local and regional economy in the long term, serving the public interest.

In discussing their personal motivations for engaging in technology transfer, faculty did not see money as primary. They stressed problem-solving or a desire to have a positive effect on society.

I have a very practical nature. I like to take basic and applied science and apply it to industry. I don't like to work on problems just for the sake of the problem. That bores me.

Nick Cavendish, professor, applied science professional school

There's the financial aspect. . . . However, I have been fascinated with the patent process and ideas and being the first one to come up with an idea and doing something, so, a patent has intrinsic value to me that way in terms of novelty.

Tyler Caulley, Jr., associate professor, applied science professional school

When faculty talked about other inventor–scientists, however, they saw economic incentives as important.

In some areas, profit is a motivator, yes. *That's not my own motivation, though it is for others I'm sure.* [Italics ours]

Laurence Threadgill, professor, basic science department

Yet profit in and of itself was not the only motivation. Commercial endeavor enabled inventor–scientists to become entrepreneurial scientists, playing a role similar to that of business leaders.

Well, I like to think the main motivation is creativity, but no question about it, there's a financial motivation that is probably largely personal—if not completely personal then certainly the development of a commercial organization in which a person can exercise his creativity, and invest his time, leadership qualities, and desire for dominance.

George Jasper, professor, applied science professional school

Entrepreneurial activity was justified to some extent by scientists' responsibility for supporting students and facilities.

Certainly it's a source of capital to run a research lab.

Leo Zazworski

The key thing is labs and graduate students.

Milton Klotz

Although the inventor–scientists acknowledged economic incentives, even if not their own, as important to the pursuit of technology transfer, there was ambivalence in their discourse about the proper relationship between science and private profit. Some thought that doing science for money tarnished the purity of the pursuit of knowledge. When talking about entrepreneurial activity, these faculty used phrases such as "dirty money," "slaves to industry," and "prostituting ourselves." Inventor–scientists thought that many of their colleagues, especially those not engaged in technology transfer, were committed to more traditional academic values that upheld the autonomy of the university and disinterestedness of science, and that these faculty looked askance at the introduction of profit to the scientific process. The inventor–scientists, too, cherished these norms, even as they acted on contradictory values. A mechanism they used to ease the tension between the two sets of values, one stressing entrepreneurial activity, the other autonomy and disinterestedness, was attributing the pursuit of profit to others engaged in technology transfer, and proclaiming their personal delight in the discovery aspect of creating patentable products and processes.

Although faculty provide complex and contradictory accounts of involvement in technology transfer, they, like central administrators, do not regard technology as problematic. Faculty on the T2C had not struggled with the question of *whether or not* they should become involved in technology transfer. Instead, the stories they told about how they became inventor–scientists were tales of serendipity and happenstance. No one spoke about a point at which they deliberated and then made a conscious choice to engage in technology transfer. Many had difficulties with transferring technology, some of which had led them away from involvement in entrepreneurial science, but these were problems of means, not ends. None questioned the long-term regional economic benefits of technology transfer, or explored possible future costs to the university and wider community.

NORMATIVE RULES INVOKED IN DISCUSSING TECHNOLOGY TRANSFER

Central Administrators

As suggested in the previous section, administrators invoked an economic development ideology, in which universities were the central players because of the contribution research made to innovations in high technology. Administrators legitimized the role universities played in this process by stressing the continuity of technology with the land-grant, public-service mission. In this section, we focus on the ideology of science articulated by administrators. Although administrators rarely used terminology that distinguished applied from basic research, they nonetheless invoked an ideology of entrepreneurial science that validated research with practical benefits.

Administrators did not challenge established academic ideologies of science. Instead of trying to replace faculty dedication to basic research with a veneration of applied work, they forged an alternative ideology. It was an instrumental ideology of science that valorized research having utility outside academe.

From time to time, whenever the academic world is discussed, the phrase "ivory tower" is used. The phrase may have had some validity at one time but that day is long since gone, certainly in the public research universities. It is impossible for us to do our job without constant interaction with the federal and state government, with business and industry, and with a thousand and one other organizations and individuals in the society that we serve.

President Grossman

The idea that Nouveau University and UPI are trying to retarget research into applied research for profit is a misconception, but we do want to help faculty recognize that there may be patentable, applied spin-offs to their research, ideas that would otherwise be wasted.

Gerald Meronick

Using the lexicon of technology transfer, administrators redefined research, so that it was evaluated in terms of what it could accomplish outside the university, not in terms of the way it was evaluated by professors within the university or by the associations of learned disciplines.

An instrumental, entrepreneurial ideology of science meant concentrating on organizational forms other than the traditional discipline-based academic departments.
Many of these things [commercialization] are the result of interdisciplinary work. Interdisciplinary groups are central, groups which bring together applied and basic in ways that will result in industrial development. This is the way we view the role of science. . . . Existing disciplines can only provide part of the answers.
Brendon Shaughnessy, dean, sciences

Central administrators did not speak frequently of "applied" research, but the ideology of science that they promoted, despite the language of technology transfer, was an ideology that celebrated applied research. In promoting applied research, administrators were challenging the ideology of science created by the academic establishment in the post–World War II period. That ideology elaborated the importance of "pure," "basic," or "fundamental science," science that was autonomous, freed from the constraints of commerce of politics, and able to follow the logic of a learned discipline to penultimate discoveries, which were finally richer in practical rewards because undistorted by demands for application (Wolfle, 1972; but for a critique of this view, see Dickson, 1984, and Greenburg, 1967). Although not directly confronting the academic ideology of basic science, the central administrators at Nouveau University nonetheless presented a substantive challenge by offering as an alternative an instrumental, entrepreneurial ideology of science that they generally spoke of as "business and university partnerships." Part and parcel of the entrepreneurial ideology of science was a commitment to interdisciplinarity, which undermined the importance of department and discipline in the ideology of basic science.

Faculty Members of the Technology Transfer Committee

The discourse of faculty suggests that they did not fully embrace the ideologies promoted by central administrators. For example, faculty interpreted the economic development and public-service ideologies invoked by central administrators somewhat differently. They also spoke to ideologies that did not figure in the discourse of central administrators. First, they spoke at length about the distinction between basic and applied science. Second, they stressed differences between university and commercial research.

As indicated in the previous section, faculty had serious questions about the short-term viability of technology transfer as the key to regional economic development, but believed that research in the long run was central to national economic prosperity.

Universities can help economic development, but in the long run, not the short.
Jeff Payne, professor and department head, information and policy sciences professional school

I personally think that technology is where our economic future may be. The West Germans have recognized this; the Japanese have recognized this.
Randall Kunkle, professor, health sciences professional school

Faculty, then, shared with the central administration the outline of an ideology of science that stressed economic development.

Faculty also spoke of the university's public-service mission somewhat differently than did central administrators. Like central administrators, faculty indicated that research and technology transfer should and did serve the public good. However, some faculty questioned central administrators' analogy between technology transfer and agricultural extension.

It is nothing like that, because in this case technology is being kept secret and privatized until a patent finally does result and in that case it's being sold to the highest bidder. Whereas agricultural extension was information developed for free, for everybody.
Barry Monroe, professor and department head, applied science professional school

Moreover, several saw difficulties in including technology transfer in the university's public-service mission. For example, faculty expressed concern about conflict between commercial and educational responsibilities in dealing with graduate students.

I don't like to support graduate students on my commercial projects, simply because I don't believe a marriage between commercial endeavor and the training of graduate students is for the best. They're here to learn to do research.
James Moneymaker, professor, health sciences professional school

Much as I'd like to encourage industrial support of research, there is an essential conflict—proprietary information. You have to be very careful about trading the intellectual freedom for the research contract. Understand, I think the main reason in my opinion for getting research contracts is the support of graduate students.
George Jasper

Embedded in these concerns were elements of two ideologies that committee members drew upon. The first is an ideology of basic science. The second is an ideology of the autonomous university, concerned primarily with education.

For many T2C members, basic science was valued as the foundation for all science.

I am a basic scientist, not an applied person. . . . Basic science is always the starting point. . . . It is the basic discovery that drives the process. . . . I would never pick a project that was purely applied and had no implications for basic science. That's not really what my function is. I am at the base of the pyramid in this technology transfer stuff, not at the peak. Basic knowledge is the foundation.

Laurence Threadgill

Generally, faculty indicated that basic research was valued over applied.

Basic research is felt to be a higher calling.

Irving Shapiro, professor, health sciences professional school

It seems that there are people around here who think applied research is less than basic.

Bjorn Larson, professor, health sciences professional school

I have heard it voiced, talking to other people: "At your stage of your career it's better." "Why don't you just publish it?" And, "There's nothing. What do you really gain by patenting something?"

Tyler Caulley, Jr.

There was a clear sense that the peer-review merit system of the university favored basic research, and that applied was regarded as a lesser endeavor.

This is a very definite consideration [for assistant professors]. They can't allow themselves to be lured by the golden fleece—away from doing what is necessary to develop themselves as researchers and teachers.

Barry Monroe

The words I've heard are that "you're prostituting yourself." . . . [That refers not just to your sources of funding but to] your attitude. You know that you're not doing basic research anymore; you're prostituting yourself to get the dollar.

Bjorn Larson

The valuing of basic over applied research was related to a second ideology invoked by faculty about the difference between universities and commercial enterprises. This ideology stressed the importance of an autonomous university, beyond profit and politics, devoted to producing knowledge and students, rather than products and processes.

I recognize that technology transfer is a necessity. Funding is becoming more difficult. The university needs money, but it's dirty; it takes away from purity. The ivory tower becomes grayer and grayer. I recognize that we have to do technology transfer, but I'm not happy with it. You hear faculty talk among themselves; academics refer to themselves as prostitutes. We feel guilty. . . . The differences between the industrial scientist and the academic are much less than they used to be. . . . Academia is becoming more like industry.

Leo Zazworski

If technology transfer became an overriding issue it would be a problem. The university exists as an institution of learning.

James Moneymaker

In sum, administrators invoked a set of ideologies that presented technology transfer as relatively unproblematic. Faculty and administrators shared some beliefs about economic development and public service. However, faculty identified points of conflict between an ideology of entrepreneurial science and more traditional academic ideologies. The basis of this conflict was rooted in conventional conceptions of basic and applied research. Although most of the faculty on the T2C had engaged in technology transfer and were moved by the ideology of entrepreneurial science, they simultaneously cherished ideologies that emphasized basic science and the autonomy of the university.

POWER: THE CONTROL AND COORDINATION OF TECHNOLOGY TRANSFER

Central Administrators

Administrators assumed that successful technology transfer was contingent upon their active guidance. They initiated formal institutional participation in technology transfer, trying to regulate the activity of the few faculty already involved and to engage more faculty in university-directed entrepreneurial science. The public discourse of Nouveau University administrators put the university at the center of the process. The administrators' insistence on the importance of institutional management of technology transfer challenged established faculty prerogatives. For years, faculty had transferred technology—consulting, contracting with private enterprises, even patenting—without institutional oversight. Prior to the inauguration of the T2C, the university had not regulated faculty technology transfer in any formal way or made any systematic claims to a share of the rewards. If the institution had been included at all by faculty involved in technology transfer, it was on an ad-hoc basis. The central administration was attempting to change faculty practice in this regard by more closely regulating faculty activity.

The public discourse of administrators shows that they used two closely related strategies to assert control over the coordination of technology transfer. First, administrators suggested in public media that faculty were naive and inept in matters of management of technology transfer, while administrators had the necessary know-how. Second, administrators legitimated their own expertise with regard to technology transfer by aligning themselves with state and national economic elites.

In order to establish a climate for entrepreneurial science, administrators suggested that they had to do no less than reshape the existing institutional culture.

The important thing is that deans and department heads who value this stuff [technology transfer] communicate this to the faculty. That's not to say that if faculty don't do technology transfer they can't stay. Rather it is to create a culture where this is valued.

Daniel Eisenbarth

Administrators were central to creating this new culture partly because faculty had to be sold on the importance and legitimacy of technology transfer activity, and partly because administrators possessed the expertise to manage technology transfer that faculty lacked.

Our job is to help them [faculty] think like business by showing them how to write business plans, conduct market research, and go through the process of identifying venture capital. We [Nouveau Technology] really have two roles: being a catalyst and providing investment dollars.

Charles Murdock

Central administrators legitimated their intervention in technology transfer management by repeatedly invoking an economic development ideology that was consistent with beliefs held by state and national elites. Central administrators cast science and the universities as key factors in the revitalization of the American economy through the development of high technology. They championed university–industry partnerships, similar to those already organized in a number of states—Massachusetts, Pennsylvania, Illinois, Ohio, New York, to name a few—as the key to economic prosperity, echoing the voices of other university presidents and CEO's of Fortune 500 companies (Fairweather, 1988; Langfitt et al., 1983). Like presidents at other Research I institutions, Nouveau University administrators aligned themselves with private-sector leaders (Edsall, 1984; Slaughter, 1990).

Cooperation [among the state's higher education institutions to benefit a communications company] extends well beyond all this. I see it as this university, state government, and our industrial enterprises work together. I have seen it in joint efforts to improve the public schools, in our effort to develop a new world class [research center] and in a remarkable team effort to bring [research facility] to the state. We are building a new state, a place in which we shall preserve the ability to work together as well as to compete. ... I want to stress in particular how cooperation with business and industry pervades our university.

President Grossman

As executive officers of a state institution, Nouveau University administrators adopted a high-technology, economic development strategy that stressed investing more public resources in the development of technology that would be transferred to the private sector. This strategy, the closer management of faculty who were or might be making commercial discoveries through their research, and the claim to the proceeds of faculty inventions were justified in terms of serving the public interest. The public interest, then, was equated with private-sector economic development. Administrative notions of entrepreneurial science and the public interest promoted the privatization of the university and research, linking them more closely to the commercial arena.

Faculty Members of the Technology Transfer Committee

Although faculty indicated that the university had a crucial role to play in facilitating technology transfer and, in the long term, economic development, they offered a somewhat different notion from that articulated by administrators of the ideal nature of university involvement. Many faculty were quite critical of Nouveau University's handling of technology transfer matters, but they offered few alternatives. In the final analysis, faculty members of the T2C accepted the formal power of central administrators as a fact of life, expressing a clear sense of what was "realistic" (that is, acceptable to administrators) in terms of policies and organizational arrangements concerning technology transfer. They did not challenge central administration by calling on a strong professional ideology of academic governance. Although faculty on the T2C saw themselves as broadly representative of all faculty at Nouveau University, they did not work to construct coalitions with the organized faculty to shape policy.

Faculty generally agreed that inventor–scientists needed the university, especially the first few times they tried to transfer technology, but they did not portray the university's role, as did central administrators, as being one of management and coordination. Instead, they spoke of the university facilitating technology transfer by providing support, information, and resources, and by getting people together.

The University has a role. I don't think managing is the right word for it. The administration is given to some terrible traps by regarding themselves as the managers, which they never should be and it leads to much grief when they think of themselves that way.

George Jasper

The major job of the university is to find ways to bring people together. Technology transfer is a people process.

Frank Krupnick

I'll tell you what would have been ideal. Had there been an office where I could have gone : . . and got professional help and advice in what would be my options. That's all I would have needed.

Randall Kunkle

Although faculty looked to the university to facilitate technology transfer, there was a general unhappiness with and mistrust of administration among faculty. Part of it was a sense that the university has not been adept at handling technology transfer.

I don't think the university is well situated to handle technology transfer. . . . It's just that they have no handle on what they are trying to do. I don't know what the goals are. It's a criticism not of [Nouveau Technology] but of higher administration officials. You know, they go to these meetings, they hear other universities talk about this stuff, and they decide suddenly, we want one, too, but they don't know what it is or what to do.

Milton Klotz

As administrators saw faculty as inept at managing technology transfer, so faculty viewed administrators as incompetent. As administrators sometimes saw inventor–scientists as demanding more than their fair share of the commercial rewards of academic science, so faculty saw administrators as using the faculty as "cash cows." In a situation where each group viewed their own activities as essential, tension and distrust may be endemic. However, administrators, as we saw previously, moved beyond this impasse, legitimating increased regulation of faculty activity by representing themselves as the custodians of public interest and economic development. Faculty seemed unable to move beyond their skepticism in a positive way.

Despite their negative attitudes toward the administration's handling of technology transfer, faculty had very little knowledge of how technology transfer and intellectual property were handled at other institutions, and did not seem concerned about acquiring such information. In response to the question of whether they had a sense of the arrangements concerning these matters at other universities, committee members usually said no.

No, no sense of what the situation is at other institutions.

Milton Klotz

No, I don't really have very much knowledge about what other universities do.

Barry Monroe

Several faculty were quite explicit about the limitations of the committee's powers and input, and about the fact that ultimately the administration would do as it wished.

We [the T2C] made our case as strong as we could. We gave our best advice. They [central administration] did what they did. That's the reality.

Frank Krupnick

The T2C has largely a puppet role. When [head of Office of Technology Transfer] says the Regents won't approve, [the Vice-President for Research] won't approve, [the President] won't approve, why bother? ... We give ideas, but are not a big part of decision-making.

Leo Zazworski

I've been happy with the committee's recommendations. I'm not so sure about the importance of the committee's voice. It seems to me that there are a couple of issues here. First is what the Regents decide. The other is what the courts decide. The playing field is bigger than the T2C.

Laurence Threadgill

T2C faculty recognized and accepted the committee's advisory role and its limited influence. There was a sense that the power lay elsewhere.

Faculty on the T2C exhibited contradictory attitudes about whom they represented. Despite the fact that T2C faculty were drawn from a narrow range of scientific and professional fields (only two from basic science units, none from social sciences or the humanities), they saw themselves as broadly representative and as protecting faculty interests in general.

I see myself representing the whole university community.

James Moneymaker

But the other reason I'm on it [T2C] is that I can act as the conscience of the faulty.

Leo Zazworski

I think the committee is trying to represent what the faculty has to say about these issues.

Randall Kunkle

However, their conception of representation was quite limited. None spoke about their being appointed by administrators rather than being nominated and elected by the faculty. None of the T2C members reported back formally or systematically to the units from which they came. They did not draw on the powerful ideology and the potentially powerful resource of faculty governance to challenge what they saw as the negative aspects of central administrators' involvement in technology transfer. They never commented on the absence of faculty representatives on the T2C from many departments and colleges, indeed, from entire sectors of the university.

In sum, administrators justified their role in technology transfer in terms of protecting and promoting the public interest, using language that had traditionally been utilized by faculty in describing their scientific activity. Although faculty were doubtful about this particular administration's capacities and actions, they too thought the university had to play a central role in technology transfer and in economic development. In formulating technology transfer policies, administrators aligned themselves with regional and national corporate elites. Faculty questioned neither this alignment, nor the positional power of administrators.

CONCLUSION

Our overriding consideration in this research is to explore the question of how professional labor is defined and controlled, a general question that comes out of critical scholars' professionalization theory. We have pursued this question in an organizational context, and in the discourse of academics and administrators of the public research I university. Of particular concern was the language of public interest in discussions of technology transfer and intellectual property rights, a language that we take at least in part to reveal a significant dimension of the organizational struggle over the conditions, process, and products of professional labor. We examined, in Giddens's terms, the structuration of academic labor in a research university, playing central administrators' public discourse against the private discourse of faculty members on the university's Technology Transfer Committee, to study the construction of public interest and the reconstitution of professional labor.

Generally, administrators articulated an organizational ideology that accounted for university involvement in technology transfer in terms of the public interest as manifested in regional (private) economic development. This ideology justified central administrators' claims to coordination and control of technology transfer. Faculty members neither challenged this belief system, nor systematically advanced a coherent ideology that ran counter to the organizational ideology of central administrators—for example, an ideology of science or of faculty governance.

Thus far, administrators have been somewhat successful in their efforts to renegotiate appropriate faculty activity and intellectual property rights. Administrators have defined technology transfer as an appropriate activity for faculty to pursue, and they have increased and formalized administrative control of this activity, in which some faculty were engaged well before the recent development of university policies. University policy now requires faculty to disclose patentable ideas to the institution, which has the right of first refusal. Intellectual property, in the form of patents and software, has been renegotiated. The administration receives a greater share of patent royalties than previously, especially in the long term, and receives the same share on software royalties as on patents, although previously the university received none on software.

Several factors may explain why faculty members on the T2C did not more actively resist and challenge the initiatives of Nouveau University's central administrators. Generally, faculty shared the broad outlines of the administrators' ideology, although they questioned the ability of this particular administration to realize the promise of the ideology. In their accounts, faculty were ambivalent about technology transfer. When they discussed involvement in technology transfer, faculty attributed noble motivations to themselves, but cited more material and ignoble motivations in discussing their colleagues, undermining any basis for making common cause with other faculty in negotiating the terms of intellectual property with the administration. Moreover, faculty were unable to appeal to an ideology of basic science to constrain administrators, because faculty were engaged in the applied work valued by administrators. Nor could faculty draw on a professional ideology, such as that expressed by the American Association of University Professors, that venerates university autonomy and faculty governance, because their participation in profit-making science undercut the social contract in which faculty were given autonomy and control over some spheres of their work in return for pursuing science in a disinterested fashion, thereby protecting the public good. If this tension was not in their minds, members of the T2C believed it was in the minds of faculty who did not sit on the T2C. They were not certain of support from their colleagues in other schools and disciplines. Indeed, they believed their peers might be more ready to restrict their commercial endeavors than the administration. As a result, they aligned themselves with central administrators in promoting entrepreneurial science while being critical and suspicious of those administrators.

In sum, the managers of professionals within the university employed professionalizing strategies. Nouveau University central administrators articulated an organizational ideology grounded in an ideal of service that not only promoted the interests of the university, but advanced central administrators' position and interests within the university. In the name of the public interest, central administrators initiated a renegotiation of the social relations among faculty and administration in redefining their right to regulate intellectual labor and increase their claims on intellectual property rights. Administrators have appropriated both the voice of the university and the public interest.

The renegotiation of professional labor is part of a continuing and contingent dynamic of struggle within organizations that reproduces and generates structure, even as it is patterned by normative and material resources and structures available to and impinging on the contending parties. Negotiations over technology transfer may open up the question of the terms of professional labor at various postsecondary institutions. We see the central project of critical constructionism in studying professional labor as: (1) the analysis of socio-political negotiations and struggles within organizations, (2) the locating of these indeterminate contests, which are immediate and in process, within larger patterns of belief and power, and (3) the connecting of these immediate struggles and larger patterns to the interests, actions, and/or privileging of particular status groups and classes in society. This project is particularly important at the present historical juncture, when the labor force in the United States is being reshaped to meet the demands of a global market. Professional as well as blue-collar and service-sector work is part and parcel of this restructuring. Transfer of technology from professors' laboratories to the marketplace is presented by administrators and the economic and state elites with whom they have aligned themselves as important to revitalizing the American economy.

Some of the more immediate issues surrounding professional labor that we need to examine are control of time, work activities, and ownership of intellectual property. Faculty may come to be defined less as independent professionals and more as full-time employees as the university attempts to induce and control faculty participation in technology transfer and the profits generated by that faculty activity. Formalizing technology transfer policies may constrain faculty's ability to engage in the wide range of consulting and commercial activities that have traditionally been viewed as faculty prerogatives. Instead, the university may attempt to direct faculty activity toward entrepreneurial science projects that it is financing and promoting. In promoting entrepreneurial science and developing technology transfer policies, the central administration may extend its claim to ownership to cover not only patents but other intellectual products, such as software and books, previously held by the faculty (Rhoades and Slaughter, forthcoming). The faculty's ability to contest administrative power may be hampered by the breakdown of departments, the traditional basis of faculty power, as administrators promote a variety of interdisciplinary structures. Faculty and administrators' readiness to privatize research might eventually result in the restructuring of funding, with a greater commercial voice in funding and a lesser faculty and university voice.

Whereas the above issues concern professional labor within the university, the reconstitution and redirection of professional labor occasioned by technology transfer activity also raise issues regarding the legitimacy of academe and the university in the external world. For example, internal redefinitions of appropriate faculty activity may lead to public redefinitions of academics from independent, disinterested professionals to self-interested business persons. Similarly, changed public perceptions may also apply to the university as a whole, with university claims to autonomy, state funds, and not-for-profit status being compromised by commercial linkages and activities (Slaughter, 1988).

Finally, the public expectations regarding economic development that are raised by the organizational ideology developed by administrators may prove problematic. Administrative and faculty support of research projects that are, in essence, transfer payments for product development in the private sector, and that generally are bought up by and benefit multinational corporations, might have negative consequences for popular support for the university if these do not create jobs and broaden prosperity in the local and regional community. The particular construction of the public interest developed by administrators, and the redirection of professional labor that is embedded in it, pose serious questions and dilemmas with regard to how academics and universities will be regarded, evaluated, and supported.

NOTES

1. In this chapter, we take technology transfer to be the movement of an idea from the laboratory of a professor to commercial product development.

2. In organizational and professionalization literature, largely written by professionals, administrators are usually cast in unflattering, bureaucratic terms that emphasize commitment to hierarchy and rigid standardization, while professionals are portrayed as committed to socially desirable values, such as autonomy and excellence. We do not find these categories particularly useful. They ignore the larger social processes that influence organizational actors. They also obscure internal differences and conflicts within each category.

3. For example, in considering committee members' accounts we focus, in Giddens's terms, exclusively on their "discursive consciousness," on their "giving of accounts" and "supplying of reasons." We attend to neither their "practical consciousness," their tacit knowledge employed in enacting conduct, nor their unconscious. Similarly, in examining the metaphors and mechanics related by committee members, we are concentrating on a delimited range of rules and resources.

4. The unit heads have generally spoken as if they were representing the interests of faculty. Indeed, most saw that as their role on the committee and, in fact, as the role of the committee in general.

5. All quotations in this and other sections are drawn from our interviews. The names have been changed, and the affiliations not fully specified.

REFERENCES

Dickson, David. (1984). *The new politics of science*. New York: Pantheon.
Edsall, Thomas Byrne. (1984). *The new politics of inequality*. New York: Norton.

Etzioni, Amitai. (1964). *Modern organizations*. Englewood Cliffs, NJ: Prentice-Hall.

Fairweather, James. (1988). *Entrepreneurship and higher education: Lessons for colleges, universities and industry* (ASHE-ERIC Higher Education Research Report No. 8). Washington, DC: Association for the Study of Higher Education.

Giddens, Anthony. (1982). *Profiles and critiques in social theory*. Berkeley: University of California Press.

———. (1984). *The constitution of society: Outline of the theory of structuration*. Berkeley: University of California Press.

Greenburg, Daniel. (1967). *The politics of pure science*. New York: New American Library.

Hughes, Everett C. (1958). *Men and their work*. Glencoe, IL: Free Press.

Kornhauser, William. (1962). *Scientists in industry*. Berkeley: University of California Press.

Langfitt, Thomas, et al. (Eds.). (1983). *Partners in the research enterprise: University–corporate relations in science and technology*. Philadelphia: University of Pennsylvania Press.

Larson, Magali Sarfatti. (1977). *The rise of professionalism*. Berkeley: University of California Press.

———. (1984). The production of expertise and the constitution of expert power. In Thomas Haskell (Ed.), *The authority of experts: Studies in history and theory* (pp. 28–80). Bloomington: Indiana University Press.

Rhoades, Gary, & Slaughter, Sheila. (forthcoming). Professors, administrators, and patents: The negotiation of technology transfer. *Sociology of Education*.

Slaughter, Sheila. (1988). Academic freedom and the state: Reflections on the uses of knowledge. *Journal of Higher Education 59*(3), 241–262.

———. (1990). *The higher learning and high technology: Dynamics of higher education policy formation*. Albany, NY: State University of New York Press.

Wolfle, Dael. (1972). *The home of science: The role of the university*. New York: McGraw-Hill.

10 TEACHING LESBIAN AND GAY DEVELOPMENT: A PEDAGOGY OF THE OPPRESSED

Anthony R. D'Augelli

As I was preparing to write this chapter, a large package from San Francisco arrived at my office. The envelope contained copies of a 16-part series of articles from *The San Francisco Examiner* entitled "Gay in America." A hand-written note explained that the mailer had been a student at the university three years earlier, and that he "used to sneak" into my class on lesbian/gay development during the weekly film or videotape that was shown. He wrote, "I remember wanting to read as much as I could about homosexuality. There didn't seem to be much literature available at Penn State. I didn't know that there were gay newspapers, gay novels, etc." He ended by hoping that the articles would be helpful to students in the class.

Later that day, I read in the campus newspaper that members of the Lesbian and Gay Student Alliance at Penn State had collected over 1,000 signatures on a petition urging the local municipality to extend legal protection against discrimination in housing to lesbians and gay men. Many of those instrumental in this initiative had just completed the most recent version of the course.

This course has enhanced the most personal part of my entire life. I now know how to handle some of these conflicting feelings that would have torn me apart months ago.

I now more clearly see the need for action. I would give money and go on marches and sign petitions and wear buttons.

One of the espoused values of higher education is to advance personal intellectual development while simultaneously developing a broader sense of personal responsibility to others. Appraisal of the degree to which the process of higher education solidifies social and economic inequities or contributes to social justice is generally determined by the ideological and political views of the observer. In the case of lesbians and gay men, however, the role of higher educational institutions is unambiguous. Few could argue with credulity that advances made in the political or social arenas for lesbians and gay men have occurred because of the role of colleges and universities in these historical processes. At best, even in 1990, lesbians and gay men, one of the largest minorities on campuses, are systematically neglected in the curriculum, are subjected to institutional indifference and prejudice, and are the most-often targeted victims of harassment and violence (Herek, 1989). A heterosexist presumption—that heterosexuality is normative as well as superior to other forms of socio-emotional relating—is deeply entrenched in the pedagogical and social structure of higher education. This presumption preserves the status quo, insuring that lesbians and gay men will have substantial difficulty achieving the personal, occupational, and political power of their heterosexual peers.

> The course helped me to realize that I can develop as a gay person—enjoying life, career, relationships, and family.

> It helped me to take a good, hard look at myself—helped me in becoming more comfortable with who I am.

While there are many approaches to the problem of heterosexism in higher education, I offer one modest solution—a course devoted to the development of lesbians and gay men. I have taught such a course for five years, educating young people who are lesbian or gay about human development and extrapolating a developmental framework to an analysis of their own lives. The underlying theory upon which the course has developed encourages personal examination, attention to family and to close relationships, and sensitivity to the social and legal policies that influence how people develop over their lifespans. When exposed to an affirmative "curriculum" on their lives, as the quotes from students that I provide throughout the chapter will attest, young lesbians and gay men undergo dramatic changes. They appreciate the nature of their own internalized homophobic views, and more clearly understand the impact of the heterosexist assumptions of their families and friends. They also become acutely aware of institutional indifference and hostility to lesbian and gay lives; it comes as no surprise, then, to discover that the university and the adjacent local community are subject to special scrutiny. By understanding the multiple constraints on their achievement of personal fulfillment, lesbians and gay men gain the freedom to affect their futures. They gain the "theory of action" Freire refers to in *Pedagogy of the Oppressed* (1984): "Just as the oppressor, in order to oppress, needs a theory of oppressive action, so the oppressed, to become free, also needs a theory of action" (p. 185).

I will start by describing the theoretical views that guide the course. Since the formal theory extends analytic concepts generally reserved for heterosexual life to lesbian and gay development, it exposes the "hidden curriculum" and propels to action for change. Then I will provide a brief portrait of the context in which the course has been offered. Finally, I will discuss some of the personal changes the course facilitates and the challenges these represent to the heterosexist status quo.

It was terrific to be gay in a class where gay was the majority.

Sometimes you present a heterophobic attitude.

THEORY

Exceptionality

Much theory concerning "homosexuality" has been dominated by perspectives conditioned by anti-lesbian/anti-gay attitudes about affectional differences. New theoretical perspectives on the development of lesbians and gay men are needed, because the conceptual vacuum that currently exists poses serious problems in the understanding of women's and men's lives. The difficulty in developing a theory is a result of both the nature of the phenomenon—complex lives over time—and the inevitable social and political consequences of models. For example, many gay activists prefer biological determinism models of lesbian/gay development, in which people are "born" with a particular affectional orientation, while opponents of gay rights prefer a voluntaristic, free-choice "model," which, in the usual rendering, removes the moral requirement of legal protections. Theoretical views are grounded in historical time: the "context of discovery" must be ideological (Kaplan, 1964). For example, a recent analysis by Kitzinger (1987) presents a strong argument for a radical feminist construction of lesbian lives, cautioning that "liberal-humanistic" views of lesbians serve to eviscerate political consciousness and action.

Without endeavoring to construct a "solution" to such dilemmas, I nonetheless must clarify my own point of departure in my work. I assume that lesbian and gay development represent *exceptional developmental processes*. In my view, women and men who express their needs for closeness and intimacy more consistently with people of the same gender have evolved within their own life histories by departing from typical heterosocial socialization patterns. Continued growth and personal fulfillment as a lesbian or gay man in our culture demands unusual competencies and special strengths. By starting with the assumption of *exceptionality*, efforts can be made to discover these adaptive talents. The exceptionality assumption transcends the discredited notion of homosexuality-as-pathology. Lesbians and gay men are not simply variants of usual (heterosexual) development ("alternative lifestyles," "natural expressions of sexual variation," and so forth); they are unique. Their lives can reveal processes with considerable generalizability, and can inform others about personal freedom, intimacy, and community. Constructing identity, relationship, and family structure, and helping communities in the face of widespread oppression, lesbians and gay men can inform others about the process of self-development.

The premise that lesbians and gay men lead exceptional lives—*the affirmative assumption*—has considerable heuristic power. Such a view redirects conceptual articulation toward the discovery of creative life solutions to the fundamental dilemmas of lesbian/gay development: *the creation of a personal life course, and "identity," that affirms one's feelings in a heterosocial society*. The normative model for lesbian/gay identity "integration" remains *social invisibility*, in which personal identity is hidden, denied, or distorted. Most social scientific research on homosexuality focuses on the minority of lesbians and gay men who disclose their orientation to researchers; earlier perspectives were built on the even smaller subgroup who sought professional services, but many other life courses exist: some lesbians and gay men remain heterosexually married; others care for children from earlier marriages; some live their lives without admitting their sexual feelings to others. In addition, while much of the research to date has been done on "adults," recent work on lesbian and gay youth (Herdt, 1989) and on older adults (Kehoe, 1989; Vacha, 1985) reveals remarkably diverse patterns of emotional and sexual unfolding. These complex patterns illustrate the human talent needed to create personal "identity" under explicitly adverse social conditions. This is not unique to lesbian women and gay men, of course, but cultural prescriptions and normlessness (except for denial, suppression, and invisibility) demand distinctive coping. Few groups develop without anticipatory socialization to this degree, and few develop a distinction that results in such intense and relentless social opprobrium.

> I started to tread through the issues that I had not yet examined. The main issue . . . had to do with societal acceptance. . . . Some of these related to childhood conditioning from my parents about how my life should be. . . . You know, husband, 2.5 kids, house with three bathrooms, lawn mower.

> My parents kind of freaked out at first when they found out about it. It took a while for my parents to really realize that being gay was not a terrible thing.

The Human Development Perspective

A powerful meta-theoretical framework for the analysis of these processes is the lifespan human development perspective (Baltes, 1987; Lerner, 1984; Riegel, 1976). This general view, which has many individual variants, involves the explication of patterns of dynamic interaction of multiple factors over time in the development of the individual. The developing woman or man must be understood in context; simultaneous descriptions of the person's social network, neighborhood and community, institutional settings, and culture are complemented by descriptions of individual physical and psychological change. A particular strength of this view is the acknowledgment of the impact of historical time on development, whether the process is observed during an individual's life, over the lives of family members, within a community, or in a culture. The human development perspective is an effort to discover variations between individuals as they move in time through diverse social situations, communities, and cultures.

One consequence of a human development view for the study of lesbians and gay men is that to describe the development of their lives without inclusion of social, institutional, cultural, and historical factors is fundamentally distorted. Indeed, to eliminate culture and historical time is to assume that lesbian and gay lives are unresponsive to social circumstances; this inevitably devolves into reductionism, generally of a biological nature. Such unidimensional perspectives have been pre-eminent in the history of "homosexuality," since scholars, theorists, and researchers have focused on either medical, biological, genetic, hormonal, psychiatric, or psychological dimensions without simultaneous analysis of current and historical context. For example, the concept of "homosexuality" as psychiatric disorder dismisses historical, community, or social factors. The deletion of homosexuality from diagnostic nomenclature of the American Psychiatric Association in 1973 (and not totally discarded by the APA until 1987) resulted from the need to incorporate a set of discordant factors—empirical findings—into traditional biological–deterministic, medical thinking. "Homosexuality" had become a treatable reification, a dysfunctional individual characteristic that exists outside social, cultural, and historical reality.

The abstraction of affectional/sexual patterns from culture so as to describe, explain, and modify "homosexuality" is the first step in this oppressive model-building. The pedagogical consequences of reductionist views are not limited to social science inquiries, although social science may provide the reference point for other analyses. For instance, I recently attended a scholarly lecture on Tennessee Williams's later plays in which the presenter linked the "self-hatred" of these later plays with Williams's lifelong insecurities. One example was Williams's capitulation to his producer's urging that references to the protagonist's homosexuality be deleted from *Cat on a Hot Tin Roof*. Castigating Williams for lifelong self-hatred, the critic never mentioned that homosexuality was literally illegal in the United States in the 1950s, that Williams's career would have ended were he to "come out," even obliquely through his plays, and that "self-hatred" is a likely reaction to a lifetime of stigma, discrimination, and hiding.

The larger implication of this perspective for higher education is that lesbian and gay lives must become integral units of analysis in many disciplines—history, political science, anthropology, cultural studies, mass communications, as well as the usual (psychology and sociology). The study of lesbian and gay lives should not be compartmentalized or tokenized; nor should such study be appropriated by those disciplines historically associated with social control (Prilleltensky, 1989; Sampson, 1977). Lesbian and gay lives are not only "hidden from history" (see Duberman, Vicinus, and Chauncey, 1989), but hidden from anthropology, political science, literary criticism, and so on, as well. A recent analysis of the work of photographers Minor White and Robert Mapplethorpe exemplifies the power of new perspectives using social and historical time in the analysis of lesbian and gay lives (Sischy, 1989). Sischy bases her critique of the photographs of these gay men—one "hidden" throughout most of his professional life (White), the other forcefully "out" in his work—on the role of very different epochs.

A human development meta-theory dictates a broad, interdisciplinary curriculum as befitting the analysis of changing lives embedded in changing cultural and historical contexts. I will now present some propositions of a human development model, and will briefly note their relevance to lesbian and gay male development.

1. *Individuals develop and change over the entire course of their lifespan.* This means that psychological, cognitive, behavioral, emotional, and physical development do not stop after the achievement of socially defined "adulthood" (usually heterosexual marriage and occupational stability). The development of affectional interests should be considered a lifelong developmental process as well. That one's sexual and affectional feelings can change in varying degrees over the course of life must be assumed; efforts to suggest otherwise are disguised social convention. Feelings of physical and emotional closeness for individuals of the same gender can evolve throughout life; they are highly conditioned by social, family, and personal expectations. A human development view allows for multiple changes over time in sexual feelings, attitudes, and behavior.

> I think I used to view lesbians and gay men only in terms of sexuality without thinking about issues in adolescence, adulthood, and aging. My scope is much more comprehensive in taking into account all of the aspects that go into lesbian or gay life.

2. *Appreciation of the plasticity or modifiability of human behavioral development is crucial.* Human functioning is responsible to environmental circumstances and changes induced by physical and other biological factors. In essence, the human development model makes few assumptions about the fixed nature of human functioning, but suggests that plasticity is a prime characteristic of human behavior. Plasticity may change over chronological time: at different ages, certain components of human behavioral functioning are more or less resistant to, or more or less responsive to, differing circumstances. Also, certain historical periods may encourage greater differentiation, whereas others may promote greater constriction of behavioral possibilities. The implication for gay and lesbian development is that some components of sexual identity may be malleable during certain parts of the lifespan and more crystallized at others. For instance, given the role of hormonal development in sexual identity development, the years temporally proximate to puberty are times in which sexual expression becomes salient. There is not an inevitable and simple biochemical process; the fundamental nature of affectional orientation appears strongly influenced by a complex pattern of neurohormonal events

and socialization experiences (see Ellis and Ames, 1987; Money, 1987). However, in our society, adolescent peer development forces a definition of sexual interests so that "expected" dating behavior can occur. Expression of emotional or sexual interest in one's own sex is simply not an option, nor is the expression of diverse emotional/sexual interests. Thus, those not conforming to the heterosexist imperative must adjust their development, whether by suppression or repression of their feelings. A plasticity assumption helps highlight those aspects of such a process that can change. The process of development for a lesbian or gay man in a society where alternatives are affirmed would be quite different than the process in our society.

I try to look at the future and I can't. Maybe that's one reason I don't tell my parents. I read about other gay communities and I think I will be part of one of these communities. Other times, I think I'll just be the way I am now—one person in a *huge* hostile society. I can't predict my future.

Even though I'm a lesbian, the topic was hard for me to discuss before I took the course, but after hearing about gay women and men all semester in class and on film, it's become easier for me to bring up the topic and voice my opinion.

3. *Individual women and men are unique in their own development over their lifespans.* The nature of the interindividual differences varies at different points in life, in different settings, and at different historical periods. In terms of gay and lesbian development, the issue of variability is essential. Indeed, the concept strikes directly at the trichotomization of sexual life in which individuals are assumed to be heterosexual, gay or lesbian, or bisexual. The human development perspective suggests the continuation of sexual feelings and experience, but would predict less variance in individuals' sexual self-definitions at certain phases of life, in certain kinds of families, in certain communities, and at certain historical times. For example, that sexual diversity increases during adulthood is not simply the result of postadolescent experiential factors, but also of exposure to less restrictive expectations, and of the availability of an increased range of behavioral models for diversity.

Because of my recently found identity, at times it was extremely painful to sit in class and just listen to everything, but personal growth and learning usually entail a certain degree of pain . . . especially when the subject breaks free of the constraints society tends to bind us into.

I was already "out," and educated on gay issues prior to enrolling in this class. I have enjoyed it, but personally, it has not affected me.

4. *Individuals have a substantial impact on their own development.*
Individuals and their families are not passive respondents to social circumstances. Individual acts and the acts of family members (in consort or in
varying degrees of coordination) have an impact on the developmental
process of the individual person and on the family unit. The acts of an
individual shape his or her development. If one assumes that development
involves increased differentiation, then individuals with refined abilities
to behave in diverse ways, whose psychoemotional responsivity allows
for behavioral complexity, and whose social skills allow for competent
performance in a wide range of social settings, are likely to be more highly
"developed."

Out of necessity, lesbians and gay men have been more self-conscious
about the need to create their own development. There have evolved over
time a series of social institutions for lesbians and gay men that have
provided partial socialization experiences. Historically, the primary social
structure for men has been the gay bar (and, to a lesser degree, gay
bath-houses, which have nearly disappeared in the AIDS era). Lesbian
socialization has occurred more often in small, nonpublic, informal groups
or in women's "communities." The nature of these socialization experiences helps create distinct norms and stereotypes: gay men are sexual
machines, whereas lesbians are relationship-oriented. Those women and
men who chose these settings became enculturated within their norms.
Women and men in future cohorts will socialize themselves under new
circumstances and will therefore create a different developmental pattern.
The increasingly diverse contexts in which lesbians and gay men can now
place themselves to explore their affective lives cannot help but promote
increased behavioral differentiation.

I had twelve years of Catholic education at an all-girl Catholic high school, and all
the morality classes were always on how it's wrong. I couldn't believe that it could be
that wrong, and I guess part of me wanted to find out for myself. I think it came about
basically from my own experiences, just finding out I have feelings for women.

The section on "coming out" was instrumental in helping me tell my sister, as well as
close friends.

Empowerment

The human development perspective provides a substantive theory by
which the development of lesbians and gay men can be discussed. Intrinsic
to the perspective is a critical analysis of context and history as influencing

personal and family development. This underscores the view that there is no universal and immutable process of development resulting in "homosexuality." Following such a conclusion, the tenet that individuals direct their own development is extraordinarily powerful, for it adds an action imperative. The process of disclosure of personal status, or "coming out," can only be discussed by taking historical time into account. For an adult in 1950 to acknowledge strong lesbian or gay feelings, and to become publicly active in the social circumstances available at that time, was extremely different from an analogous behavioral sequence in 1990. Disclosure to family is now facilitated by increased cultural acceptance, more positive imagery in media, and far more gay-affirming resources. In earlier days, families could literally fear their offspring's arrest, loss of employment, social censure, and isolation. Prior to 1973, disclosure of lesbian/gay status was admission of psychopathology as well. This "universal" process of lesbian and gay development is thus highly dependent on circumstances. However, the process of disclosure is under the person's control, since lesbian/gay status is not a visible characteristic. One's action related to disclosure influences one's future in many ways. An appreciation of the process leads to empowerment, the understanding of how individual action stimulates social change when action emerges from an appreciation of social oppression.

A human development perspective also demands a precise review of the constraints on behavior that are *not* within the person's control. In understanding the patterns of current lesbian and gay life, for instance, legal barriers to behavioral choices need to be delineated. Indeed, lesbians and gay men *cannot* direct their own development and that of their intimates because of the lack of legal protection in fundamental domains of personal development—housing, employment, family life, spiritual practice, and so on. In nearly half of the United States, consensual sexual activity (between lesbians and between gay men) is illegal. In only one state (Wisconsin) is protection from discrimination guaranteed; in only a handful of municipalities are such rights extended to lesbians and gay men. Maintenance of institutional homophobia in this way reaffirms the status quo, and directly interferes in how lesbians and gay men live their lives and make important life choices. These inequities influence family life and relationship development. Most importantly, the lack of legal protection prevents integration into society and maintains the marginality of lesbian and gay lives.

A developmental analysis provides a foundation for an agendum for change. Women and men who come to define themselves as lesbian or gay create their own identities in the face of two powerful barriers—their invisibility in our culture and the social and legal penalties attached to public expression. The process of delineation that is a *sine qua non* of a developmental analysis accomplishes the first critical step in personal and social change—the proclamation of *existence*. Elaboration of a developmental model further propels action in that the majority "identity" template is deconstructed. Such an analysis creates a point of "no return," in which barriers to personal change and social action are articulated and the need for action emphasized. A developmental analysis leads lesbians and gay men to a personal "breaking point" that involves *becoming an ex-heterosexual*, to use Ebaugh's (1988) analysis. Exiting from heterosocial reality is the first developmental task for a lesbian or a gay man, but understanding the parameters of this reality is exceedingly difficult. The subsequent task—the creation of an affirming lesbian and gay life—is difficult in a different way: it involves confrontation with the formal barriers to development that abound in our society. The study of lesbians and gay men that does not address homophobia, heterosexism, discrimination, harassment, and violence is the study of development steeped in oppression. Majority culture seeks to retain the most powerful tool to maintain the status quo—*the right to describe the process of "normal" development and the description of achieved identity*. These tools need to be appropriated to affirm lesbian and gay lives.

My previous courses in human development had never allowed for a full look at lesbians and gays from a life cycle perspective, or, from any perspective, for that matter.

I have learned a lot about how to understand what I went through (and still am going through!), and how to be content with just exactly who and what I am.

CONTEXT: HOMOPHOBIA AT THE UNIVERSITY

An appreciation of the context in which the course developed is critical to understanding its impact on individual students. I have described the community in which the university is located elsewhere (D'Augelli, 1989a). Perhaps the most relevant aspect of the context is its rural location and its distance from major metropolitan areas. These factors make lesbian and gay life much more difficult: There are few sources of support available locally, and there are intense fears attached to disclosure (D'Augelli and Hart, 1987). Nonetheless, during the mid-1980s, several new groups emerged, and the climate for lesbians and gay men in the local area modestly improved. By the time the first offering of the course occurred, in the spring of 1985, groups serving both women and men in the community were complemented by a new telephone help line. A student organization at the university, which had gone into decline, was reorganized, and showed much promise as a support system for the many lesbian and gay students presumably in attendance. This constellation of factors, which I have called the "development of a helping community for lesbians and gay men" (D'Augelli, 1989a), had direct and indirect impact on the university, the predominant institution and employer in the community.

The evolution of informal support systems for lesbians and gay men in the community inevitably brought into focus the climate at the university itself. During the mid-1980s, little overt support existed for lesbians and gay men at the university. There had never been educational or cultural events related to lesbian/gay issues; there were no self-acknowledged faculty or staff; there was no coverage of any relevant material in courses. Essential campus services, such as the health center and the mental health unit, made no explicit effort to offer services to lesbians and gay men. No one on the staffs of these important facilities was openly lesbian or gay, or even willing to state a special interest in helping this population. Lesbians and gay men were officially invisible in the formal administrative structure of the university.

The only public "acknowledgment" was through the student organization, one of hundreds of student organizations on campus. This organization, however, was unique in that its constituency was generally hidden and fearful; even attending a meeting was a courageous act. The invisibility functioned in a self-reinforcing way: afraid to attend meetings and disclose sexual orientation, few lesbian and gay students could emerge to create a presence. Without the support of an informal community, lesbians and gay men remained victimized by the myths of the culture and by the silence of the heterosexual majority. Their voices could not be raised to insist that the university address lesbian and gay lives. Such insistence does not come readily to young people who are lesbian or gay.

I'm going to try to have an effect on the amount of homophobic comments I hear. I will no longer keep silent.

So often we don't have enough information, and, we never have any positive reinforcement.

When some lesbian and gay students overcame their own hesitancies and made their orientation public, they met with hostility and violence. In

1985–86, I conducted a survey of lesbians and gay men on campus, distributing a questionnaire at meetings, dances, and other social events of the student group (D'Augelli, 1989c). Of the 125 women and men who described themselves as lesbian, gay, or bisexual, more than 25 percent had been verbally insulted at least once, and 50 percent had experienced verbal harassment more than once. Over a quarter (26 percent) had been threatened with physical violence, and 22 percent reported that they were chased or followed. Most reported hiding their sexual orientation, especially from other students (who were the perpetrators of most of the harassment and violence), but also from faculty and job supervisors. To avoid harassment, many lesbians and gay men made changes in their daily routine, and 64 percent reported fearing for their personal safety. When asked their general expectation of harassment on campus, 94 percent said that they expected harassment at the university in the future.

These findings of widespread victimization were corroborated in late 1988, when the university released its own report on harassment and campus "climate" for minorities. Of all incidents reported to the university, 70 percent of the harassment targeted lesbians and gay men (Penn State University, 1988). In addition, another study I conducted, this time among students in training to be resident assistants, confirmed that lesbians' and gay men's predictions of harassment were not unique to them. Every one of the 103 future RAs felt that harassment of the "average" lesbian or gay man was likely. Interestingly enough, many of these students had contributed to the negative climate themselves: 77 percent admitted having made anti-lesbian/anti-gay comments (D'Augelli, 1989b).

Needless to say, the climate for lesbians and gay men on this campus was very negative and threatening. Similar results have been found on every campus in which systematic research has been conducted (see Herek, 1989, for the most current review of this literature and other data on hate crimes against lesbians and gay men). Despite this situation, little formal protection against harassment and discrimination existed at the university. The official equal opportunity policy of the university did (and does) not include "sexual orientation" among its protected classes, providing a symbolic commentary on institutional commitment to protecting this population. Only in the spring of 1988 were lesbians and gay men acknowledged at all, when a student policy defining "acts of intolerance" against members of the university community was amended by adding "sexual orientation" to its list of groups. However, this action, an important step in itself, serves a limited institutional function, since it covers only student conduct.

The hostile climate and the minimal official response created tensions within the groups both on campus and in the local community. As the groups developed increased strength and confidence, evidence of explicit discrimination and institutional indifference still occurred. While it might seem inevitable that conflict would result, the risks for lesbians and gay men to engage in social action was considerable, including possible job loss, loss of friendships, family rejection, and so forth. Perhaps most fundamental, however, is internalized homophobia and doubts of self-worth, consequences of exposure to the "hidden curriculum" of heterosexual culture in general and the local context in particular. For students in the course, this alternative curriculum proved an antidote.

I now see a very large number of US out there. We come from all walkways of life and have the same problems. I see other lesbians and gays as needing the same kind of love as I need. This course was worth gold to me!

As a gay man, this course has given me a better understanding of myself and the opportunities available to me. Aspects of my life I had considered liabilities are no longer so, and some are real benefits.

The fact is I've seen more homophobia in action since I've come into the course. Reading the negative articles has inspired me even more than a lot of the positive ones.

CREATING A CLIMATE FOR DEVELOPMENT

I have offered the course since 1984, and it is currently a routine offering at the university. It draws 25–35 undergraduates from many majors. Most (approximately 80 percent) of the students are lesbian/gay; they typically divulge this information in the first class, although I never ask. No heterosexual male has yet taken the course, although several have attended initial meetings. The heterosexual women in the class give two reasons for enrollment: most have a lesbian/gay close relative (usually a sibling), and the rest are planning to enter a helping profession. Of the lesbian and gay majority, most have attended lesbian/gay functions on campus before enrolling in the course. Very few—though there are some—use the course as a way to "come out" publicly. Rather, the lesbian/gay students use the course to integrate more fully their orientation into their lives. Most are not open with their parents and families; some have avoided the issue; some have lied. All of the lesbian/gay students seem highly aware of their parents' and families' views, although some of their conclusions remain untested. I have little doubt that entrance to the course represents a turning point, both in terms of self-consciousness and social disclosure, and also in terms of commitment to change.

Just the fact that I took this course allowed me to talk to others about lesbian and gay issues.

The course helped me "come out of the closet" faster and more confidently than if I hadn't taken it. It has been especially helpful with my relationship with my family. For so long, I was afraid there would be a trade-off between my "gay liberation" and my relationship with my family, but with bold discussion, education, love, and understanding, I am achieving both.

Change occurs in diverse ways in class members, but it is facilitated because the class provides a supportive climate for development. Students report that this is the only course at the university in which lesbian/gay lives are acknowledged in such an extensive way. Most, on the other hand, have experienced homophobic remarks by faculty in courses in which "homosexuality" is mentioned. Many report irrelevant derogatory jokes and remarks about lesbians and gay men. Few describe efforts to assert themselves in these situations, either by requesting more detailed coverage or more accurate presentations, or by confronting a faculty member about a prejudicial remark. Most acknowledge feeling demoralized by these events, and occasionally this feeling emerges as anger. More often, attributions of worthlessness occur, reinforcing years of earlier "socialization."

Thus, an explicitly lesbian/gay classroom environment is an emotionally startling event, with no precedent in their lives. Most say that they have never been in a social situation in which they could freely discuss their lives; the only exceptions have been conversations held with small numbers of lesbian/gay friends. For many, the simple experience of being asked to read lesbian/gay materials—especially the several novels that are part of the required readings—opens up an entire world of information that they did not know existed. (One man told me that he had no idea that there were "gay" novels, except for pornography.)

I've come to realize that the word "homosexual" has some nasty connotations when used by many heterosexuals.

There are common personal changes observed in the students in this course. Most become acutely aware of their own internalized homophobia, appreciating how they too have believed the many myths of the culture. Most begin to understand that lesbian/gay status involves special challenges and that there are far more supportive resources available than they suspected. Many become active in social settings for lesbian/gay people, and others in the class help with anxieties about attending lesbian/gay activities. They realize that they must take initiatives to chart their own development, since little assistance will be provided by heterosexual society. There is a gradual acknowledgment of the pain of their earlier years. This is especially true of youths who had been harassed during adolescence, although resentment about lost opportunities occurs even if the young people were "closeted" in adolescence. On the other hand, when they realize that their earlier experiences were not unique, there is a relaxation of self-judgment and a hopefulness for the future. Some anger motivates commitment to "make up for lost time."

> The course has put me in touch with some of the greater injustices that will prevent me from ever just fading back into the closet.

This hopefulness often takes the form of efforts to develop relationships and to become more direct with families about affectional status. Many students initiate first relationships, often with considerable emotional intensity. Readings on couplehood help prepare students for the turmoil of first relationships, which are far more intense for lesbian/gay youth than for their heterosexual counterparts, in my experience. Another common movement is toward greater closeness with parents. If parents are valued sources of support and affection, students share their lives with them, although there is always considerable fear attached to this process. If parents seem likely to reject, students tend to approach others in the family. These efforts become more direct and assertive over the semester, under-taken after the students have a stronger sense of personal security and a better-grounded background in lesbian/gay life. Since the course is offered in the spring, many plan to discuss these issues during the mid-semester break. Some report leaving copies of the books for the course in conspic-uous places, hoping to spur a discussion. Over the years, those who have disclosed to parents have been surprised at parents' support, after some initial surprise and denial. Few have reported parental rejection; most students expect this refrain from disclosure, at least at this point in their lives.

In addition to greater openness with families, there is clearly momentum to extend their newly found strengths into their proximal social world on campus. Students become hyperconscious of the heterosexist assumptions of other students and faculty. Several students verbally challenged faculty when lesbians and gay men were totally ignored in class materials; one student confronted a faculty member inappropriately railing against gay male "promiscuity" during a lecture on the AIDS epidemic. They also become sensitive not only to exclusionary efforts, but also to overt homophobia. One student complained to a department head when a faculty member said he would likely kill his son were he to "come out." Since the course describes the richness of lesbian/gay lives, personal vigilance about others "knowing" is slowly replaced by personal affirmation. The many opportunities provided by routine academic life (doing papers, asking questions in class, seeking additional reading, and the like) for acknowledgment of lesbian/gay status provoke students to "test the waters"; they are now "armed" with current information and the knowledge that they can turn to others in the class (and to other resources now more accessible) to process the results of disclosure. Most want to disclose to all of their friends. They also seek to let others in their classes know. Often such a declaration comes in the form of raising questions in classes about lesbian/gay issues. (I encourage this, noting how important—and *legitimate*—this process is, suggesting that many faculty are unaware of their heterosexist views and can be encouraged to change.) Responses to these comments help categorize, albeit imperfectly, the supportiveness of others. More commonly, disclosure occurs with several in the class who have already been "proven" to have supportive views. The end result is a heightened awareness of the role of one's social network in affirming one's lesbian/gay status. Students no longer perceive "others" as an undifferentiated group of hostile individuals, but understand the need to determine sources of support and affirmation within their networks. This process helps students avoid developing exclusively lesbian/gay social networks, and encourages the integration of lesbian/gay status into "conventional" social circles, while also strengthening lesbian/gay pride.

> It has allowed me to broaden my awareness of other gay people and what they have gone through. It has allowed me to form new friendships.

Because the course focuses on how social networks and social structures facilitate and/or impede development, it inevitably elicits attention to legal and political issues central to lesbian/gay lives. Very few students have any understanding of the complex legal barriers that exist. When asked about the status of various lesbian/gay rights, few even understood that these were relevant to their lives. They were unaware, for instance, that they could be fired from a job because of sexual orientation at the university, in the town, and in the state, since no formal legal protection existed. They did not understand that discrimination in housing was legally permissible in the local municipality, and that landlords could evict lesbian and gay tenants. Most expected to live hidden lives or, in a very innocent way, assume a fulfilling life in an urban area after graduation. Interestingly enough, personal legal issues were of most concern, and readings on wills and power of attorney were met with shock and surprise (especially the ability of even hostile natural parents to supplant long-term partners in legal matters). Similarly, readings on experiences in parenting, generally concerning custody problems after divorce, and in creating families via donors, found students fascinated at the possibilities for their lives and simultaneously furious at arbitrary legal barriers. For most, this process evolved into heightened awareness of law; for others, it led to attempts at political action.

> About the only effect on my personal life would be a more focused outlook on gay rights.

> I was beginning to appreciate issues facing the gay community and the more I learned, the more I wanted to get involved to improve the situation. The knowledge gained here can only help in both my personal life and in my political life.

In moving toward legal and political action, most inevitably turned to the university, scrutinizing its formal and informal policies regarding lesbians and gay men. Because one of the course's themes encourages consideration of the social systems that influence one's development, much student activism has been directed toward administrative units concerned with the campus' residence halls. Training of RAs on concerns of lesbian/gay issues was an important concern, as well as policies about harassment, but this focus readily shifted to concern about broader policy—specifically about the lack of formal protection for lesbian/gay students, faculty, and staff in the official affirmative action policy of the institution.

As the entire domain of lesbian/gay legal matters crystallized, the stance of the municipality surrounding the university also became a focus. Few were aware of the minimal formal protections in basic life resources—housing, accommodations, employment—that existed in the borough in which the university is located. Indeed, in spring 1989, students in the class attended hearings on a municipal law that would extend protection from discrimination in housing to lesbians and gay men. The refusal of the local authorities to extend these protections—despite the strong support for such extensions by the mayor of the town—was met with incredulity by students who had not directly observed the machinations of legalized homophobia in their own setting. Their experiences in higher education had not prepared them to address legal barriers to their own lives. Moreover, they had never been so directly exposed to the process by which prejudice and bias rebuffed efforts of lesbians and gay men to obtain basic legal rights. In earlier course offerings, these issues were discussed, but the examples were not local, since no local action was occurring. Observing the legal process firsthand, particularly after discussions of the impact of such decisions on efforts of lesbians and gay men to become fully integrated into their communities (so as to, among other things, break the cultural chain of stereotyping) was experiential learning of the highest order.

The positive attitude toward gay people in the class (the way it should be) was wonderful. I have never felt so good about life, particularly hearing about everything in such a positive manner, and laughing at the ludicrous conclusions of others.

I began thinking about things I had pretty much ignored until now. Lesbian issues, gay minorities, gays and religion, etc.

CONCLUSION: A PEDAGOGY OF THE OPPRESSED

My experiences over the last five years have convinced me that teaching this course in the manner I have described is an act of empowerment. In fact, delineating the multiple impacts of personal factors, social process, and culture on lesbian and gay lives for young people at a critical point in their own development is a political act, an act that can provoke turbulent personal reactions to conditions of institutional and community oppression. My analysis of the process has been conditioned by Paolo Freire's *Pedagogy of the Oppressed* (1984). Although Freire's examples are from the history of oppression in South and Central America, his articulation of the radical consequences of informing oppressed men and women of the structure and parameters of their oppression is directly relevant to the experiences of young lesbians and gay men who are shown the sociopolitical conditions that will dictate their futures unless change occurs. This awareness releases strong anger; such education can unintentionally push individual gay men and women to confrontation with the sources of their oppression. There are tremendous personal risks in this process, since often these young people move forward in their personal development as a consequence of confrontations with homosexist "authority"—their parents, their teachers, their university.

Based on my role in this complex process, I feel that young lesbians and gay men must be informed of barriers to their development. They must be encouraged to appreciate their exceptionality, and to take steps to plan their own development in an active and assertive manner. The educational process that I have observed has elicited considerable strength in this group, and has unveiled possibilities for the creation of rich lives and partnerships as well as activism for social justice. Unless lesbians and gay men in colleges and universities are offered such pedagogical opportunities, they will remain victimized by the "hidden curriculum" of homophobia in higher education and will remain uninformed about the legal and political processes that directly shape their future.

I wonder how I'll end up. I'll just probably be like someone I know who never socialized, did her job, went home, slept, and basically became a hermit. I know it won't happen, though—I know myself too well. I may be against the norm, but it's what I am and what I stand for. I'm going to make myself known. I've already started doing that, in more ways than one.

I see more of a need to deal with issues outside of myself. I have to work on both a personal and a public level. I have gained much more sympathy for those who are at an earlier developmental stage than me.

REFERENCES

Baltes, P. B. (1987). Theoretical propositions of lifespan developmental psychology: On the dynamics between growth and decline. *Developmental Psychology, 23,* 611–626.

D'Augelli, A. R. (1989a). The development of a helping community for lesbians and gay men: A case study in community psychology. *Journal of Community Psychology, 17,* 18–29.

———. (1989b). Homophobia in a university community: Views of prospective resident assistants. *Journal of College Student Development, 30,* 546–552.

———. (1989c). Lesbians' and gay men's experiences of discrimination and harassment in a university community. *American Journal of Community Psychology, 17,* 317–321.

D'Augelli, A. R., & Hart, M. M. (1987). Gay women, men, and families in rural settings: Toward the development of helping communities. *American Journal of Community Psychology, 15,* 79–93.

Duberman, M. B., Vicinus, M., & Chauncey, G. (Eds.). (1989). *Hidden from history: Reclaiming the gay and lesbian past.* New York: New American Library.

Ebaugh, H. R. F. B. (1988). *Becoming an ex: The processes of role exit.* Chicago: University of Chicago Press.

Ellis, L., & Ames, M. A. (1987). Neurohormonal functioning and sexual orientation: A theory of homosexuality–heterosexuality. *Psychological Bulletin, 101,* 233–258.

Freire, P. (1984). *Pedagogy of the oppressed*. New York: Continuum.

Herdt, G. (Ed.). (1989). *Adolescence and homosexuality*. New York: Harrington Press.

Herek, G. M. (1989). Hate crimes against lesbians and gay men: Issues for research and policy. *American Psychologist, 44*, 948–955.

Kaplan, A. (1964). *The conduct of inquiry*. San Francisco: Chandler.

Kehoe, M. (Ed.). (1989). *Lesbians over 60 speak for themselves*. New York: Harrington Press.

Kitzinger, C. (1987). *The social construction of lesbianism*. London: Sage.

Lerner, R. M. (1984). *On the nature of human plasticity*. Cambridge: Cambridge University Press.

Money, J. (1987). Sin, sickness, or status? Homosexual gender identity and psychoneuroendocrinology. *American Psychologist, 42*, 384–399.

Pennsylvania State University. (1988). *Campus reports of acts of intolerance*. Unpublished manuscript.

Prilleltensky, I. (1989). Psychology and the status quo. *American Psychologist, 44*, 795–802.

Riegel, K. F. (1976). The dialectics of human development. *American Psychologist, 31*, 689–700.

Sampson, E. E. (1977). Psychology and the American ideal. *Journal of Personality and Social Psychology, 35*, 767–782.

Sischy, I. (1989, November 13). White and black. *The New Yorker*, 124–146.

Vacha, K. (1985). *Quiet fire: Memoirs of older gay men*. Trumansburg, NY: Crossing Press.

SELECTED BIBLIOGRAPHY

Apple, M. (1979). *Ideology and curriculum*. Boston: Routledge & Kegan Paul.

Apple, M. (1982). *Education and power*. Boston: Routledge & Kegan Paul.

Aronowitz, Stanley. (1988). *Science as power: Discourse and ideology in modern society*. Minneapolis: University of Minnesota Press.

Bourdieu, Pierre. (1977). Cultural reproduction and social reproduction. In J. Karabel & A. Halsey (Eds.). *Power and ideology in education* (pp. 487–510). New York: Oxford University Press.

Brint, S., & Karabel, J. (1989). *The diverted dream: Community colleges and the promise of educational opportunity in America, 1900–1985*. New York: Oxford.

Burrell, G., & Morgan, G. (1979). *Sociological paradigms and organisational analysis*. Exeter, NH: Heinemann.

Carnoy, Martin. (1984). *The state and political theory*. Princeton, NJ: Princeton University Press.

Carnoy, M., & Levin, H. M. (1985). *Schooling and work in the democratic state*. Palo Alto, CA: Stanford University Press.

Clark, Burton. (1983). *The higher education system: Academic organization in cross-national perspective*. Berkeley: University of California Press.

Clark, Burton. (1987). *The academic life*. Princeton, NJ: The Carnegie Foundation for the Advancement of Teaching.

D'Augelli, A. R. (1989). The development of a helping community for lesbians and gay men: A case study in community psychology. *Journal of Community Psychology, 17*, 18–29.

Dewey, John. (1926). *Democracy and education*. New York: Macmillan.

Duberman, M. B., Vicinus, M., & Chauncey, G. (Eds.). (1989). *Hidden from history: Reclaiming the gay and lesbian past*. New York: New American Library.

Fay, Brian. (1987). *Critical social science: Liberation and its limits*. Ithaca, NY: Cornell University Press.

Foucault, M. (1980). *Power/knowledge*. New York: Pantheon.

Freire, Paolo. (1984). *Pedagogy of the oppressed*. New York: Continuum.

Geertz, Clifford. (1973). *The interpretation of cultures*. New York: Basic Books.

Giddens, Anthony. (1982). *Profiles and critiques in social theory*. Berkeley: University of California Press.

Giddens, Anthony. (1984). *The constitution of society: Outline of the theory of structuration*. Berkeley: University of California Press.

Giroux, Henry A. (1983). *Theory and resistance in education: A pedagogy for the opposition*. South Hadley, MA: Bergin & Garvey.

Giroux, Henry A. (1988a). *Schooling and the struggle for public life*. Minneapolis: University of Minnesota Press.

Giroux, Henry A. (1988b). *Teachers as intellectuals: Toward a critical pedagogy of learning*. South Hadley, MA: Bergin & Garvey.

Giroux, Henry A., & McLaren, P. (1986). Teacher education and the politics of engagement: The case for democratic schooling. *Harvard Educational Review, 56*(3), 213–238.

Gramsci, Antonio. (1971). *Selections from the prison notebooks of Antonio Gramsci*. (Quintin Hoare & Geoffrey Nowell Smith, Eds. and Trans.). New York: International Publishers.

Grubb, W. N. (1984). The bandwagon once more: Vocational preparation for high-tech occupations. *Harvard Educational Review, 54*(4), 429–451.

Habermas, Jurgen. (1975). *Legitimation crisis*. Boston: Beacon Press.

Holland, Dorothy, & Eisenhart, Margaret. (forthcoming). *Schooling, romance, and resistance: University women and the gender status quo*. Chicago: University of Chicago Press.

Keller, Evelyn Fox. (1985). *Reflections on gender and science*. New Haven, CT: Yale University Press.

Kitzinger, C. (1987). *The social construction of lesbianism*. London: Sage.

Larson, Magali Sarfatti. (1977). *The rise of professionalism*. Berkeley: University of California Press.

Lerner, R. M. (1984). *On the nature of human plasticity*. Cambridge: Cambridge University Press.

MacIntyre, A. (1984). *After virtue: A study in moral theory* (2nd ed.). Notre Dame, IN: University of Notre Dame Press.

McLaren, Peter. (1989). *Life in schools*. New York: Longman.

Mouffe, C. (1988). Radical democracy: Modern or postmodern? In A. Ross (Ed.), *Universal abandon? The politics of postmodernism*. Minneapolis: University of Minnesota Press.

Noble, David W. (1977). *America by design: Science, technology and the rise of corporate capitalism*. New York: Alfred Knopf.

Pincus, F. (1980). The false promises of community colleges. *Harvard Educational Review, 50*, 332–361.

Rosaldo, Renato. (1989). *Culture and truth: The remaking of social analysis*. Boston: Beacon Press.

Sears, J., Marshall, J., & Otis-Wilborn, A. (1989). The political economy of teacher training: Attracting high-ability persons into teaching, a critique. *Teacher Education Quarterly, 16*(4), 5–72.

Siegel, H. (1987). Rationality and ideology. *Educational Theory, 37*(2), 153–167.

Silva, Edward T., & Slaughter, S. (1984). *Serving power: The making of the academic social science expert.* Westport, CT: Greenwood Press.

Slaughter, Sheila. (1990). *The higher learning and high technology: Dynamics of higher education policy formation.* Albany, NY: SUNY Press.

Tierney, William G. (1989). *Curricular landscapes, democratic vistas: Transformative leadership in higher education.* New York: Praeger.

Weis, Lois. (1985). *Between two worlds: Black students in an urban community college.* Boston: Routledge & Kegan Paul.

Wexler, P. (1987). *Social analysis of education: After the new sociology.* New York: Routledge & Kegan Paul.

Willis, Paul. (1981). *Learning to labour: How working class kids get working class jobs.* New York: Columbia University Press.

INDEX

ABOUT THE EDITOR AND CONTRIBUTORS

WILLIAM G. TIERNEY is associate professor and senior research associate at the Center for the Study of Higher Education at The Pennsylvania State University. He is the author of *Curricular Landscapes, Democratic Vistas: Transformative Leadership in Higher Education*. His other works include *The Web of Leadership* and *Collegiate Culture and Leadership Strategies* (with Ellen Chaffee). He is currently at work on a book utilizing critical theory for the analysis of Native American students in higher education. He has recently traveled in northern Thailand.

ANTHONY D'AUGELLI, a community/clinical psychologist, is associate professor of human development at The Pennsylvania State University.

WILLIAM FOSTER is associate professor of education at the University of San Diego. He is the author of *Paradigms and Promises: New Approaches to Educational Administration*.

PATRICIA J. GUMPORT is assistant professor of education and, by courtesy, of sociology at Stanford University. She is also deputy director of the Stanford Institute for Higher Education Research.

KEN KEMPNER is assistant professor of higher education and research at the University of Oregon. He is co-author of *Sex Equity in Education*.

YVONNA S. LINCOLN is associate professor of higher education at Vanderbilt University. She publishes extensively on constructivism and methodological inquiry and is currently Vice-President of Division J of the American Educational Research Association.

J. DAN MARSHALL is associate dean for teacher education at the National College of Education and assistant professor of curriculum. He is co-editor of *Teaching and Thinking About Curriculum*.

AMY K. OTIS-WILBORN is assistant professor at the University of Wisconsin-Milwaukee specializing in exceptional education.

GARY RHOADES is associate professor of higher education at the University of Arizona. He publishes in the *Review of Higher Education* and *Sociology of Education*.

JAMES T. SEARS is associate professor at the University of South Carolina and senior research associate at the South Carolina Policy Center. He is co-editor of *Teaching and Thinking About Curriculum*.

SHEILA SLAUGHTER is professor at the Center for the Study of Higher Education at the University of Arizona-Tucson. She is the author of *The Higher Learning and High Technology: Dynamics of Higher Education Policy Formation*.